MAKE STRAIGHT THE WAY OF THE LORD

ISBN 9781522080671

First Edition - August 2017

Cover photo taken of Mount Washington from Paradise Meadows walking trail, British Columbia, Canada.

Foreword

Hail to the King!

Lord Jesus is "the Vine" and Tom Walker, as every born-again, is a "branch". It has been my habit to consider fellow branches – what motivates them and what doesn't, their degree of loyalty to Christ, the strength of their connection to the Vine – things like that.

I had befriended the Tom Walker branch several years ago. A very unusual branch this branch, laden with much fruit.

Much fruit doesn't just happen. It takes grace, yes, but also tenacity. Years of hanging in there. Repentance, repentance, repentance. Recommitment, recommitment, recommitment. Christ as Lord, Christ as shepherd, Christ as teacher, Christ as "first love".

I notice that though the fruit just keeps increasing, the Walker branch doesn't feel the strain. Strength flows freely from Vine to branch. Not only is Tom well connected to the Vine, you see, but the Vine is well connected to the branch. He will never leave us or forsake us. He will never disconnect Himself. He is faithful. He is good.

Hail to the King!

"He who loves Me will be loved by My Father, and I will love him and manifest Myself to him." Every Christian loves Lord Jesus. But there are degrees of love. That's why there are degrees of success and joy and peace. And degrees of His manifested Presence.

We are talking relationship. All-important relationship. The value of relationship determines one's calibre of Christianity. The value of a book is determined by its ability to draw its reader into deeper, stronger alliance. Many books just don't do that. Some actually have an adverse effect.

And some books are keepers, to be considered now and reconsidered later. Which brings us to *'Make Straight the Way of the Lord'*. This is not a book merely to be read, but one to be studied. It is for the serious seeker of God's will and ways. It will better your connection to Christ and thus enrich your eternity.

You may notice that Tom's "first love" leaks out of every chapter. Tom speaks Christ and writes Christ. Few love Him so thoroughly.

It has been said that the love of Brother Lawrence (1614 – 1691) for Lord Jesus almost consumed him. Better be careful, Tom Walker.

Hail to the King!

Larry J. Jones
Kelowna, B.C.

Author's Prologue

We need often to be reminded of our debt to the past, for without the knowledge and wisdom gained by countless seekers of fundamental truth we would have nothing to build on. Yet, as human beings created in the very image of God, we find within us an inherent need to advance our understanding on a broad front, that we may probe ever deeper and unveil truths that are yet to be discovered.

No heart search can be more vital to the dwellers on this wonderful earth than that they individually and in company with others grow in their awareness and delve ever deeper into the knowledge of the Divine Being. For, as Paul proclaimed to those deity-speculating Athenians who were gathered on Mars Hill so long ago, *'He is not far from each one of us; for in Him we live and move and exist'*. Acts 17:27-28.

This three part compendium has been dedicated to this most vital of all heart searches. For this life we have been mystically launched upon was given us that we might be active participants in God's eternal purpose. Not only so, but that we mortals might be taken from our lowly estate and be raised up to the highest heights in Jesus, who is the one and only Son of the Father. Not only so, but that we might sit forever in the heavenly places as joint heirs with Him in glory as *'His bride, the wife of the Lamb'*.

It is the desire of the writer that we not only receive glorious cameos of divine truth composed and penned by human hearts (of which there are many), but that such expressions of heavenly wisdom be garnered and linked together to define a pathway of truth that shall enlighten our journey, that we may with confidence progress along it, visualizing with divinely afforded insight the ultimate destiny that lies ahead of us.

'....but just as it is written, "things which eye has not seen and ear has not heard, and which have not entered the heart of

man, all that God has prepared for those who love Him." For to us God revealed them through the Spirit; for the Spirit searches all things, even the depths of God'. 1 Corinthians 2:9-10. God's greatest cameos of divine wisdom are contained within the Scriptures and it is upon the revelation of the Holy Spirit that we completely depend for an unveiling of *'things which eye has not seen and ear has not heard and which have not entered the heart of man'*.

In presenting these small offerings of his heart's overflow the writer places them wholly into the hands of the Master that He may bless them, break them and distribute them to all who have a deep heart hunger for Him.

Tom Walker
August 2017

Kindly note that unless otherwise stated all Scriptural references are from the NASU Version of the Bible. Direct quotations from Scripture are shown in italics.

PART ONE
WELL PLEASING TO HIM

Introduction to Part One

Poem: 'Come Unto Me'

Chapter 1 – So Great a Salvation 4
Chapter 2 – You are to be Perfect 8
Chapter 3 – Take My Yoke upon You 13
Chapter 4 – I will Build My Church 17
Chapter 5 - The Church which is His Body 23
Chapter 6 – Jesus Christ is Lord 27
Chapter 7 – Do this in Remembrance of Me 32
Chapter 8 – Making the most of Your Time 38
Chapter 9 – He gave some Prophets 43
Chapter 10 – Where there is no Vision 48
Chapter 11 – The Word of Truth 52
Chapter 12 – You cannot Serve God and Wealth 57
Chapter 13 – You are All Brothers 61
Chapter 14 – Members One of Another 66
Chapter 15 – Prepare the Way of the Lord 71
Chapter 16 – This Gospel of the Kingdom 76
Chapter 17 – I Will Come Again 81
Chapter 18 – Your Will be Done 86
Chapter 19 – The Testimony of Jesus 90

Introduction to Part One

The enjoyment of the Lord Jesus and freedom in the Spirit that characterized the early church is hard to find in Christendom today. The mighty power of God demonstrated through His people in those former days often seems so distant a memory that reference to it should simply be on a purely historical basis. It is easy to assume that life and conditions in the world today are responsible for this loss of the church's vitality.

Thus it is that a burden has been placed on the writer's heart to search afresh in the Scriptures to identify many elements of church life, belief and practice that provided the pattern the Lord intended His people to follow, not only then but until His return in glory.

Over the past decades many individuals have simply walked away from their church communities. Many of these have been drawn to gather in homes, where they have found greater freedom in the Spirit and interpersonal warmth and acceptance which has made their spiritual journey more meaningful. However, after a while, the same tendencies of control and formality may have begun to creep into their gatherings that were characteristic of their former fellowship in the mainline churches.

The aim of Part One is to identify from the Scriptures the first principles and practices that the Lord ordained in establishing Spirit directed, self-administering communities of believers throughout the Roman world and beyond. It advocates a return to the basics of the faith as practiced in the first century church that made it the dynamic force that shook the whole Roman world of the time.

If we would *'Make straight the Way of the Lord'*, surely we must come fully into His thought concerning what the church should be in order to bear His testimony before the world and *'against the rulers, against the powers, against the world forces of this darkness, against the spiritual forces of wickedness in the heavenly places'*. Ephesians 6:12.

Thomas Walker
August 2017

COME UNTO ME

Come unto Me calls Jesus, O hear His urgent cry;
So many church traditions are part of Satan's lie,
Leave compromising methods, divisive worldly ways;
Turn to Him with all your heart, let Jesus fill your gaze.

These are the times long-waited, the age is turning fast,
The coming tribulation for seven whole years will last;
Soon comes a time of shaking, believers first to test,
To prove their faith is real, perfect them for His rest.

If we would overcome him, then Satan cannot stay
Right at God's throne accusing the brethren every day;
God waits the male child's birthing from out the woman stood
Before the great red dragon, who's poised to drink his blood.

Immediately the male child is caught up to the throne,
The woman tall who bore him remains on earth alone;
No place is found for Satan in heaven he's known so long,
For Michael and his angels cast out the demon throng.

Some other overcomers for whom the heavens wait
Are those of Philadelphia, its name describes their state,
They have but little power, His name they've not denied,
His open door before them, a crown He'll them provide.

Cast down to earth is Satan, whose time is growing short,
He gives the beast his power, his antichrist cohort;
Then greatest tribulation the world has ever known
Will come upon all nations till Jesus takes the throne.

Come unto Me says Jesus, in Me your race to run,
Find brotherhood with others where all in Me are one;
Where all may freely function, express their unique role,
And all as one in Spirit unite to meet My goal.

Thomas Walker
Revised August 2017

CHAPTER 1
SO GREAT A SALVATION

Scripture references: Revelation 21:4-5, Philippians 2:12-13, Hebrews 2:1-4, Luke 21:36, Revelation 12:10-11, John 3:14-21, Romans 8:19-21, 1 Peter 2:1-5.

When the topic of salvation comes to mind, we are apt to consider what it means to us as individuals, yet pay far less attention to the immensity of what the Lord Jesus accomplished through His death on the cross. We may rightly rejoice in the greatness of our personal salvation, yet we must never forget that *'The Son of God appeared for this purpose, to destroy the works of the devil'*. 1 John 3:8. His was an immense victory beyond our human capacity to comprehend.

'So great a salvation' has ensured that all creation will be restored back to the perfection at the beginning, as though evil had never existed. *He will wipe away every tear from their eyes; and there will no longer be any death; there will no longer be any mourning, or crying, or pain; the first things have passed away." And He who sits on the throne said, "Behold, I am making all things new." And He said, "Write, for these words are faithful and true."* Revelation 21:4-5. All Satan's destructive work has been dealt with through the cross. In the life hereafter there will be no remembrance of Satan, of the fall of man, of death and destruction, nor even consciousness of Hell. It will be as though none of this had ever been. *'The first things have passed away'...."Behold, I am making all things new."*

'....how will we escape if we neglect so great a salvation?' All those who have come to the Lord Jesus in repentance and faith have been given responsibility to participate in the work of salvation. We read in Philippians 2:12-13, *'work out your salvation with fear and trembling; for it is God who is at work in you, both to will and to work for His good pleasure'*.

'For this reason we must pay much closer attention to what we have heard, so that we do not drift away from it. For if the word spoken through angels proved unalterable, and every transgression and disobedience received a just penalty, how will we escape if we neglect so great a salvation'? Hebrews 2:1-3. This urgent message

is not to the unsaved, but for those who have already entered upon their journey of eternal life in Christ. It cautions us against drifting away from what we have heard. The escape described is not to escape damnation, but of escaping *'a just penalty'*. Those who *'escape'* will be greatly honoured for their faithfulness to the Lord. Those who *'neglect so great a salvation'* will receive *'a just penalty'*. Galatians 6:7. *'Do not be deceived, God is not mocked; for whatever a man sows, this he will also reap'*.

What it will mean to escape can be found in the words of Jesus in Luke 21:36, "*But keep on the alert at all times, praying that you may have strength to escape all these things that are about to take place, and to stand before the Son of Man.*" Those who *'pay much closer attention'* to what they have heard and who *'keep on the alert at all times'* will not only *'escape all these things that are about to take place'* but will be caught up to the throne of God *'to stand before the Son of Man'*.

The *'just penalty'* will be, for instance, to remain on earth during the great tribulation or to be denied participation in *'the marriage supper of the Lamb'*. Revelation 19:7.

All those who have come to Jesus for grace and salvation have a vital part to play in His recovery of all things. Their role is to bear the living testimony of Jesus in the face of God's enemy, Satan, in opposition to all his works. *'Then I heard a loud voice in heaven, saying, "Now the salvation, and the power, and the kingdom of our God and the authority of His Christ have come, for the accuser of our brethren has been thrown down, he who accuses them before our God day and night. "And they overcame him* (Satan) *because of the blood of the Lamb and because of the word of their testimony, and they did not love their life even when faced with death'*. Revelation 12:10-11.

John 3:16 has been rightly and blessedly used to bring unbelievers to real life-changing faith in Christ; *'that everyone who believes into Him would not perish, but would have eternal life'*. Recovery Version. This translation *'into Him'* is supported by 1 John 5:11. *And the testimony is this, that God has given us eternal life, and this life is in His Son*. *'Eternal life'* is *'in His Son'* so all must believe *'into Him'* in order to receive it.

How easy it is to read those well-known and much loved words of John 3:16 yet miss the real importance of the context. *'God so loved the world'*. It wasn't only to the sinner that God determined to bring newness through the death of His Son, but to all His creation, including this earth and even the remotest galaxies. All that Satan had despoiled, the Father determined to recover to perfection.

A failure of much of the Christian church has been to limit the meaning of salvation. Once individuals have accepted Christ they are all too often informed that they are now 'saved'. The impression given is that, at the close of life's journey, heaven awaits all who have come to Jesus in repentance and faith. The saved (and often those who are yet unsaved) are encouraged to participate actively in church meetings and other events. This has resulted in the creation of multitudes of largely passive church members. In this spiritually limiting and controlled environment even the most passionate of newly born again believers are likely to lose their first love for Jesus.

Though the step of individual repentance and faith is of vital importance to God and to each one who takes it, nevertheless it is simply the entrance into the kingdom of heaven and the beginning of a process through which the Holy Spirit will transform each surrendered life into the likeness of Jesus. This is God's ultimate goal for every believer.

Concerning the suffering of creation and the means of its rescue, we read in Romans 8:19-21, *'For the anxious longing of the creation waits eagerly for the revealing of the sons of God. For the creation was subjected to futility, not willingly, but because of Him who subjected it, in hope that the creation itself also will be set free from its slavery to corruption into the freedom of the glory of the children of God'*. The *'sons of God'* referred to here are the very ones who *'have strength to escape all these things that are about to take place, and to stand before the Son of Man'*. When these overcomers are revealed, Satan will be cast out of heaven and will have but little time in which he will create 'hell on earth' during the three and a half years of the great tribulation.

It is God's intention that we take His pathway to perfection *'with fear and trembling'*, wholly trusting that *'it is God who is at work in you, both to will and to work of His good pleasure'*.

The verses in 1 Peter remind us that *'like new born babies'* we must take in *'the pure milk of the word'* that we may by it *'grow in respect to salvation'*. If we will faithfully do so we will be constituted *'as living stones'* for the building up of a spiritual house to perform the functions of *'a holy priesthood, to offer up spiritual sacrifices acceptable to God through Jesus Christ'*. That we become, with others, a holy priesthood to offer up spiritual sacrifices indicates considerable growth in life from our first state of being new born babies. How important it is to regularly read our Bible, as God's living word, in an attitude of prayer and worship. How rich an experience it is and how precious are the revelations that the Lord graciously gives us.

'...he who practices the truth comes to the Light, so that his deeds may be manifested as having been wrought in God'. John 3:21. And *'If we walk in the light as He is in the light'*, 1 John 1:7, it will be recognized that our works have been *'wrought in God'*. Even if we have already been blessed with many revelations from the Lord, these verses remind us that we must practice what we have been shown. To do so will result in God giving us more revelation of His Son, the Lord Jesus, for everything we need is in the Son. He Himself is all that we lack in our fallen self. If we cannot love others, He will be the love of God in us, expressed through us to others. Whatever we need, Jesus is.

The ultimate goal of this *'so great a salvation'* is the full and final accomplishment of the eternal purpose of God which goes far beyond what Satan hampered and tried to destroy. Transformed and united believers will one day comprise *'the bride, the wife of the Lamb'* and the eternal dwelling place of God.

CHAPTER 2
YOU ARE TO BE PERFECT

Scripture references: Matthew 5:48, Philippians 3:7-15, 1 Thessalonians 5:23-24, Matthew 7:13-14, Matthew 11:28-30, 2 Timothy 4:6-8, Hebrews 12:1-2, 1 John 3:2.

In the latter part of the first century A.D. and over many centuries that followed, the church of Jesus Christ became Christianity as we know it today. It became debased from the living organism it had been from its beginnings at Pentecost in the power of the Spirit to become an organization, or a series of organizations under human authority. No longer was Jesus unrivalled and supreme Lord among great numbers of His people, but He must be represented and His will must be interpreted and communicated to common folks by layers of ecclesiastical people. However, during the many centuries since that first Pentecost, the Lord maintained His true testimony through many scattered communities of the faithful: the Bogomils, the Waldenses, the Albigenses, the Moravians, the Anabaptists and more recently the Brethren among these. The list is long.

Martin Luther, born in 1483, was used of God to release millions of captives held in bondage, not only by sin, but by an indulgence-dispensing religious body that purported to possess divine authority over the entrance to heaven's bliss.

However, it was one thing for Martin Luther to bring the great truth of salvation by grace through faith to the forefront, yet what has been largely neglected is that salvation is both an event and a process. It has its entrance by faith and its completion is by faith. If God's full work of transformation is to be completed during the time allotted to us on earth, we must permit the Holy Spirit to be Lord over all our thoughts, our words and our actions. He will surely complete His work in us if all our hours, days and years are yielded to Him.

The damage done by partaking of the fruit of the tree of knowledge must be eradicated, not controlled. The full work of transformation through partaking of the fruit of the tree of life must be allowed to progress until completed. Adam and his believing seed must be as though they had never partaken of the tree of the knowledge of good and evil. The new creatures in Christ, who together comprise the new Jerusalem, must be brought to the same state of perfection as their Saviour and coming Bridegroom.

Among evangelical Christians there is rightly great emphasis on 'justification on the basis of faith'. This is perhaps their central theme. There is also increasing emphasis on a catching away of the justified believers and the soon return of Christ. Both themes are scriptural, glorious and filled with anticipatory hope. What is largely missing, however, is the pathway the same Scriptures clearly reveal to be the essential elements that lie between the new birth and the resurrection of the redeemed. There seems to be a lack of awareness of the significance of the Lord's command *'You are to be perfect as your heavenly Father is perfect'*, Matthew 5:48.

As an eager young believer some sixty or so years ago, the writer recalls being urged to seek 'the second blessing'. This was, as he understood it, the baptism in the Holy Spirit with a new language accompanying – speaking in tongues. But what did this have to do with the uncompromising admonition of the Lord Jesus *"Therefore you are to be perfect, as your heavenly Father is perfect"*? Those who received the baptism of the Holy Spirit on the day of Pentecost, and all those who have received this blessing since, were not perfected by the experience. Surely the baptism in the Holy Spirit was bestowed so that those upon whom He fell might be clothed with power from on high, that they might be equipped to fulfil the great commission to *'preach the gospel to all creation'*.

The example of the apostle Paul provides some key answers to our Lord's command *"Therefore you are to be perfect, as your heavenly Father is perfect."* In his letter to the assembly in Philippi he writes *'that I may know Him and the power of His resurrection and the fellowship of His sufferings, being conformed to His death; in order that I may attain to the resurrection from the dead. Not that I have already obtained it or have already become perfect, but I press on so that I may lay hold of that for which also I was laid hold of by Christ Jesus'*. Philippians 3:10-12.

Paul was pressing on that he might become perfect. To perfect Paul was the purpose for which Christ had laid hold of him. How was this being accomplished? He set aside and discounted his natural assets and abilities. He counted them all as worthless compared with gaining Christ. Paul's ultimate goal was *'that I may lay hold of that for which also I was laid hold of by Christ Jesus'*. Surely Paul's goal was to *'be perfect as our Father in heaven is perfect'*.

Paul's prayer for the members of the assembly in Thessalonica addresses this matter in a unique way: *'Now may the God of peace Himself sanctify you entirely; and may your spirit and soul and body be preserved complete, without blame at the coming of our Lord Jesus Christ. Faithful is He who calls you, and He also will bring it to pass'*. 1 Thessalonians 5:23-24. These verses tell us that we are tripartite beings. We are spiritual beings, for we have a spirit. We are thinking, feeling and decision-making beings, for we have a soul. We are physical beings, for we have a body. From an objective point of view what is perfection according to the Lord? Perfection is that God Himself sanctify (make us holy as He is holy) and preserve our spirit and soul and body *'complete, without blame at the coming of our Lord Jesus Christ'*.

God gives every human being a spirit. *'Thus declares the Lord who stretches out the heavens, lays the foundation of the earth, and forms the spirit of man within him'*, Zechariah 12:1. The human spirit is the organ into which the Holy Spirit comes at the instant of the new birth. John 3:6 "That which is born of the flesh is flesh, and that which is born of the Spirit is spirit." On our passing from this human life *'the spirit shall return to God Who gave it'*. Ecclesiastes 12:7, AMP. The spirit God gives is perfect and returns to God perfect. Sin cannot affect our spirit.

Our bodies are subject to deterioration, decay and death, yet at the coming of the Lord Jesus a perfect spiritual body will be ours to replace our earthly body. We shall then be physically perfect. 1 Corinthians 15:42-44.

During this earthly life the soul of a believer - that is our mind, our emotions and our will - forms the battleground for the conflict between Christ and Satan. Each individual believer must make frequent decisions whom to serve. That our *'soul....be preserved complete, without blame at the coming of our Lord Jesus Christ'* will prove to have been the outcome of making wise decisions and choices along life's journey.

When we first believed we received *'the mind of Christ'*. 1 Corinthians 2:16. Our responsibility is to *'bring every thought captive to the obedience of Christ'*. 2 Corinthians 10:5. We must make it our choice to allow the Spirit to be Lord over our mind, emotions and will so that He may exhibit His fruit in all the circumstances of our daily life. Yes, we are gifted by God with freedom of choice. May we be given grace to respond wisely to all our choices, *"Your will be done"*. Matthew 6:9.

That we may be perfect as our heavenly Father is perfect will demand an unconditional surrender to Him of all we are, spirit, soul and body, and all we have, including the gifts He has bestowed upon us.

In Matthew 7:13-14 is a very significant parable of Jesus. Hidden within this parable is the pathway to becoming perfect in Christ Jesus. Within it lie the secrets of living the victorious life for all who desire to be well pleasing to the Lord Jesus and to follow Him fully. Jesus exhorts those who would be His disciples to *"Enter through the narrow gate....For the gate is small and the way is narrow that leads to life, and there are few who find it."*

It is only those who are willing to take up their cross daily to follow Jesus who will find the narrow gate. Only Jesus may enter through this gate and He must usher us through it in Himself. All the things that were gain to us must be left behind. To pass through the narrow gate in Jesus is to count all things as loss just as Paul did. *'Whatever things were gain to me, those things I have counted as loss for the sake of Christ'*. Philippians 3:7.

Having entered through the narrow gate we discover that *'the way is narrow that leads to life'*. Only the Lord Jesus can walk that narrow way and He invites us, *"Come to Me, all who are weary and heavy-laden, and I will give you rest." "Take My yoke upon you and learn from Me, for I am gentle and humble in heart, and you will find rest for your souls. "For My yoke is easy and My burden is light."* Matthew 11:28-30.

So many try and try to live their life separated unto Christ. Failure after failure will be their experience until they simply allow His easy yoke to rest upon their neck so that they may find their rest in Him. Philippians 2:8 tells us that Jesus *'humbled Himself by becoming obedient to the point of death, even death on a cross'*. The narrow way is the way of the cross. Although it will be our cross that we are carrying, He will be bearing most of its weight. As we are yoked with Him we will learn *'of'* or *'off from'* Him. Thus we shall increasingly be getting to know Him. We shall know too, in our experience, the fellowship of His sufferings and we will be conformed to His death. Paul's great goal *'That I may know Him'* will be our goal too.

Paul expressed to Timothy his confidence that his course was now completed. By this time he had 'become perfect' or he was very close to becoming perfect. He states, *'I have fought the good fight, I have finished the course, I have kept the faith; in the future there is laid up for me the crown of righteousness, which the Lord, the righteous Judge, will award to me on that day....'* 2 Timothy 4:7-8. The crown of righteousness that will be awarded to Paul will be the Lord's recognition that Paul has pressed on and become perfect in Him. As Paul did so long ago, *'let us run with endurance the race that is set before us, fixing our eyes on Jesus, the author and perfecter of faith'*. Hebrews 12:1-2.

The final words of Paul's statement must surely encourage us. He says, *'....and not only to me, but also to all who have loved His appearing'*. The crown of righteousness will be our award too if we faithfully press on in Christ, yoked to Him, along the narrow way that leads to life. Then, through the transforming work of the Holy Spirit, we too may echo Paul's words, *'I have fought the good fight, I have finished the course, I have kept the faith'*.

'Beloved, now we are children of God, and it has not appeared as yet what we will be. We know that when He appears, we will be like Him, because we will see Him just as He is'. 1 John 3:2. *'We will be like Him'* for we shall have been transformed into His likeness. Then we shall indeed be perfect as our Father in heaven is perfect.

CHAPTER 3
TAKE MY YOKE UPON YOU

Scripture references: Revelation 21:2, Matthew 11:28-30, Matthew 1:18-19, Revelation 19:7 NKJV, 1 Peter 2:2-3, 1 John 3:2-3, Ephesians 4:14-15.

'Come to Me....' These seemingly simple words of Jesus usher us through a gateway into the most profound experience ever brought into the consciousness of man. The goal of this simple invitation is that, at the close of time, all who have come to Him, all who have taken His yoke upon them and journeyed with Him, might participate as His *'bride, the wife of the Lamb'*, being glorified together with Him.

His message is for those who are willing to *'cease striving and know'* that He is God. Psalm 46:10. It is for those who recognize that it is God who is at work in them *'both to will and to work of His good pleasure'*. Philippians 2:13. It is for those who know that they need to be *'made ready as a bride adorned for her husband'*. Revelation 21:2. Those who are yoked together with Jesus will be conscious that they are undergoing the process of being made ready to be His wife, which will culminate in their being yoked together with Him for eternity.

Surely it is no accident that the prime example of being yoked together that exists among mankind is Christian marriage. No doubt members of other faiths, and many of those of no faith, would substantially agree that marriage is, or should be, the highest earthly example of union. As believers in Jesus we understand that earthly marriage is the type of which Christ and His bride is the heavenly eternal reality. Matthew 19:5-6. *'....for this reason a man shall leave his father and mother and be joined to his wife, and the two shall become one flesh'? "So they are no longer two, but one flesh'*.

It is not until we have come to Jesus, acknowledged Him as Lord, surrendered to Him every aspect of our life and of ourselves, and have willingly taken His yoke upon us, that we shall know the joy of being betrothed to Him. To be betrothed to Jesus is to be unbreakably pledged in marriage to Him.

Consider the example of Joseph and Mary. The word tells us in Matthew 1:18-19 that when *'Mary was pledged to be married to Joseph, but before they came together, she was found to be with child through the Holy Spirit. Because Joseph her husband was a righteous man and did not want to expose her to public disgrace, he had in mind to divorce her quietly'*. NIV. In other words, so binding was even the pledge *'to be married'* that to break it would have been like getting a divorce.

To be yoked with Jesus is to be pledged for eternity to Him as though we are already His wife. *"Let us be glad and rejoice and give Him glory, for the marriage of the Lamb has come, and His wife has made herself ready."* Revelation 19:7, NKJV. How has His wife made herself ready? She has consistently and willingly been *'led by the Spirit of God'* in the performance of righteous acts that are well-pleasing to her future Husband. Only those who, during their life on earth, have entered the experience of being consistently *'led by the Spirit of God'* will be invited to the marriage supper of the Lamb.

The Holy Spirit through Peter in 1 Peter 2:2-3 urges new believers, *'like newborn babies, long for the pure milk of the word, so that by it you may grow in respect to salvation, if you have tasted the kindness of the Lord'*. As we take in the pure milk of the word we shall press on from being babies to become children.

Ephesians 4:14-15 informs us that *'we are no longer to be children, tossed here and there by waves and carried about by every wind of doctrine, by the trickery of men, by craftiness in deceitful scheming; but speaking the truth in love, we are to grow up in all aspects into Him who is the head, even Christ'*. As we press on to know and speak the truth in love, leaving the uncertainties of our thoughts and emotions we shall *'grow up in all aspects into Him who is the head, even Christ'*. This important step will lead us on to become sons of God as we yield ourselves to Jesus to be yoked together with Him.

That we prove to be *'heirs of God and fellow heirs with Christ'* in experience is surely a further step on the way to His ultimate purpose for us. It comes with the requirement that *'if indeed we suffer with Him....we may also be glorified with Him'*. As we walk yoked with the Lord Jesus He will grant us the privilege of suffering with Him that we may learn of Him who is *'meek and lowly of heart'*. We shall then enter into His rest and, as time passes into eternity, we shall be glorified together with Him.

In taking upon us the yoke of Jesus we shall place ourselves wholly under His lordship and direction. He alone will be our Lord and Master. Ambition to be prominent and have control over others will fade away, to be replaced by a deep desire to do what is pleasing in the eyes of the Lord and to honour Him above all. Our focus will be upon exercising the gift He has given us in harmony with other members of our Christian community. All who are likewise yoked to Jesus will be acutely aware of His every move and thus will be actively using their gift as He calls upon them to do so, yet will be equally willing to welcome the gifts of others as He shall speak and act through them also.

Christendom largely operates under layers of spiritual authority and control. Thus, the vast majority of the members of the body of Christ are rendered silent, deferring to those with special training who have been approved by human institutions in accordance with human standards. Sad to say, large numbers who have genuinely come to Jesus have placed themselves under the yoke of man. In their dependence on spiritual 'experts' and 'professionals' there are few members within these hierarchical institutions who will labour regularly to take in the pure milk of the word, even in the quiet of their own homes, thus they may remain spiritual infants for five, ten, twenty or, sadly, even more years. How then can it be possible for them to be led moment by moment by the Spirit of God?

There has never been a more significant time than now to hear and respond to these timeless words of Jesus - *"Come to Me, all who are weary and heavy-laden, and I will give you rest. "Take My yoke upon you and learn from Me, for I am gentle and humble in heart, and you will find rest for your souls. "For My yoke is easy and My burden is light."* As we make it our deliberate and firm commitment to come to Jesus and to take upon ourselves His easy yoke, we shall enter upon a future far beyond the comprehension of the human mind. *'....just as it is written, "things which eye has not seen and ear has not heard, and which have not entered the heart of man, all that God has prepared for those who love him."* For to us God revealed them through the Spirit'. 1 Corinthians 2:9-10.

As individuals take Christ's yoke upon them and join together with others of like mind to become a company of those yoked to Him, they will fulfil the prayer of the Lord Jesus *"....that they may be one, just as We are one"*. John 17:22. This will not only be their living experience but it will be their testimony to all around.

CHAPTER 4
I WILL BUILD MY CHURCH

Scripture references: 1 Kings 6:7, 1 Peter 2:4-8, Matthew 16:18-19, Ephesians 2:19-22, 1 Corinthians 1:11-13, 1 Corinthians 3:3-11, Matthew 23:8-10, Ephesians 4:11-13, John 16:13, 2 Corinthians 3:17-18.

God is completely consistent in all He does. Thus, in order to better understand the role and function of Jesus as builder of His church, it will be helpful to refer back to the account of the construction of the temple in Jerusalem during the reign of King Solomon.

Although God had given David the design of the temple and it was he who gathered much of the material for the building of it, yet it was God's will that it would be David's son Solomon, whose name means 'peaceable', who would direct and oversee the temple's construction. 1 Chronicles 28:1-19.

The temple on Mount Zion was to be the permanent dwelling place of God among His people Israel, so it was constructed of stone. *'The house, while it was being built, was built of stone prepared at the quarry, and there was neither hammer nor axe nor any iron tool heard in the house while it was being built'.* 1 Kings 6:7. We note that the stones were *'prepared at the quarry'*. On arrival at the building site each stone had been shaped to fit exactly in the place selected for it. *'....there was neither hammer nor axe nor any iron tool heard in the house while it was being built'*. No work was done at the site of the building even to add finishing touches to any stone.

We may say that the quarry, in which the stones for the temple were being prepared, is a type of the various settings and circumstances in which the Lord places His people during their earthly life. The Master stonemason in the quarry is the Spirit of the Living God for it is He *'who is at work in you, both to will and to work for His good pleasure'*. Philippians 2:13. The Holy Spirit will perform His perfecting work in each one of us as we allow Him to do so.

When we read in 1 Peter 2:5 *'....you also, as living stones, are being built up as a spiritual house....'* we must realize that *'living stones'* for the building are perfected stones. As in the case of the building of the temple in Jerusalem, only perfected stones will be ready to be fitted into their allotted place in God's building.

In Matthew 16:15-18 we read of an occasion when Jesus questioned His disciples, *"But who do you say that I am?"* Peter gave an inspired answer, *"You are the Christ, the Son of the living God."* In response Jesus informed him, *"I also say to you that you are Peter, and upon this rock I will build My church...."* Only One can be *'this rock'* (petra – a mass of rock) and only one will build His church and that One is Jesus.

That Jesus is the foundation for the building is affirmed in Ephesians 2:20: *'Christ Jesus Himself being the corner stone'*. Jesus is not only the builder of His church but He is also the corner stone to which the whole building is aligned and on which the whole building depends.

"Therefore you are to be perfect, as your heavenly Father is perfect." Matthew 5:48. Just as the corner stone is perfect so all that is built upon this stone must also be perfect. When Jesus commanded His disciples to be perfect He spoke to them individually and also as a community of His followers, for it is the Father's intention that perfected individuals be built together into a perfect community of believers, His ekklesia, that will one day be His Son's perfect bride. *'And I saw the holy city, new Jerusalem, coming down out of heaven from God, made ready as a bride adorned for her husband'*. Revelation 21:2.

All true believers in *'Christ Jesus'* are fellow citizens with all other believers of all the ages right back to Adam. *'....So then you are no longer strangers and aliens, but you are fellow citizens with the saints, and are of God's household'*, having been built on the foundation of the apostles and prophets'. Ephesians 2:19-20. In Revelation 21:14 we read, *'And the wall of the city had twelve foundation stones, and on them were the twelve names of the twelve apostles of the Lamb'*. Peter's name (petros – a piece of rock) is surely one of these.

'According to the grace of God which was given to me, like a wise master builder I laid a foundation, and another is building on it. But each man must be careful how he builds on it, 'For no man can lay

a foundation other than the one which is laid, which is Jesus Christ'. 1 Corinthians 3:10-11. The foundation that Paul built upon had already been laid, Jesus Christ. Paul, *'according to the grace of God'*, was a master builder in the hands of the Lord Jesus.

Regrettably, over the centuries, countless other foundations have been laid, no doubt with good intentions at the time; Anglican, Presbyterian, Lutheran, Methodist, Baptist, Pentecostal to name but a few.

1 Corinthians 11:11-13. *'For I have been informed concerning you, my brethren, by Chloe's people, that there are quarrels among you. Now I mean this, that each one of you is saying, "I am of Paul," and "I of Apollos," and "I of Cephas," and "I of Christ." Has Christ been divided? Paul was not crucified for you, was he? Or were you baptized in the name of Paul?'* The jealousy and strife among the believers in Corinth was focused on human heroes; Paul, Apollos, Cephas. Those who said they were *'of Christ'* were also doing so out of partisanship.

When any company of Christians exalts and identifies with its own versions of Paul, Apollos and Cephas an unimaginable consequence must follow - the Person, absolute authority and sovereignty of the Lord Jesus Christ among His people will be set aside. God has said, *'My glory I will not give to another'*. Isaiah 42:8.

If what has been built, or is being built, is on the foundation of Jesus Christ there will be no names, no heroes, no exalted ones to follow, no pet doctrines and no divisions. All will focus upon Christ. Believers must heed Paul's caution that they build alone on the foundation of Jesus Christ. All that is a substitute for Christ, or competes with Christ for focus and attention; all that is not built directly upon the one foundation of Christ will form part of *'Babylon the great, the mother of harlots'*.

This should present a real warning and admonition to believers everywhere. If, as the body of Christ, we would bear His testimony and carry out His great commission in the power of the Spirit, then He must be lifted up among us, central and supreme, as builder of His church. That *'at the name of Jesus every knee will bow, of those who are in heaven and on earth and under the earth, and that every tongue will confess that Jesus Christ is Lord, to the glory of God the Father'.* Philippians 2:10-11.

Matthew 23:8,10. *"But do not be called Rabbi; for One is your Teacher, and you are all brothers....One is your Leader, that is, Christ."* There are no titles or positions in the kingdom of heaven. All are gifts to the one body; some greater gifts and some lesser gifts. There is only one Rabbi, one Teacher and one Leader. All His true followers throughout the ages, including the apostle Paul, are all brothers. Acts 21:18-20.

In Ephesians 4:11 the original Greek text reads *'....And He gave some apostles, and some prophets, and some evangelists, and some pastors and teachers';* not as most translations incorrectly state, *'And He gave some* 'as' *apostles....'* etc. The greater gifts to the body listed here are exactly that – gifts. They are not titles or positions. They are greater gifts and, as such, more is required of them. We may recall the admonition, *'Let not many of you become teachers, my brethren, knowing that as such we will incur a stricter judgment'.* James 3:1.

The role of the greater gifts is to equip believers to better perform their work of service so that, by the operation of each and every member, the body may continuously be built up *'until we all attain to the unity of the faith, and of the knowledge of the Son of God, to a mature man, to the measure of the stature which belongs to the fullness of Christ'.* Ephesians 4:13.

"But when He, the Spirit of truth, comes, He will guide you into all the truth'. Who is referred to as *'you'* here? Surely it is everyone in whom the *'Spirit of truth'* dwells. *"He will guide you into all the truth....He will disclose to you what is to come...."* John 16:13. When believers offer allegiance to their version of Paul or Apollos and give prominence to such ones above the rest this will inevitably lead to great spiritual loss. What will be lost? The right and freedom of every member of Christ's body to contribute their gift to build up the body of Christ in speaking, teaching, exhorting, admonishing and encouraging their fellow members as led by the Holy Spirit. 1 Corinthians 14: 31-32. Living stones must be worked on and shaped to fit perfectly into God's eternal dwelling place, yet how can they

be worked on and shaped if they are not permitted or enabled to express the life of God with others of like mind?

'But we all with unveiled face, beholding and reflecting like a mirror the glory of the Lord, are being transformed into the same image from glory to glory, even as from the Lord the Spirit'. 2 Corinthians 3:18, Recovery Version. By the time Paul wrote his second letter to the church in Corinth it is evident that they were experiencing meetings such as these. If in our gatherings together today we are not *'beholding and reflecting like a mirror the glory of the Lord'* we must be prevented from doing so by the greatest of all errors. We must be beholding someone other than Christ, for the glory of God which transforms cannot be mistaken.

The good news is that we may indeed enjoy and benefit from glorious meetings such as these if *'He, the Spirit of truth'* who *'....will guide you into all the truth'* is truly Lord.

In His day the Pharisees had Jesus standing right in front of them, yet they did not recognize Him. Sadly, there are times when believers may be unaware that Jesus is outside their assembly knocking on the door. *'Behold, I stand at the door and knock; if anyone hears My voice and opens the door, I will come in to him and will dine with him, and he with Me'.* Revelation 3:20. Anyone in that assembly who hears His voice may open the door of his heart to Jesus and He will come into that one and will dine with Him.

Many who long for more than is available to them in their local assembly find enjoyment in a very personal and private relationship with Jesus. They have invited Him to make His home in their heart. Yet how such ones must long to be among a whole company of those whose eyes are filled with their glorious Lord as He is in the midst?

As Jesus takes His rightful place as the builder of His church, those who place themselves together under His Lordship will experience glorious transformation together into His image and likeness. As we, His people, come to Him, meet with Him, listen to Him, obey Him, praise and worship Him, glorify Him and speak as the Spirit leads and prompts, in His full authority and power, this will be our experience - *'....But we all, with unveiled face, beholding as in a mirror the glory of the Lord, are being transformed into the same image from glory to glory, just as from the Lord, the Spirit'.*

The glory the Father gave His Son has been given to us that we may all be one. John 17:22. The proper functioning of each individual member will cause *'the growth, of the body for the building up of itself in love'.* Ephesians 4:16.

Paul may have recognized that he was a master builder, yet he will have been acutely aware that the one doing the building through him was He who assured us, *"I will build My church."*

CHAPTER 5
THE CHURCH WHICH IS HIS BODY

Scripture references: Matthew 18:19-20, Mark 6:7-13, Luke 10:1-21, Mark 6:7, Luke 10:1, Acts 13:1-4, 1 Corinthians 12:18-27, Ephesians 2:14-22, Hebrews 12:1-2.

The words of the Lord Jesus quoted from Matthew 18:20 are among the best known and most treasured by believers. They are His words of comfort that assure us that He is present in the midst of even two who meet together in His name. Yet within this statement is contained much more than comfort. Jesus is providing the simplest expression of what constitutes the church, which is His body and that will one day be His bride.

The words *'I am there in their midst'* leave no doubt of Jesus' central place whenever believers meet in His name. All power in heaven and on earth resides in Jesus. In His name even two believers in Jesus may call upon heaven to act in response to their joint request; *"Again I say to you, that if two of you agree on earth about anything that they may ask, it shall be done for them by My Father who is in heaven."* Matthew 18:19.

In these brief statements the Lord Jesus is describing the simplicity of what constitutes His church on earth. In fact, if we comprehend the significance of what He is saying we shall have to acknowledge that what most of Christendom practices is far, far removed from Almighty God's desire and what He has freely made available to us.

The word in the Greek for 'church' is 'ekklesia'. This Greek word is used 119 times in the New Testament. On at least 92 occasions it refers to a 'local' assembly of believers. The implication of the word 'ekklesia' is of 'called out ones gathered unto Him'. In other words whenever two or more believers meet together under the lordship of Jesus Christ then, right there, is an expression of the whole church, His body. The place of their meeting, the occasion of their meeting, and their position relative to each other is immaterial. He is Lord and those gathered unto Him are brothers. Matthew 23:8.

When two or more meet together in His name there is no requirement of intermediaries or experts. Jesus is their intermediary and He is the source of their wisdom. As we accept this basic truth we will realize how impossible it would be to eradicate every expression of the church on earth. However difficult life on earth may become it will only take one brother meeting with another, with Jesus in their midst, to represent the united testimony of Jesus, His church.

When two or more meet in Jesus name He is in their midst as Lord and they constitute the smallest viable expression of the church. Two who ask anything in agreement can call upon more power than all this world's rulers who rely upon their fleshly wisdom.

The record of the Lord sending forth the twelve is found in each of the first three Gospels, but Mark 6:7 informs us that the Lord sent them out in pairs. In Luke 10:1 we read of the seventy being commissioned by Jesus' and also being sent forth in pairs. In neither case is there inference or mention of one or other taking precedence, simply that He sent them out with a clear purpose and gave them His authority. He bestowed upon them for these missions the authority of the Holy Spirit.

In Acts 13 is the account of the sending forth of Barnabas and Saul *'for the work to which I have called them'*. The Holy Spirit spoke through a prophetic utterance and the believers unitedly laid hands on the two of them to confirm their agreement with the Holy Spirit's injunction. Having been commissioned as apostles they immediately set out in obedience. Although Barnabas is mentioned first by name there is no inference that he was in charge. Later it is noteworthy that Paul's name is mentioned first yet still with no connotation of precedence.

When Paul and Barnabas disputed about the inclusion of John Mark as a companion for their next journey, it came about because Paul perceived the mind of the Lord and Barnabas 'leaned on his own understanding'. Barnabas departed to Cyprus with Mark and the Lord chose Silvanus, i.e. Silas, to accompany Paul.

In God's arrangement it appears that He desires balance between those He uses and sends forth. In the kingdom of God there is no place for individualism. Two united together in Jesus' name, meeting under the authority of the Holy Spirit, represent that vital and indivisible basic unit of the church.

How little heed is paid by the vast majority of assemblies today to 1 Corinthians chapters 12 and 14, considering their great significance. Whether two members, or two hundred, are gathered unto Jesus, they will be members one of another, in mutual dependence on that which each member supplies. Honour is to be bestowed upon all, but titles shall be accorded to none. One is our Master and His title is Lord.

'But now in Christ Jesus you who formerly were far off have been brought near by the blood of Christ. For He Himself is our peace, who made both groups into one and broke down the barrier of the dividing wall....' Ephesians 2:13-14. These verses from Ephesians 2 are an important reminder that Jews and Gentiles have been reconciled together to be the one body of the Lord Jesus Christ. Through the blood of Christ the believing Gentiles have been made one with the believing Jews. This wonderful reality has not only brought together believing Jews and Gentiles but it has also sealed the unbreakable unity between all believers, in all assemblies, in all communities, in all the nations, in every age. To live in division by acting contrary to this great unalterable reality is a terrible sin.

It is important to remember that should any two or more who meet together not be in unity in the Spirit they will not be able to call down the mighty power of God, nor will they be granted authority to act together in His name. This was the situation that Paul was facing in the Corinthian assembly where each one was saying, "I am of Paul," and "I of Apollos," and "I of Cephas," and "I of Christ." To which Paul responded 'Has Christ been divided'?

To be in agreement of heart must precede agreement concerning any specific matter. Surely this spirit of division is what is rendering the church on earth so impotent today. God has one 'household' to which all those who have believed in His Son Jesus are members, in love, undivided, and of one purpose, for through Him we all have *'access in one Spirit to the Father'*.

Ephesians 2:16 *'.... And might reconcile them both in one body to God through the cross....'* This passage from Ephesians expresses the wonders of what His people shall experience together as they enter into the peace that He has wrought for them through the cross. When the building is complete, they all will have been *'built on the foundation of the apostles and prophets, Christ Jesus Himself being the corner stone'*. This great building of God's design will, one day, be displayed as *'the holy city, new Jerusalem, coming down out of heaven from God made ready as a bride adorned for her Husband'*. Revelation 21:2.

'Therefore, since we have so great a cloud of witnesses surrounding us, let us also lay aside every encumbrance and the sin which so easily entangles us, and let us run with endurance the race that is set before us, fixing our eyes on Jesus, the author and perfecter of faith....' Hebrews 12:1-2. These verses provide an extraordinary picture of the immensity of the household into which believers have entered. For, not only may the two or more meet together with the supreme and exalted person of Jesus in their midst, but they will be surrounded by the whole company of those who have run their race and have finished their course. These ones are actively and unitedly encouraging all those who are still running their race to press on with urgency. It is impossible to imagine a stadium so immense that it could contain such a vast company of cheering spectators; the faithful ones of all the ages, not only from Pentecost and onwards, but encompassing all of the faithful back to Adam.

In this greatest of all races those who are running are not rivals of each other but, on the contrary, are wholly encouragers of each other, that all must keep running, looking away to He who is positioned at the finishing line – Jesus.

May the Lord give us a fresh vision of what He has given us to be an eternal part; *'the church which is His body'*.

CHAPTER 6
JESUS CHRIST IS LORD

Scripture references: Philippians 2:5-13, Isaiah 14:14-15, Matthew 28:18-20, John 14:8-18, Hebrews 12:7-10.

In Philippians 2:5-11 we have a very unique description of humility, the humility of the Son of God made Son of Man: *'Have this attitude in yourselves which was also in Christ Jesus'*. Only the power of God and His unrestricted operation in us could bring us to such a humble attitude as this; yet, were it impossible for us to *'have this attitude'* it would not be commanded of us. Surely, though, in this exhortation lies the secret of living out our earthly life and fully accomplishing our part of the Father's will.

The Lord Jesus *'existed in the form of God'* but He *'did not regard equality with God a thing to be grasped'*. He forever has the highest place with the Father and the Holy Spirit. He is the creator of all things that exist, yet He willingly set aside all the honour due to Him for a while, in order to do His Father's will. Even more than that, *'He emptied Himself, taking the form of a bond-servant ....being made in the likeness of men'*.

The attitude of the Lord Jesus is in direct contrast with the attitude of Satan. *'....you said in your heart, "I will ascend to heaven; I will raise my throne above the stars of God, and I will sit on the mount of assembly in the recesses of the north'. I will ascend above the heights of the clouds; I will make myself like the Most High."'* Isaiah 14:14. Satan's intention was to elevate himself above *'the stars of God'*, the angels, and make himself equal with God.

'Being found in appearance as a man, He humbled Himself by becoming obedient to the point of death, even death on a cross'. Satan's rebellion and all its consequences were dealt with completely and forever through the cross of Christ. God's sentence upon Satan is *"Nevertheless you will be thrust down to Sheol, to the recesses of the pit."* Isaiah 14:15.

Because Jesus *'humbled Himself by becoming obedient to the point of death, even death on a cross'*, God highly exalted Him, and bestowed on Him the name which is above every name, so that at *the name of Jesus every knee will bow'*. All mankind, the living and the dead, the redeemed and the lost, young and old, all will bow the knee confessing *'that Jesus Christ is Lord....'*

Men and women of every nation and language bow down with awe and wonder before Him; even at the mention of His name! The Son's Almighty Father does not simply suggest we do this, He commands it. May we who love Him *'have this attitude'* of utter humility. Jesus Christ is Lord!

In verses 5 through 11 is a description of what the Lord Jesus laid aside, and the pathway of suffering He willingly endured in obedience to His Father's will. Every knee will bow to Him; every tongue will confess His Lordship *'to the glory of God the Father'*. As we read these words we are inclined to linger in the wonder of it all. However, what comes next is of vital importance to us because, in light of what we have just read, Paul exhorts us to apply ourselves to urgent action.

'So then, my beloved, just as you have always obeyed, not as in my presence only, but now much more in my absence, work out your salvation with fear and trembling; for it is God who is at work in you, both to will and to work for His good pleasure'. *'So then'* he says (these two words carry great emphasis). What Paul is implying is this – 'in response to what the Holy Spirit through me is telling you, this is what you must do'.

Paul exhorts us to diligently work out our salvation *'with fear and trembling'*. Why? Because the One He has just been describing, Jesus the Lord, before whom every knee will bow, is the one who is at work in us *'both to will and to work for His good pleasure'*.

Why might so many of us be experiencing this awesome and all-prevailing Presence so fleetingly in our daily life? Is it perhaps because our vision is cluttered with the cares of this world? Why might we be experiencing this awesome and all-prevailing Presence so rarely in our assemblies? Might it be because He, the Lord Jesus Christ, is not filling our vision? Are we so used to looking to substitutes that we are perhaps unaware that we have settled down complacently into a state of apostasy?

What disrespect is shown to Almighty God if we deny His Son Jesus Christ His rightful place as Lord. Surely, if Jesus was visibly present in our local assembly or gatherings, would those attending have eyes and ears for anyone else but Him? There would be no planned order of service and no on-stage music leadership team; His would be the sole and absolute authority to speak or act through whomever He would choose to anoint.

When the Lord Jesus was manifested in the flesh, His followers had no doubt that He was Lord. Peter's great revelation echoes down the ages, *"You are the Christ, the Son of the living God."* Matthew 16:16. When He sent out the twelve, and later the seventy, He gave them His authority to carry out His instructions. His very last command to His disciples, before He returned to glory, contains the unequivocal phrase *"All authority has been given to Me in heaven and on earth. Go therefore...."* Matthew 28:18-19a. All authority in heaven and on earth is invested in Jesus and He shares His authority only with those to whom He is truly Lord.

A short time before His atoning death Jesus told the disciples of His departure, while assuring them *"I will ask the Father, and He will give you another Helper, that He may be with you forever; that is the Spirit of truth, whom the world cannot receive, because it does not see Him or know Him, but you know Him because He abides with you and will be in you. I will not leave you as orphans; I will come to you"*. John 14:16-18.

We may ask how was the Holy Spirit abiding with them? He abode with them in the person of Jesus. Who was the one who was going to be with them forever? The Spirit of truth. Yet Jesus assured them that He in person was also going to come to them – in the Spirit. He later comforted His disciples with the words *"lo, I am with you always, even to the end of the age."* Matthew 28:20.

A careful study of John Chapter 14 will reveal that it is the Godhead that is at work in us, to will and to work of His good pleasure; the Father, through the Son, by the Spirit. This unimaginable flow of power into us is available to perform God's full and complete work in us as individuals. His authority has been given to us that we might present His testimony before the world and before Satan and his minions.

At Pentecost the first believers were *'clothed with power from on high'* in the blessed person of the Holy Spirit that He might, through them and through all following generations of believers, perform and complete the full work of God. *'For we are His masterpiece, created in Christ Jesus for good works, which God prepared beforehand in order that we would walk in them'*. Ephesians 2:10, Recovery Version. His masterpiece, *'the bride, the wife of the Lamb'* was created in Christ Jesus for a purpose; namely, *'good works, which God prepared beforehand in order that we would walk in them'*. How awesome that the deeds that God purposed and planned in eternity past were to be carried out by those whom He called and chose to be His disciples.

Concerning the church in Laodicea we read that the Lord Jesus was outside knocking on the door. Revelation 3:20 *'Behold, I stand at the door and knock; if anyone hears My voice and opens the door, I will come in to him and will dine with him, and he with Me'*. He was not knocking to be let into that assembly but, rather, that if anyone in the assembly was listening to His voice and would open the door of his heart to Him, He would come into that one and He would dine with him. *'He who has an ear, let him hear what the Spirit says to the churches'*. Revelation 3:22.

If Jesus, in the Spirit, is not the supreme and central focus and the director over all the proceedings when we meet together then we are 'playing' church and attempting to organize Him into our plans. I well remember, long ago, a dear brother in Christ put the issue like this – "If He is not Lord of all He is not Lord at all".

Throughout all the Scriptures, including the pre-incarnation appearances of Jesus in the Old Testament, He is displayed consistently as Lord. By Jericho He was revealed as Captain of the Lord's host before whom Joshua removed his sandals. He was the fourth one whom Nebuchadnezzar saw walking in the midst of the fiery furnace with Hananiah, Mishael and Azariah. It is the Father's determined will that to mankind and to all creation Jesus be accorded unquestioned and unchallenged pre-eminence. Nothing we think, plan or do will have any value whatsoever unless the Lord Jesus is the author of it, the focus of it, and the director of it. Jesus Himself said *"apart from Me* [cut off from vital union with Me] *you can do nothing"*. John 15:5, AMP.

In the world today, and throughout past history, measurements of success are common. For example, 'Hers was a fine performance' or 'He did his best'. In the kingdom of heaven there are only two outcomes; namely victory or defeat, life or death, depending on whether the mind is set on the flesh or on the Spirit; if the mind is set on the Spirit then the evidence in the individual and in the assembly will be *'life and peace'*. Furthermore, those who are fully yielded to the will of God, being continually led by His Spirit, *'are sons of God'*. His measure of our success is that we become sons of God.

Both male and female believers are proven to be sons of God through yielding themselves to His discipline. *'It is for discipline that you endure; God deals with you as with sons; for what son is there whom his father does not discipline? But if you are without discipline, of which all have become partakers, then you are illegitimate children and not sons. Furthermore, we had earthly fathers to discipline us, and we respected them; shall we not much rather be subject to the Father of spirits, and live? For they disciplined us for a short time as seemed best to them, but He disciplines us for our good, so that we may share His holiness'*. Hebrews 12:7-10

The work of the Father, through the Son, in the Holy Spirit, is to bring *'many sons to glory'*, as the increase of His Son, to be His body, the church, His bride. The body of Christ is one (not an array of disorganized fragments). It carries His image, it exercises His authority, it performs His will upon this earth; it is God's living and united testimony to an unbelieving world that *'Jesus Christ is Lord'*.

CHAPTER 7
DO THIS IN REMEMBRANCE OF ME

Scripture references: 1 Corinthians 11:23-29, 1 Corinthians 10:16-17, Acts 2:46, Acts 20:7-12, 1 Peter 4:12-13, John 6:53-58, Romans 8:18.

Long after the event itself, Paul received from the Lord an exact account of His sharing the bread and the wine with His disciples *'in the night in which He was betrayed'*. In his first letter to the church in Corinth Paul provides valuable additional insights into the meaning and significance of the Lord's Supper, which many refer to as Communion.

In 1 Corinthians 11:23-25 we read that the Lord Jesus *'took bread and when He had given thanks, He broke it and said, "This is My body, which is for you; do this in remembrance of Me." After He had taken the cup He said "This cup is the new covenant in My blood; do this, as often as you drink it, in remembrance of Me."* Jesus' heart's desire is that, through this simple yet profound act, His disciples (and all who would become His disciples) would remember what He has made available to them through suffering; that they would remember Him often in this special way by participating together in the bread and the wine.

Is not the cup of blessing which we bless a sharing in the blood of Christ? Is not the bread which we break a sharing in the body of Christ? Since there is one bread, we who are many are one body; for we all partake of the one bread. 1 Corinthians 10:16-17. Paul describes a symbolic aspect of the Lord's table in making the point that the *'one bread'* represents *'one body'* (the body of Christ that comprises all from the past and all from the present who have truly believed in God's redemptive act in Jesus). He brings to the attention of the Corinthians that this *'one bread'* signifies unbreakable unity. In 1 Corinthians 1:13 Paul had put this question *'has Christ been divided'?* As the Father, the Son and the Holy Spirit are one so is the body of Christ one and indivisible.

It is certain that, following Pentecost, the Holy Spirit was exercising unquestioned Lordship over the growing number of believers. At that time we read, *'breaking bread from house to house, they were taking their meals together with gladness and sincerity of heart....'* Acts 2:46. Remembering the Lord's death and, above all, remembering Him with joy was a regular happening and formed part of the believers' sharing their meals together. There was no one officiating over these joyful and grateful remembrances except the blessed Lord Jesus Himself, in whose presence these early believers lived and functioned.

Many years later, assemblies of believers had been established throughout much of the Roman Empire, largely through the apostolic ministry of Paul and his companions. In Acts 20:7 we have an example of the assembly in Troas remembering the death of the Lord Jesus: *'On the first day of the week, when we were gathered together to break bread....'* The emphasis of the words *'gathered together to break bread'* strongly suggests that this was the central purpose of their meeting together and also that the Lord's table meeting was a weekly practice celebrated on the day of the week on which our Lord rose from the dead. For this purpose the assembly in Troas met to *'proclaim the Lord's death until He comes'*. 1 Corinthians 11:26.

In the Jewish calendar the first day of the week commences at sundown, which is 6 p.m. on our Saturday. This provides perspective to the fact that Paul *'prolonged his message until midnight'*. Acts 20:7.

So Jesus said to them, "Truly, truly, I say to you, unless you eat the flesh of the Son of Man and drink His blood, you have no life in yourselves. "He who eats My flesh and drinks My blood has eternal life, and I will raise him up on the last day. "For My flesh is true food, and My blood is true drink. "He who eats My flesh and drinks My blood abides in Me, and I in him. John 6:53-58. How wonderfully these precious words of Jesus describe the value of His people gathering unto Him to celebrate the Lord's Supper, Communion. His body given for us made His divine life available to us. His blood shed for us brought us redemption. Thus to eat the flesh of the Son of Man and to drink His blood is to receive an abundance of His life into us; His redeeming life, His transforming life, the very divine life of God.

In 1 Corinthians 11:27-29 Paul mentions judging the body rightly; that the body is one and indivisible. All who partake of the Lord's table must hold dear and inviolable their unity in Christ with all other believers present, and with all communities of believers across the face of the earth. John 11:51-52 makes plain that Jesus not only died for the Jewish nation but *'that He might also gather together into one the children of God who are scattered abroad'*.

In view of what the elements of bread and wine signify, one of the saddest of conditions in Christendom is its present state of disunity. How can we *'proclaim the Lord's death until He comes'* if we do not approach the elements of bread and wine in a true spirit of unity and reconciliation?

From the early accounts it is certain that celebrating the Lord's table, or Communion, has fallen into much lower significance in the visible church today and is, for the most part, conducted among companies of people who are divided on the basis of doctrine and organization. Yet, might there also be an even deeper reason for the neglect of gathering together to remember Him?

Much attention is paid in the Scriptures to the necessity and benefit of sharing in Jesus' sufferings on the part of those who love Him and wish to follow Him fully. Consider the following quotations and ponder on the very special joy that comes from our willingness to suffer for Jesus sake.

'....For you have been granted [the privilege] *for Christ's sake not only to believe in* (adhere to, rely on, and trust in) *Him, but also to suffer in His behalf'*. Philippians 1:29, AMP. Suffering on behalf of Christ is a gift from God and a privilege to those to whom it is given.

In 1 Peter 4:12-13 we read, *'Beloved, do not be surprised at the fiery ordeal among you, which comes upon you for your testing, as though some strange thing were happening to you; but to the degree that you share the sufferings of Christ, keep on rejoicing'*. In this statement Peter emphasizes the collective sharing in the sufferings of Christ *'that also at the revelation of His glory you may rejoice with exultation'*. This example also demonstrates that, just as suffering was the pathway to glory for the Lord Jesus, so it will also be for those of His own who willingly choose this path to glory. *'....For I consider that the sufferings of this present time are not worthy to be compared with the glory which shall be revealed in us'*. Romans 8:18, NKJV.

Of the Lord Jesus we read, *'who for the joy set before Him endured the cross, despising the shame, and has sat down at the right hand of the throne of God'*. If we connect these words which refer to Jesus with 2 Timothy 2:11-12 we shall see that, similarly, suffering for His sake will bring with it an amazing reward: *'It is a trustworthy statement: For if we died with Him, we will also live with Him; If we endure, we will also reign with Him...'*

In all the instances mentioned, suffering is connected with joy, glory, reigning with Jesus. In Colossians 1:24 Paul expresses joy in being called upon to suffer, *'Now I rejoice in my sufferings for your sake, and in my flesh I do my share on behalf of His body, which is the church, in filling up what is lacking in Christ's afflictions'*. He shows that an amount of suffering has been left to fill up *'what is lacking in Christ's afflictions'* on behalf of His body, the church. Herein is an amazing truth. Surely, to fill up what yet remains of the sufferings of Christ has been left as a very special privilege for those who love Him.

We may look at today's situation and note with sadness the widespread complacency and worldliness, yet are not all who have come to Christ for salvation part of Christ's one body? Knowing this deplorable condition among so many believers, are we willing to suffer for His sake on their behalf? Some of us have perhaps already suffered more from members of the body of Christ than from unbelievers. Yet *'consider Him who has endured such hostility by sinners against Himself, so that you will not grow weary and lose heart. You have not yet resisted to the point of shedding blood in your striving against sin'*. Hebrews 12:3-4.

Let us consider a few examples of the sufferings of the Lord Jesus.

- *'He was in the world, and the world was made through Him, and the world did not know Him. He came to His own, and those who were His own did not receive Him'*. John 1:10-11

- During the last supper the disciples argued among themselves who was the greatest. The Lord demonstrated to His disciples that He who is greatest is truly servant of all, by washing their feet.
- Shortly before His betrayal, the travesty of His trial and His unjustified cruel treatment and crucifixion, the Lord Jesus asked His disciples to watch with Him while He prayed. They fell asleep.
- When the mob came to capture Him in the garden of Gethsemane, all His disciples forsook Him and fled. Jesus was left utterly alone in what was to follow.
- He was falsely accused and condemned as a criminal. The multitude of *'His own'* demanded that He be crucified, although Pilate was willing to release Him.
- He not only endured the cruel agonies of the cross, but He took upon Himself the sin of the whole world; suffering far beyond that which anyone has ever been called upon to bear.

Sad to say, the most plausible reason for the neglect of *'doing this in remembrance of Me'* is because so few know what it means to suffer for Jesus' sake. The path of suffering will only be followed by those who have willingly taken up their cross to follow Jesus. Accepting God's free gift of salvation is not so hard; taking up our cross to follow Him is costly. Singing the happy songs of what the Lord Jesus has wrought for us may be light hearted and comforting; but walking the blood-stained trail that leads to pleasing Him is often filled with pain and rejection. James exhorts us: *'Consider it all joy, my brethren, when you encounter various trials'*. James 1:2.

To enter into the reality of communion with Jesus will take a completely new mind-set. As we are yoked with Jesus and share in His sufferings we shall more and more embrace Paul's overwhelming desire *'that I may know Him'*. The introversion of self-love will incrementally give place to divine love. For love of Jesus we will go to any length to seek and to save what is lost, or to pay the ultimate price to restore what has been damaged or destroyed through the evil operations of Satan. To be in communion with Jesus is to be in a state of unity in heart and attitude with He who *'For the joy set before Him endured the cross despising the shame'*.

On the first day of every week it is so good to meet together in company to remember and to pour out our gratitude and praise to the Lord; for the work of God in our lives; for special blessings received; for revelations from the Word; for His unfailing care and provision. At a high point of that special Spirit-led experience there will be a moment when the unleavened bread may be broken and distributed and the cup be shared. Oh! What a joy there is in remembering together in unity, identified with Him through suffering, in overflowing love and praise, *'the Lord's death until He comes'*.

CHAPTER 8
MAKING THE MOST OF YOUR TIME

Scripture references: 1 Peter 4:17-19, Matthew 24:44, NKJV, Hebrews 10:24-25, James 4:4 NKJV, Ephesians 5:15-17, 1 Corinthians 6:19-20, 2 Timothy 3:1-5.

"For those days will be a time of tribulation such as has not occurred since the beginning of the creation which God created until now, and never will." Mark 13:19. These are the words of Jesus about the days that are now so fast approaching, *'a time of tribulation'*. These will be days of judgment on mankind to try men's hearts.

Judgment begins with the household of God according to 1 Peter 4:17. Why would God's judgment begin first with believers? We who believe unto salvation have been entrusted with God's authority to act on His behalf as His representatives before an unbelieving world as the testimony of Jesus. We must confess on behalf of ourselves and of our brethren in Christ that, at best, that testimony has not been as it was in the church at its inception.

For those who know not the Lord the tribulation will be a time of turmoil, a time of chaos, *'....men fainting from fear and the expectation of the things which are coming upon the world'*. Luke 21:26. On the other hand, for those who will *'entrust their souls to a faithful Creator in doing what is right'*, 1 Peter 4:19, this will be an intense time of refining and purification that they may be transformed into the likeness of their beloved Master. Only those who entrust their souls to a faithful Creator will be ready when the Bridegroom comes. *"Therefore you also be ready, for the Son of Man is coming at an hour you do not expect."* Matthew 24:44. NKJV.

On every hand today there is a sense that our world is heading into some very difficult and challenging times. Among believers there is a deepening sense, not only of testing times ahead, but that the *'day is drawing near'*. Not the day that many misinformed Christians have been told about, a catching away of all believers before the time of tribulation begins, but the day when the kingdom of this world will become *'the kingdom of our God and of His Christ'*; the day that will be preceded by seven years of tribulation, the last three and a half years of which will be 'the great tribulation'.

The words of Hebrews 10:24 admonish us, as we *'see the day drawing near'*, that we should *'stimulate one another to love and good deeds'*; not forsaking *'our own assembling together'*, but we should meet together *'all the more'*. Believers are a gathering people, a meeting people around their Lord. We are to display the glories of *'Him who has called us out of darkness into His glorious light'*.

In view of these facts presented we must not misuse or waste the time allotted to us either as individuals or as a community of God's people. For instance, as is the case in the western world, can it be His will that members of *'the household of God'* forsake many of their regular gatherings together for a three month summer break?

Our individual and corporate testimony to Jesus is displayed in the constancy of our love for Him, for one another, our concern for the lost who need Christ and for the lonely who can always be found among, or close to, our Christian communities. The latter are often of limited financial means who will have no opportunity of travel or visiting family and friends. If they lose their support group for such a long while they may feel very alone and vulnerable.

How stark is the comparison between this typical loosely knit church community and those gathered during the first century AD in a local ekklesia in Jerusalem, or in one of the many assemblies throughout the Roman world.

How urgent and all important was 'the great commission' to the first apostles and to all those early believers in Jesus who were on fire to play their God-ordained part to carry it out. In the church in Jerusalem they sold their homes and possessions in order to share in a common life of faith and love for Jesus. They did so that they might go *'and make disciples of all the nations....baptizing them.... teaching them'*. Thus they were ready to go as soon as the Lord should send them forth.

All those who followed Jesus were active in fulfilling their part in this all-consuming task. It is also clear that the family life of believers at that time was lived in the broader context of the local community of Christians.

How easy it is for many, when regular sources of fellowship are suspended, to drift away and join hands with the world in following the same worldly pursuits and interests. *'Adulterers and adulteresses! Do you not know that friendship with the world is enmity with God? Whoever therefore wants to be a friend of the world makes himself an enemy of God'.* James 4:4, NKJV. These are strong words, yet much of what Christians today accept as normal and acceptable is in sharp contrast with the behaviour and standards those early believers held dear. Many, like Stephen, paid the ultimate price of martyrdom because of their uncompromising faith.

The admonition in Ephesians 5:16 is quite specific; *'making the most of your time, because the days are evil'*. We might well ask whether the days in which we live are any less evil than they were in Ephesus in Paul's day. Those who profess and call themselves Christians have no business serving Satan and his tempting distractions. If Jesus is indeed Lord among us may we recognize that our time belongs wholly to Him. We are to be the shining forth to the world of the great light of God, the *'city that is set on a hill which cannot be hidden'*.

Taking this a step further; distraction occurs on each and every occasion that the Holy Spirit is not Lord, whether in our individual lives or in our assembling together. *'....do you not know that your body is a temple of the Holy Spirit who is in you, whom you have from God, and that you are not your own? For you have been bought with a price: therefore glorify God in your body'.* 1 Corinthians 6:19-20.

From the instant of the new birth not one single second of one single minute of one single hour of one single day of one single month of one single year belongs to a believer in Jesus. All we are, all we have, all the past and all the future belong solely and wholly to Him!

In the quotation from Ephesians the words *'making the most of your time'* (or *'redeeming the time'* in the original Greek) signify 'buying back the time' or 'rescuing the time from loss'. The time allotted to us on this earth is a limited resource and none of us knows how much time we have. Every idle moment or misused opportunity is lost for Jesus, lost for His kingdom, and lost for the one who wasted it. 1 Corinthians 3:11-13.

We are already living in the days described in 2 Timothy 3:1-5. In fact we have been living in them for some while now. Especially is this true in our western world. The words of Paul to Timothy spell out in detail God's evaluation of our civilization: '....*men will be lovers of self, lovers of money, boastful, arrogant, revilers, disobedient to parents, ungrateful, unholy, unloving, irreconcilable, malicious gossips, without self-control, brutal, haters of good, treacherous, reckless, conceited, lovers of pleasure rather than lovers of God....*' Those who have lived through the past several decades have watched a very evident and widespread descent into immoral, unethical and self-centred behaviour. All of the characteristics described above are very evident in our society today.

Note these words in verse 5, *'holding to a form of godliness, although they have denied its power....'* The literal translation of the Greek is 'holding to the mere form of a godly life' or as we sometimes say, 'going through the motions'. We may think this does not apply to believers, yet evidence of this lukewarmness is endemic. Complacency is everywhere in Christian communities today. Gatherings are frequently designed to cater to the preferences of those attending rather than to give the Lord the praise and worship due to Him. In simply *'holding to a form of godliness ....they have denied its power....'* to transform them into the living, genuine and undeniable testimony of Jesus.

In this respect verse 12 of this chapter in the Amplified text is informative, *'Indeed all who delight in piety and are determined to live a devoted and godly life in Christ Jesus will meet with persecution'*. Literally speaking, 'those who live righteously will be made to suffer because of their unwavering faith in Jesus'. How aptly do the words *'are determined to live a devoted and godly life in Christ Jesus'* describe the behaviour of those who commit themselves to Jesus and 'make the most of their time'.

If in Paul's era *'those who have wives should be as though they had none.... and those who use the world, as though they did not make full use of it'*, then should not this be so among us in our day, as the time of Jesus' sure return draws near? Family attachments and worldly concerns must be, for many of His people, where rescuing time from loss must begin.

At this point in our review of the Scriptures it is to be hoped that excuses for the summer break have been rendered insupportable.

In our materialistic, economy-driven western world we should take special note of these admonitions, *'those who buy, as though they did not possess; and those who use the world, as though they did not make full use of it; for the form of this world is passing away'*. 1 Corinthians 7:30. Add to these words the quotation from 1 John 2:15, *'Do not love the world nor the things in the world. If anyone loves the world, the love of the Father is not in him'*.

As we spend each day and as we spend the time allotted to us on this earth in the presence of Jesus, gazing into His wonderful face, running our race looking unto Him, hand in hand with others of undistracted gaze, what unparalleled joy will fill our hearts. Yet what will be most important is that we shall be using our time in carrying out the will of our Father and being well-pleasing to the Lord Jesus.

CHAPTER 9
HE GAVE SOME PROPHETS

Scripture references: Acts 13:1-2, Acts 11:19-20, 1 Corinthians 14:26-33, Jude 14, Ephesians 4:11-13, Matthew 24:37-38, Isaiah 40:3-5.

In both Old and New Testament times prophets have been raised up by God. In fact, from the New Testament era onwards, all the greater gifts - apostles, prophets, evangelists and pastor teachers have been chosen and empowered by God. The church of Jesus Christ knows no human design, no titled officials, nor hierarchy of control. The Holy Spirit may speak through whomever He chooses in order to issue a divine decree or to empower with His authority. For instance, God assigned Elijah to anoint Hazael king over Aram, Jehu king over Israel and Elisha as prophet in his place.

Prophets bring the instant word of God to whomever He sends them. This instant word may have an immediate or extended time application. In order to carry out their vital role prophets must spend much time in the presence of God that they may know the mind of the Lord. What He shows them and directs them to say, to whom He sends them, when He wants the message given, they must faithfully and precisely follow and carry out. We may recall the story of the prophet Jonah whom God dealt with very severely because he attempted to avoid going to Nineveh to proclaim God's message of destruction and compassion to the people of that great city.

In the first few verses of Acts 13 there is an account of the anointing and sending forth of two members of the assembly of believers in Antioch. The message from God that two of their number be sent forth as apostles came almost certainly through one of three prophets. This proved to be a key turning point in God's move to make disciples of all the nations. Why did this take place in Antioch? Because in Antioch at that time there were a people that closely represented God's full thought for His church in their operation, harmony and obedience.

'Now there were at Antioch, in the church that was there prophets and teachers....' Antioch appears seemingly out of nowhere to be the most prominent place in the Lord's move throughout the Roman

Empire and beyond. We do know from Acts 11:19-20 that believers *'came to Antioch'* following the persecution that arose at the time of the stoning of Stephen; and that, while some of these spoke to the Jews only, some men of Cyprus and Cyrene *'who came to Antioch....began speaking to the Greeks also....and a large number who believed turned to the Lord'*. It was to this assembly in Antioch that Barnabas brought Saul some eleven years after the stoning of Stephen. It is significant that, from the time of their arrival, the centre of God's operations moved from Jerusalem to Antioch.

What is of key importance is that there were prophets (who were also teachers) in the assembly in Antioch. From ancient times prophets had been termed seers, and with good reason, for they were the 'eyes' to see the will of God and to proclaim fully and accurately *"Thus says the Lord"* to His people.

"Set apart for Me Barnabas and Saul for the work to which I have called them." We cannot identify the prophet through whom the command came by the Holy Spirit, yet, because of its great importance, the word most likely came through Simeon, Lucius or Manaen. Yet we must remember that the Holy Spirit is free to speak through whomever He will, *'For you can all prophesy one by one, so that all may learn and all may be exhorted....'* 1 Corinthians 14:31.

We note that Paul in his letter to the assembly in Corinth, when enumerating the gifts God gives to His body, places apostles first, then prophets and thirdly teachers. In his letter to the Ephesian assembly evangelists are placed third with pastors and teachers fourth. Right here it must be reiterated that even the greater gifts are not positions that bear titles and none of these greater gifts hold a position of authority over others. All control resides with the Holy Spirit until Jesus returns to reign forever.

The current situation in the churches today is that there seem to be an inability and unwillingness to recognize God's prophets who have been sent by the empowering Holy Spirit to speak His instant word directly from Him. A prophet's role is to bring those who will listen into God's plans and what are His commands, His standards and His timetable.

The earliest prophet in the Bible that we know about is Enoch. He is referred to as a prophet in Jude 14. Until Israel and Judah became apostate, the prophets were a functioning part of the Jewish nation but, when the people departed from the Lord, His prophets were found outside, standing alone, calling the people back to God, warning of His coming judgments and foretelling their fate if they disobeyed.

The special calling of the prophet Isaiah is described in detail in Isaiah 6:1-9. *Then I heard the voice of the Lord, saying, "Whom shall I send, and who will go for Us?" Then I said, "Here am I. Send me!" He said, "Go, and tell this people: 'Keep on listening, but do not perceive; Keep on looking, but do not understand.'*

The call of the Lord to Jeremiah is found in Jeremiah 1:4-10. *'Now the word of the Lord came to me saying, "Before I formed you in the womb I knew you, And before you were born I consecrated you; I have appointed you a prophet to the nations. "Then I said, "Alas, Lord God! Behold, I do not know how to speak, Because I am a youth."* Apparently, Jeremiah was quite young when God spoke to him.

The prophet Ezekiel's call is contained in Ezekiel 2:1-7. *'Then He said to me, "Son of man, stand on your feet that I may speak with you!" As He spoke to me the Spirit entered me and set me on my feet; and I heard Him speaking to me. Then He said to me, "Son of man, I am sending you to the sons of Israel, to a rebellious people who have rebelled against Me'...."As for them, whether they listen or not - for they are a rebellious house - they will know that a prophet has been among them'.*

When His people are in a fallen and rebellious state the Lord chooses His prophets directly. They are found outside the spiritual community with which the Lord is displeased. So it is today. One of Christendom's great failures is to respond to the word of His prophets to repent and become the true united testimony of Jesus before an unbelieving world. If these warnings go unheeded much of Christendom will participate in religious Babylon and will share its ultimate fate.

Consider the words of Jesus in His lament over Jerusalem; *"Jerusalem, Jerusalem, who kills the prophets and stones those who are sent to her! How often I wanted to gather your children together, the way a hen gathers her chicks under her wings, and you were unwilling. Behold, your house is being left to you desolate!"* Matthew 24:37-38. Jesus expressed condemnation at the treatment given by Jerusalem to the prophets *'sent to her'*. They had killed the prophets and stoned God's messengers. He then assumed the role of a prophet as He foretold the fate of their centre of worship, the temple: *"....Behold, your house is being left to you desolate!"*

The church in Antioch was approved by the Lord, thus Barnabas and Saul had the hands of the members of that assembly laid upon them and they went forth in full obedience to the work.

Today, Christendom is so fragmented that the divisions and splits cannot be counted. Many churches have accepted the standards and practices of the world. In these last days the Lord is raising up prophets directly commissioned by Him. These know who they are; some within the church recognize who they are; some of those who recognize the significance of their role rely upon their word, *"Thus says the Lord"*; yet the vast majority seem to be unaware of what the Spirit is saying to the churches.

God's true prophets today are warning His people of their departure from what He desires and the dire consequences of disobedience. They are standing unitedly against all the works and wiles of the devil. God's prophets are aware of the times in which they live, they receive insight into His timetable that those who hear and respond may get ready to meet their Bridegroom and may *'prepare the way of the Lord'*.

The cry of John the Baptist is again going forth through many chosen vessels, in many languages, in many settings, far and wide, in preparation for the second coming of the Messiah. A voice is calling, *"Clear the way for the Lord in the wilderness; Make smooth in the desert a highway for our God. "Let every valley be lifted up, And every mountain and hill be made low; And let the rough ground become a plain, And the rugged terrain a broad valley; Then the glory of the Lord will be revealed, And all flesh will see it together; For the mouth of the Lord has spoken."* Isaiah 40:3-5.

Because of the nature of their message and its strict demands prophets (also known as seers) tend to be subject to rejection, ridicule and persecution. This often comes most severely from the very ones to whom God has sent them. At times they suffer from a sense of aloneness that few can comprehend who have not experienced it.

May the Lord grant us discernment. May we listen to the Spirit through His servants the prophets in these last days. May we hear and understand what the Spirit is saying to His church so that we may come out from all that does not give the Lord Jesus the central and supreme place which is His by right.

May we be recognized by both believers and the world as the unshakable and unmistakable testimony of Jesus. May prophets be found and nurtured in our midst, that the Lord may freely speak His urgent messages to His people through such as He raises up, for without the function of the seers, the prophets, who are the eyes of His body, the church will be blind.

CHAPTER 10
WHERE THERE IS NO VISION

Scripture references: Proverbs 29:18, Ecclesiastes 3:11 CJB, Hebrews 11:9-10, Psalms 132:1-5, Revelation 21:2-3, Hebrews 3:5-6, John 14:2, Ephesians 2:22.

'Without a prophetic vision, the people throw off all restraint'. Proverbs 29:18. (Complete Jewish Bible). Unless prophets are raised up and are active among God's people there can be no vision, for prophets are the eyes of the church. Unless prophets are operating freely within an undivided Christian community a lack of focus will develop which will grow and spread like a great blanket of confusion, as individuals and groups do what they think is right. This is a reminder of the time of the judges, *'In those days there was no king in Israel; everyone did what was right in his own eyes'*. Judges 21:25.

What keeps people moving forward together is a compelling vision. In any aspect of human endeavour and indeed, within civilization itself, a sense of direction and a joint common purpose is a great motivator. From earliest times, through selected ones, God has given His people a vision of His ultimate goal, His great eternal purpose in Christ. *'He has given* (placed within) *human beings an awareness of eternity'*. Ecclesiastes 3:11. CJB.

The Lord is a God of purpose. He sees the end from the beginning. From eternity past the Lord Jesus is the alpha and the omega, the beginning and the end. Jesus was the Father's foreordained answer to the sin of Adam. As soon as Adam fell into disobedience and *'sin reigned unto death'* God's plan of redemption was put into action. When Jesus was on earth He knew that on *'the third day I reach My goal'* Luke 13:32. On the day of His resurrection from the dead the sin issue would be fully dealt with and the future perfection of everything in accordance with God's plan would be assured.

The reference in Hebrews 11 to Abraham is interesting in that it explains why he himself, and then Isaac and Jacob, were tent dwellers. They recognized they were strangers and pilgrims on the earth, and Abraham's vision was so clear, *'he was looking for the city which has foundations, whose architect and builder is God'*.

Hebrews 11:10. If we catch this vision of the eternal city we shall hold the things of this earth much more lightly. We will live the simple life in which attachments are few and our faith in the future rests entirely in the Lord.

From the beginning of time it was God's intention to dwell among mankind whom He had created. Through the seed of Abraham He chose a people. This people, in God's foreknowledge, lived and multiplied in Egypt to more than a million souls. Following the Exodus, they became tent dwellers again; their God-given vision being to return to the land promised by God to Abraham. However, because they did not trust Jehovah to drive out the inhabitants of the land ahead of them, they were destined to wander for forty years in the great wilderness.

Jehovah called Moses up to the mountaintop and gave him the law and an exact design for a tabernacle (a large and magnificent tent) wherein He, Jehovah, would dwell in glory at the very centre of His people. Moses took the vision God had given Him and faithfully communicated it to the people. He oversaw the construction of the tabernacle and its furniture; he initiated the role of the priesthood and the offerings God had ordained; and the glory of the Lord filled the tabernacle.

Some four hundred or so years later, after King David had conquered all the territory that had been promised so long before to Abraham, God gave him a vision of the temple and stirred his heart to gather the raw materials for the building of it as a permanent dwelling place for Jehovah on Mount Zion. *'Remember, O Lord, on David's behalf, All his affliction; How he swore to the Lord And vowed to the Mighty One of Jacob, "Surely I will not enter my house, Nor lie on my bed; I will not give sleep to my eyes Or slumber to my eyelids, Until I find a place for the Lord, A dwelling place for the Mighty One of Jacob."* Psalm 132:1-5.

This Psalm precedes the very short Psalm 133: *'Behold how good and how pleasant it is for brothers to dwell together in unity....For there the Lord commanded the blessing — life forever'*. God will only make His dwelling place, His home, where there is unity. At the time that David's son Solomon built the temple the nation of

Israel was at peace and in unity as one people. As with the tabernacle, the glory of the Lord filled the temple on the day of its dedication.

During the next almost four hundred years Jehovah continued to dwell among His people, until the Babylonian captivity, when the temple was destroyed under Nebuchadnezzar. At around that time the ark-of-the-covenant disappeared and the Shekinah glory of God departed from the holy of holies, never to return.

The prophets of the Old Testament received many visions which applied to their own times and to later times. Many of these visions have only partially been fulfilled as yet, and their conclusion lies in the future. Nebuchadnezzar's dream, for which the Lord gave Daniel the interpretation, has largely been fulfilled and we are now approaching the time of the feet and toes of the great image. Daniel 2:41-43. The final week of the vision of the seventy weeks, which the archangel Gabriel gave to Daniel, is still to come. Daniel 9:21-27. We, in our day, are right on the brink of entering this last week, the final seven years of tribulation.

As the pastor-laity system has become more deeply entrenched and God's people have become increasingly divided, a state of spiritual paralysis and stagnation is prevailing. No part of Christendom shares a common vision with the other parts. *'Without a prophetic vision, the people throw off all restraint'*. Schisms are doomed to do their own thing. All too easily they become enmeshed in fleshly opinions. They gather around a belief system rather than to the Saviour.

The holy of holies in the tabernacle and the temple were types of what shall yet forever be – the Holy City, new Jerusalem. Between the types and their fulfilment there are two significant steps. Firstly, John 1:14 informs us that *'the Word (Jesus) became flesh and tabernacled (pitched His tent) among us'*. When Jesus was incarnated to be the Son of Man He was God's dwelling place on earth. Secondly, Hebrews 3:6 informs us, *'but Christ was faithful as a Son over His house - whose house we are, if we hold fast our confidence and the boast of our hope firm until the end'*. From

Pentecost onwards God's house is a unified people gathered unto Jesus.

"In My Father's house are many dwelling places; if it were not so, I would have told you; for I go to prepare a place for you." John 14:2. Who or what are these dwelling places? The answer lies in Ephesians 2:22. We *'are being built together into a dwelling of God'*. These dwelling places are individual believers in whom the Spirit of God is at work to transform them into the image and likeness of Jesus, and to fit them together perfectly to be the Holy City, new Jerusalem - His bride. This is confirmed by 1 Peter 2:5, *'....you also, as living stones, are being built up as a spiritual house'*.

Under the inspiration of the Holy Spirit John the apostle wrote the Book of Revelation based on visions given to him. These and other relevant visions need to be unveiled and understood by all true and faithful followers of the Lord Jesus. In fact, all need to see what is the eternal purpose and plan of God which unfolds from Genesis 1 and culminates in Revelation 22, and to understand how those who believe in Jesus fit into this vast eternal plan.

As world history is winding down and the time is growing short, those who love the Lord Jesus and who give themselves fully to follow Him need a fresh vision of His pathway that leads to perfection and glory.

If, by the Spirit, we have caught a glimpse of *'the holy city, new Jerusalem....made ready as a bride adorned for her husband'* and, if we realize that we have been betrothed to the Lord Jesus, how then shall we continue to consort with others any longer in the sin of division? Shall we not desire passionately to leave the counterfeit, coming together simply as brothers to receive a fresh vision of our Bridegroom? *'Therefore, come out from their midst and be separate," says the Lord, "and do not touch what is unclean; And I will welcome you. And I will be a father to you, And you shall be sons and daughters to Me," says the Lord Almighty.* 2 Corinthians 6:17-18. May our compelling vision be, as was Abraham's *'the city which has foundations, whose architect and builder is God'* - of which we shall, by grace, be an eternal part.

CHAPTER 11
THE WORD OF TRUTH

Scripture references: John 1:1-4, John 17:17, Hebrews 4:12-13, John 6:57-58, Matthew 4:4, 1 John 2:27, John 16:13-14, Jeremiah 15:16, 2 Timothy 2:15, 1 Corinthians 14:26, AMP.

No symphony composed by man can match the sonorous and majestic opening of the Gospel of John. Even in the Scriptures there is little to compare with it. *'In the beginning was the Word, and the Word was with God, and the Word was God. He was in the beginning with God. All things came into being through Him, and apart from Him nothing came into being that has come into being. In Him was life, and the life was the Light of men'*. John 1:1-4. Yet these spiritual words of poetic and literary merit can pay only limited honour to the One announced through them. It is to Him, Christ Jesus the Lord, before whom our hearts spontaneously bow down in worship and adoration.

Jesus is the truth. He is the Logos, the Word. His word is truth. *'Sanctify them in the truth; Your word is truth'*. John 17:17. His word, His truth, sanctifies us, making us holy. If by the Spirit we take in His word it will carry out His transforming work in us. Without a regular intake of the living word we will remain spiritual paupers. Rejection of He who is the Word spells a forever lost eternity. *'Your word is truth'*.

Jesus, *'the word of God, is living and active...there is no creature hidden from His sight....all things are open and laid bare to the eyes of Him with whom we have to do'*. Hebrews 4:12. Without His penetrating gaze upon us which is sharper than any surgeon's knife, we might simply compare ourselves with others and think we are quite good. Yet those same eyes that see the sinful destitution and depravity into which we were born also see the finished work He intends to accomplish in us if we will let Him.

Jesus, who is the Word, is *'the bread which came down out of heaven'*. He told His disciples *"he who eats Me, he also will live because of Me."* John 6:41,57. The very life of God flowed to earth in the Person of the Word. It flowed constantly into Him and flowed freely and purely from Him in accordance with the Father's will. To eat Him is to allow Him as the Word, Who is the very essence and substance of the living God, to flow into us that it may to do its transforming work in us and that it may flow forth from us to perform His perfect will on this earth.

This brings us to one of the greatest and most sinister causes of the lack of impact the church is having upon the communities around them; namely a systematic and sustained limitation of the flow of the word of truth. This flow that comes from the throne of God should be the lifeblood of the body of Christ on earth and the source of a powerful outflow of the gospel of the kingdom. Should this life flow be restricted then the health of the body will be jeopardized and its effectiveness will suffer greatly. *"To the angel of the church in Sardis write: He who has the seven Spirits of God and the seven stars, says this: 'I know your deeds, that you have a name that you are alive, but you are dead."* Revelation 3:1. What an indictment!

Neglect of regular personal labouring on *'the word of truth'* is a widespread characteristic among Christians today, as is the anointed sharing of words of wisdom, knowledge, exhortation and prophecy. All too often it seems that believers are satisfied to rely upon the weekly messages of a paid professional as their sole encounter with the word of God found in the Scriptures. How can spirits which are barely surviving on such a restricted diet of the living word of God be equipped to *'go into all the world and preach the gospel to all creation'*? Mark 16:15.

If a man was very thirsty and he found himself beside a pond whose perimeter bore traces of green slime, yet, within a hundred feet or so of the pond he discovered a living spring, from which would he quench his thirst? Jesus told the woman at the well of Samaria *"....whoever drinks of the water that I will give him shall never thirst; but the water that I will give him will become in him a well of water springing up to eternal life."* John 4:14. That which is given us by the Holy Spirit, through personal experience and revelation will be the purposeful, practical and timely word of God for us. As we obey the Spirit's speaking we shall know what it means to be living *'by every word that proceeds out of the mouth of God'*. Matthew 4:4.

'As for you, the anointing which you received from Him abides in you, and you have no need for anyone to teach you'. 1 John 2:27. Who or what is this anointing? He is the indwelling Holy Spirit who is given to every believer as a pledge, or down payment, at the instant of the new birth. *"But when He, the Spirit of truth, comes, He will guide you into all the truth."* John 16:13. It is God's intention that all believers be led by the Spirit *'into all the truth'*. There is a place for studying the word of God with others and there is a case for studying the word on our own, yet without the anointing of the Holy Spirit upon the word it will simply remain dead knowledge.

After Saul encountered the resurrected Jesus on the road to Damascus he did not sit at the feet of even the apostles who had lived and walked with Jesus. Instead, God took him to His private 'theological college' of the Arabian desert, where He revealed His Son Jesus into Paul. There He unveiled to him all he would later require to spread the gospel of the kingdom far and wide throughout the Roman world, and to write almost half our New Testament.

"He will glorify Me, for He will take of Mine and will disclose it to you." John 16:14. The Spirit's disclosure to us will always glorify the Lord Jesus. The Spirit will reveal Jesus into us and He will reveal Him into others as we speak under His anointing. Unless God reveals His Son into us we will not be equipped to go forth to share Him with others.

'There is a river whose streams make glad the city of God, The holy dwelling places of the Most High'. Psalm 46:4. As the river of God is composed of many *'streams that make glad the city of God'*, so it is that many Spirit-filled human vessels, as they allow the divine life to flow into them and to flow forth from them, will contribute to the river of God. No man, however seemingly spiritually gifted, can be a source of anything larger or more significant than a living stream. Here then is the fallacy of so much of the Christian church and a source of its poverty - the one man ministry. Even Peter, John or Paul, though highly gifted apostles and contributors to our New

Testament, could not individually be counted as more than living streams within the whole body of Christ.

The river of God has a characteristic not found in the rivers of earth. It flows back to its source. It flows from the throne into each human vessel that is open to it. It flows as a living stream from each one, as prompted by the Spirit's anointing. Then all these streams contribute to the flow of divine life as it flows back to the throne of God, *'the holy dwelling places of the Most High'*.

When Jesus, the Logos of God, was on earth He was the river of God, confined in its flow to a comparatively limited geographical area. When the Holy Spirit, the Spirit of Jesus, was poured out on the believers at Pentecost, each indwelt vessel became a part of the body of Christ and a tributary to the river of God. So it continued in the assemblies of God's people until one stream exalted itself, claiming to be a larger stream than the others and lording itself over the rest. Where this began to occur, or when it occurred we do not know, but it occurred within the lifetime of the apostle John. *'I wrote something to the church; but Diotrephes, who loves to be first among them, does not accept what we say'*. 3 John 10. Diotrephes exalted himself above others in the assembly and even ignored the message given to the church through the apostle John.

In our personal walk with Jesus may we share in the cry of Jeremiah, *'Your words were found and I ate them, And Your words became for me a joy and the delight of my heart; For I have been called by Your name, O Lord God of hosts'*. Jeremiah 15:16. And may we also heed the words of Paul to Timothy *'....Be diligent to present yourself approved to God as a workman who does not need to be ashamed, accurately handling the word of truth'*. 2 Timothy 2:15.

If all who meet together regularly as a local assembly of the body of Christ have been steeped in the Spirit-revealed word, the Logos, the richness of their meetings will be inexpressibly glorious as they exalt the Lord Jesus and supply life to one another. *What then, brethren, is* [the right course]? *When you meet together, each one has a hymn, a teaching, a disclosure of special knowledge or information, an utterance in a* [strange] *tongue, or an interpretation of it. [But] let everything be constructive and edifying and for the good of all*. 1 Corinthians 14:26, AMP.

As we faithfully follow Jesus and regularly take in the living Word we shall be nurtured by the flow of His divine life. As we continue faithfully to do so, He will equip us to share His words of life for the encouragement of our fellow believers and to deliver His message to others who know Him not. *'Your word is truth'*.

CHAPTER 12

YOU CANNOT SERVE GOD AND WEALTH

Scripture references: Luke 16:13, Mark 10:17-22, Luke 12:32-34, Matthew 13:18-23, Matthew 7:13-14, Luke 14:26-27.

Luke 16:13 makes a sharp distinction between *'God and wealth'* with no middle ground between them. Let us make no mistake, *'you cannot serve God and wealth'*.

Wealth is far more than money. It may be described as access to the 'good life' which embraces all the many things that provide freedom from want, freedom from discomfort, freedom from fear and the sense of security. Wealth perhaps is best described as all that competes with God to provide human satisfaction. What God offers is real; all else is counterfeit. All our choices and all our decisions are made on the basis of two alternatives; to seek His will and do what He desires, or to follow the desires of self.

"Good Teacher, what shall I do to inherit eternal life?" There was seriousness and genuineness in this young man's question. The word says, *'Looking at him, Jesus felt a love for him'*. In response, Jesus offered the rich young ruler a clear choice; continue with the comfort of owning much property, or sell all and become My disciple. *'But at these words he was saddened, and he went away grieving'*. His heart was where his treasure was. There is no room for compromise in what Jesus demands of those who would be His disciples. Mark 10:17-22.

"Do not be afraid, little flock, for your Father has chosen gladly to give you the kingdom...." Luke 12:32. If we come to the Father, through Jesus the Son, the Father will reveal His Son into us as He did into the apostle Paul. Embodied in Jesus is the kingdom. God's complete gift to His people is to be found in Christ. His ultimate desire and purpose is that all the transformed and perfected saints shall be constituted to be *'the bride, the wife of the Lamb'*. This is the Father's choice. He does it gladly and He gives it freely to all who will come out of Satan's fake 'good life' and receive the Father's *'indescribable gift'*, Christ.

Rampant materialism has spread across the western world since World War II, which has created an illusion that wealth is within the reach of large numbers of its citizens. This great illusion has become evident among believers and in church communities to an alarming extent. In its acquisition and ownership of property and financial assets, and its lack of separation from the world, the church on earth has laid up for itself treasure on earth and has adopted many worldly pursuits and practices, simply adding a religious flavour to them. Consequentially much of Christendom exists today in a state of compromise and has become increasingly fruitless. *'You cannot serve God and wealth'*. This is the unchangeable and unalterable word of God. But what Satan said to Eve in the Garden of Eden he continues to say to us today, *"Indeed has God said...?"*

Over many decades, now, believers have felt increasing discomfort as ethical and moral standards have declined, especially in the western world. While believers have tended to draw back from the world's excesses there has been a major shift towards accepting the new mores without necessarily endorsing them. To be laid back is cool. However, Satan's lie has led to a steady erosion of the principles and practices that our forefathers held dear and inviolable. Though religiosity pervaded much of Christendom in those times, yet there was a clear line drawn, across which the majority of God's people would not cross. Certainly, many believers were branded as narrow minded in those former days, yet a sense of living under the all-seeing gaze of an omnipotent God was widely evident, even among those of no professed faith. Now, the excesses of this world and active hostility towards moral restraint, are leading to changes in societal behaviour and flagrant disregard for God's edicts and standards for mankind. An example is the almost worldwide dishonour of God's sacrament of marriage. The world ever desires to have its evil practices accepted, even sanctioned, by so-called Christians.

The parable of the sower is one of the best known and best loved parables of Jesus. In it the *'word of the kingdom'* is likened to seed which the sower, the Lord, sows in a variety of conditions - *'beside the road....on the rocky places....among the thorns....on the good soil'*. In our western world great numbers of believers and churches are aptly described in these words of Jesus concerning seed that fell among thorns, *'the worry of the world and the deceitfulness of wealth choke the word, and it becomes unfruitful'*. Matthew 13:22.

Another parable of Jesus reminds us, *'For the gate is wide and the way is broad that leads to destruction, and there are many who enter through it'*. Matthew 7:13-14. Those who represent the seed sown among thorns have chosen the wide gate through which they pass easily, together with all their worldly baggage. Among such ones a prosperity gospel finds ready adherents.

The end for all who choose the broad way is destruction. Not perdition, as some have affirmed, but terrible loss and shame at the judgment seat of Christ when all unworthy works will be burned up. Note, though, that *'If any man's work is burned up, he will suffer loss; but he himself will be saved, yet so as through fire'*. 1 Corinthians 3:15. *'If any man's work is burned up....'* what will be the consequences? Let no one be deceived. When the Bridegroom comes, those who have failed to *'work out their salvation with fear and trembling'* will have to go and buy oil under unknown circumstances. God is not mocked. Serving wealth will, in the end, incur a much greater penalty than can be imagined. *'Choose for yourselves today whom you will serve....'* Joshua 24:15.

By contrast, those few who find the narrow way, who pass through the constricted gate, do so in Christ. Such ones are no longer caught up with *'the worry of the world and the deceitfulness of wealth'*. Their eyes are fixed on their beloved Master. His yoke is upon their neck. They follow Him wherever He goes. Yes! Thanks be to God for these faithful ones who represent the good soil *'who hear the word and understand it; who indeed bear fruit and bring forth, some a hundredfold, some sixty, and some thirty'*. These are the overcomers whom Satan fears because they will be the means of his final casting out from heaven. Revelation 12:11.

"If anyone comes to Me, and does not hate his own father and mother and wife and children and brothers and sisters, yes, and

even his own life, he cannot be My disciple." Luke 14:26. How shocked must many Christians be to know that these relationships included in Jesus' words are also liable to be a part of 'wealth'. We must not try to please those close to us at the expense of doing His will. To serve God involves absolute commitment to find and to do what He wishes, as opposed to following our own desires or the desires of those who are nearest and dearest to us. *"No servant can serve two masters...."*

"Whoever does not carry his own cross and come after Me cannot be My disciple." Luke 14:27. It is only those who carry their own cross who can enter through the constricted gate. All that represents wealth to them is found wholly in Christ. *'You will seek Me and find Me when you search for Me with all your heart'*. Jeremiah 29:13.

We cannot maintain one foot in the kingdom and one foot in the world. We cannot serve God and wealth. As the prophet Elijah challenged the people of Israel so long ago, *"How long will you hesitate between two opinions? If the Lord is God, follow Him; but if Baal, follow him."* 1 Kings 18:21. The pathway of life in Christ ever was and always will be *"Follow Me."* No excuses; no delays; no half-heartedness.

Oh! May we be among those who have gazed deep into the eyes of 'the One of peerless worth', who have been wrecked forever from seeking substitutes, soothers or short cuts. Hebrews 12:1-2: *'....let us run with endurance the race that is set before us, fixing our eyes on Jesus'* while also holding out both our hands for others of like mind to join in a great chain converging together towards the finishing line, where our beloved Bridegroom is waiting with His *'Well done, good and faithful slave. You were faithful with a few things, I will put you in charge of many things; enter into the joy of your master'*. Matthew 25:21.

CHAPTER 13
YOU ARE ALL BROTHERS

Scripture references: Matthew 23:8-10, Galatians 3:26-28, Acts 21:17-25, Galatians 5:1, Acts 13:1-31, Ephesians 5:23-24, Corinthians 11:3.

"But do not be called Rabbi; for One is your Teacher, and you are all brothers. "Do not call anyone on earth your father; for One is your Father, He who is in heaven. "Do not be called leaders; for One is your Leader, that is, Christ." Matthew 23:8-10. The meaning of this statement of Jesus could hardly be more specific. One is your Teacher and Leader, One is your Father, He who is in heaven, and you are all brothers. The Triune God is exalted far above all, and those who are His own are all on the same level or plane as *'brothers'*. In stating *"do not be called Rabbi"* Jesus is telling His followers that positions and titles shall not be adopted.

'One is your Teacher and you are all brothers'. Whenever Jesus is accorded His rightful place as Lord all those who attend upon Him take the position of brothers gathered unto Him. Are the women included? Yes, all who believe have been baptized into Christ. For this reason women have the standing as brothers in the gatherings together with the Lord, yet as members of the human believing community they are sisters. Romans 16:1.

'....For you are all sons of God through faith in Christ Jesus....there is neither male nor female; for you are all one in Christ Jesus'. Galatians 3:26-28. In Christ Jesus all are sons of God, Jew or Greek, slave or free man, male or female. This is the standing of both male and female in the kingdom. We are all sons.

However that may be, within the body of Christ, His church, there are roles and functions. There are delegated authorities (which carry no titles). There are greater gifts and there are lesser gifts, yet all these gifts are to harmonize together as the Holy Spirit directs. Thus the whole body, under the direction of the Head, may fulfil the plan and purpose of God.

In the churches today there is widespread disregard paid to the absolute sovereignty of the Lord Jesus in respect to His church, its gatherings and its ministry. Sadly, this grave and fundamental error has led to misapplication of His delegated authorities and to the creation of many bogus authorities.

The roles and authorities that God has established for this present age are not changeable or negotiable to suit this world's, or Christendom's, fads or fancies. As things now stand, there are defined levels of bogus authority and control over the general company of believers. Some are clergy and some are laity. There are vast church bodies and organizations. There are boards and directors.

At the birth of the church at Pentecost the Holy Spirit fell upon around one hundred and twenty persons. Twelve of these were apostles, including Matthias who had been chosen to fill the place of Judas. Three thousand came to faith in Jesus that day and were baptized. From that time forward there were increasing numbers rejoicing in their newfound faith in Christ, living a communal life of shared resources and living arrangements. We read such things as *'....the Lord was adding to their number day by day those who were being saved'.* Acts 2:47. *'And when they had prayed, the place where they had gathered together was shaken, and they were all filled with the Holy Spirit and began to speak the word of God with boldness'.* Acts 4:31. These accounts really stir our hearts.

We might think that, since the Jerusalem church was God's new beginning, it would forever remain the perfect example of what churches ought to have been throughout the Roman Empire and, later, what they should be throughout the whole earth. Yet there are some important lessons to be learned from the Jerusalem church. There are events that demonstrate how easy it is to drift away from the purity of God's intention. The first questionable instance was when the Greek widows were not receiving a proper allocation of food. The apostles rightly established deacons to take care of this situation. Among those selected were Stephen and Philip. However the statement of the apostles at the time demonstrates that they held themselves above such involvement. *"It is not desirable for us to neglect the word of God in order to serve tables."* Acts 6:2.

In Acts 21:18-24 there is an example of the church in Jerusalem using fleshly wisdom, making an unwise decision, and not seeking the mind and will of the Lord. (In passing, we note that members of the church in Jerusalem are referred to as *'the brethren'* and Paul is referred to by them as *'brother'*.)

James, half-brother of Jesus, and all the elders were present when Paul gave an encouraging report of the Lord's ministry through him and His companions. Yet, after glorifying God for this news, those present expressed concern about Paul's apparent neglect of the requirements of the Law. *"Therefore do this that we tell you...."* they told Paul. What emerged from the discussions was a plan they hoped would set the minds of the Jewish believers at rest. Surely this was a fleshly and retrograde step because, to use Paul's own words, *'It was for freedom that Christ set us free; therefore keep standing firm and do not be subject again to a yoke of slavery'*. Galatians 5:1.

Contrast this with the scene in the church in Antioch, many years earlier, described for us in the first few verses of Acts 13. *'Now there were at Antioch, in the church that was there, prophets and teachers: Barnabas, and Simeon who was called Niger, and Lucius of Cyrene, and Manaen who had been brought up with Herod the tetrarch, and Saul. While they were ministering to the Lord and fasting, the Holy Spirit said, "Set apart for Me Barnabas and Saul for the work to which I have called them."* Who was in control of this meeting? The Holy Spirit. Who was being consulted through the prayer and fasting? The Holy Spirit. From Whom came forth the directive that Barnabus and Saul be set apart for the work? The Blessed Person of the Holy Spirit!

No special prominence is given in these verses to any one of the five prophets and teachers. Their mention has significance because, the fact of them being a part of that assembly, enabled the Holy Spirit to give a special command *"Set apart for Me Barnabas and Saul for the work to which I have called them."* Acts 13:2. This was to prove so significant to the forward move of God throughout the whole Roman world. No mention is made of the prophet through whom the Holy Spirit spoke this word.

What a monumental lesson this is concerning the Holy Spirit being Lord in the assembling together of God's people. What a demonstration, too, of the importance to the Lord's agenda of prophets being raised up in local assemblies. At this very juncture God moved the centre of His plans and operations from Jerusalem to Antioch.

We must turn now to the important matter of the position of women within God's eternal plan and purpose. Before sin entered the world it was God's intention that man should be the head of the woman as Christ was destined to be over His bride. *'For the husband is the head of the wife, as Christ also is the head of the church'*. Ephesians 5:23. This order of things is eternal and not the result of sin. Christ will still be *'the head of the church'*, His bride, in eternity future.

In the Lord the husband is to provide leadership to his wife. In a marriage where the wife is more gifted and wiser than her husband he may learn much from her and be greatly helped through her advice and counsel. Her respect for him as her *'head'* should encourage him to be an appreciative husband who welcomes his wife's sound judgment, and he will lead lovingly and in harmony with her.

The Lord created man and woman with distinctly different yet complementary qualities. Thus in life and in the church they are suited to distinctly different roles. Adam is a type of Christ. Eve, the woman who was taken out from the man is a type of the bride of Christ. Christ, *'the last Adam was made a life giving Spirit'*. Out from Him His bride has been taken, that one day she may be presented to Him as *'His bride, 'the wife of the Lamb'*.

1 Corinthians 11:3: *'I want you to understand that Christ is the head of every man, and the man is the head of a woman, and God is the head of Christ'*. This concise and precise statement expresses man collectively as, *'the man'*, being *'the head of a woman'*. This in effect means that no woman, however spiritually gifted, may take authority over any man. God's blessing will only rest upon strict obedience to the roles and authorities that He has ordained. Scripture informs us that in the assembly a woman, under the

anointing of the Holy Spirit, is just as free to pray or to prophesy as a man, yet with her head covered.

All who are saved by grace have a place within the body of Christ, a role to play, and works *'which God prepared beforehand so that we would walk in them'*. Ephesians 2:10. If we will simply surrender ourselves fully into the hands of the Lord Jesus and allow Him, in and through us, to fully perform those fore-ordained works, we shall have accomplished as much as the greatest saint who ever walked this earth.

CHAPTER 14
MEMBERS ONE OF ANOTHER

Scripture references: 1 Corinthians 12:4-14, 19-30, Romans 12:3-13, John 6:57-58, Galatians 6:2,5.

In the Scriptures God has given us much information concerning the operation and organization of the whole Christ; He the Head, and His body the church. The picture is one of many members who have been gifted by the Spirit with a variety of attributes and functions so that each and every one may contribute to the well-being and life of the body under the control and direction of the Head. If the members don't maintain a vital relationship with the Head and function in accordance with His leading the body will be paralyzed.

Every earthly example we can find falls short in describing the formation, operation and co-ordination of *'God's masterpiece'* the church. But consider the following example.

A symphony orchestra, from humble beginnings, has become world renowned. The mention of its name and its famous and esteemed conductor bring instant recognition and respect. It was brought together over a period of time by careful selection of skilled and dedicated musicians. This orchestra developed and grew in size and skills through each member's commitment to its aims and complete trust in the direction and vision of the conductor. Each musician and instrumental group now combine together to produce the most moving renditions of famous compositions in accordance with the conductor's interpretation of the music. Its reputation as a world class orchestra brings deserved credit to the maestro who has overseen its transformation.

'Now there are varieties of gifts, but the same Spirit. And there are varieties of ministries, and the same Lord. There are varieties of effects, but the same God who works all things in all persons'. 1 Corinthians 12:4-6. These verses describe for us how the Father and the Holy Spirit operate through the Head, Christ, to direct, control and empower every member of the body in performing its unique function in a co-ordinated and harmonious manner to carry out the full will and purpose of the Godhead.

What are some of these gifts and what is their function within the body of Christ, His church? *'But to each one is given the manifestation of the Spirit for the common good. For to one is given the word of wisdom through the Spirit, and to another the word of knowledge according to the same Spirit; to another faith by the same Spirit, and to another gifts of healing by the one Spirit, and to another the effecting of miracles, and to another prophecy, and to another the distinguishing of spirits, to another various kinds of tongues, and to another the interpretation of tongues. But one and the same Spirit works all these things, distributing to each one individually just as He wills'.* 1 Corinthians 12:7-11. Note that *'To each one is given the manifestation of the Spirit for the common good'*. The word of wisdom, the word of knowledge, faith, gifts of healing, the effecting of miracles, prophecy, the distinguishing of spirits, various kinds of tongues, interpretation of tongues. These gifts are given that they may be expressed within the gatherings of the saints in their meeting place, in homes, or anywhere that two or more are gathered in His name. Each one is given a gift.

Later in 1 Corinthians 12:27-28 more of the gifts of the Spirit are described. *'Now you are Christ's body, and individually members of it. And God has appointed in the church, first apostles, second prophets, third teachers, then miracles, then gifts of healings, helps, administrations, various kinds of tongues'*. Note that apostles, prophets and teachers are members of the body, not rulers over it.

God has set up and established His church to be His representative and His testimony on this earth, in which all the members, co-ordinating together under the Head, execute His eternal purpose and plan. Under the Head, Christ, the whole body is equipped to go forth, bearing His authority, going where He sends it, proclaiming the messages He gives it, and carrying out His perfect will throughout the whole earth. Jesus expressed the goal for the members of His body as follows *'This gospel of the kingdom shall be preached in the whole world as a testimony to all the nations, and then the end will come'*. Matthew 24:14.

Looking again at the orchestral example, imagine what would happen if almost all the musicians ceased to exercise their gifts, and simply joined the audience. The orchestra now might consist only of a solo pianist, a violinist and a clarinettist. The skills of the many would decline and become virtually useless. If the solo pianist took the lead in attempting to perform Chopin's 2nd Piano Concerto with the two other musicians following his lead, what an incomplete and disappointing rendering this would be.

Now let us take the analogy of this orchestra and apply it to what takes place within many church communities. Sunday after Sunday individual soloists take the stage to create their own rendition, although they do not have, nor can they have, more than a part of the score. Only the Holy Spirit knows the full musical score and how to interpret the piece. Only He has an intimate knowledge of each individual whom He has gifted to contribute a part that will blend together harmoniously to compose a symphony of divine life that will be pleasing to our Father's ears.

Christian denominations on the earth today are numbered in the tens of thousands. The great majority of them allow little or no freedom to those who might be impelled by the Holy Spirit to speak or function in their meetings in accordance with their gifts. If functioning is limited to the few, then life in the Spirit is stifled and the non-functioning members will be rendered incapable of gaining confidence to proclaim their faith, as the Lord commanded us to do *'to all creation'*. This lack of freedom to function on the part of the members is one of the most serious impediments to the spread of the gospel of the kingdom and has over many centuries hampered the plan and purpose of God.

In place of the operation of spiritual gifts countless programs, designed and organized by church authorities, are developed and put in place to carry out the plans of their organization. Goals are established and funds are allocated for approved programs. Church members are often selected to lead such programs in accordance with their human abilities and willingness to serve. These organizational networks may largely operate in a similar manner to secular businesses.

Church organizations such as the ones described are formed around doing things right instead of doing the right things. The right things can only be done by looking to Jesus alone and relying on Him to direct, control and empower all that is said, all that is done, how it is done, and where and through whom action should be taken.

The Lord Jesus described Himself as the true, or real, vine and those who are His own as the branches. He said, *"I am the true vine, and My Father is the vinedresser. "Every branch in Me that does not bear fruit, He takes away; and every branch that bears fruit, He prunes it so that it may bear more fruit."* John 15:1-2. This parable of the vine offers a wonderful example from which we may learn much about the operation and composition of God's masterpiece, His church.

Jesus is the vine in which are many branches; referred to these days as 'fruit spurs'. The fact that there is only one vine clearly demonstrates that the church is one and cannot be divided. Jesus' Father and ours is the vinedresser who looks for fruit from each little fruit spur. Each one has its unique place in the vine that it may bear fruit. If it does not fulfil this function the Father removes it. How serious it must be to be cut off from the life of the vine.

We are reminded of the seed that fell among thorns spoken of in Jesus' parable of the sower. This was fruitless because the cares of this world and the deceitfulness of riches choked the word. Jesus made it quite clear that *"You cannot serve God and riches."*

In order to bear fruit we must have an undivided heart and be grafted firmly into the vine. In other words we must abide in Jesus. If we will abide in Him we shall bear fruit and the Father will prune us in order that we may produce more abundant fruit; remaining fruit.

As the living organism of the body of Christ consistently receives direction from the Head and obeys the Head, then the true body life will be experienced by all the members. Then they will function and act in perfect co-ordination, care for one another, and experience great mutual enjoyment under the anointing of the Holy Spirit.

The main points to be drawn from Romans 12 and 1 Corinthians 12 are that there are diverse gifts among the many members of the body of Christ. Some are greater gifts and others, by inference, are lesser gifts. None of these gifts carry titles. All members have a gift that must be allowed to contribute to the building up of the body of Christ. *'To each one is given a manifestation of the Spirit for the common good'*. 1 Corinthians 12:4. *'Since we have gifts that differ according to the grace given to us, each of us is to exercise them accordingly'*. Romans 12:6. Every member is necessary. Each member must bear his own load, yet all must be aware of and share in carrying the burdens of those who are weighed down under their loads. Galatians 6:2,5.

May the Lord be gracious to us that we may freely exercise our own gift in love for one another. May we encourage all the members to exercise their individual gifts too; that the Lord may be glorified among His own and for *'the building up of the body of Christ'*.

CHAPTER 15
PREPARE THE WAY OF THE LORD

Scripture references: Isaiah 40:3-5, Luke 3:4-6 NLT, John 17:20-21, Matthew 23:5-12, 3 John 9-10, 1 Corinthians 14:26, 31, Revelation 2:15-17, 2 Peter 3:9-13, Ephesians 4:16.

The message to Israel at the Lord's first coming was *'Prepare the way of the Lord'*. Now, as the second coming of the Lord Jesus fast approaches, the message is the same *'Prepare the way of the Lord'*. It comes with great urgency to the members of Christ's body, His church, who have ears to hear.

The New Living Translation brings out clearly the underlying meaning of two passages, one in Isaiah 40 and the other in Luke 3. The passage in Isaiah applies to both the first and second comings of the Lord Jesus, while the passage in Luke describes how John the Baptist was *'a voice shouting in the wilderness: 'Prepare a pathway for the Lord's coming'!* Luke 3:4 NLT.

John lived and preached in the wilderness of Judaea where the people flocked to hear his message, *"Repent for the kingdom of heaven is at hand"*. Many were baptized by him in the River Jordan, Jesus Himself among them. John faithfully prepared the way for the Lord Jesus for His first coming, yet Israel did not repent, and *'those who were His own did not receive Him'*. John 1:11. *'Those who were His own'* ended up by crying out for His crucifixion.

At first sight the passage from Isaiah 40:3-5 appears to be very mysterious. Why does the Lord want a smooth highway prepared? What or where is the wilderness? However, one thing is certain, when the valleys have been filled and the hills levelled to provide this smooth highway, *'then the glory of the Lord will be revealed, and all people will see it together; For the mouth of the Lord has spoken'*. Isaiah 40:5.

"Make a highway for the Lord through the wilderness." What is a wilderness? A wilderness is where there is a scarcity of water and life. It is a wild place, a desert. In John Bunyan's 'The Pilgrim's Progress', he clearly portrays the evil state and sinful ways of this world and of its people. The opening line of his very widely

acclaimed book reads, 'As I walked through the wilderness of this world...' The wilderness is this world's wicked system and ways under the authority of Satan, the fallen angel Lucifer.

'Make a straight, smooth road through the desert for our God.' In our day and age a highway might be likened to a runway on which an airliner, or perhaps a space shuttle might land; long, straight, level and smooth. To construct such a runway would require filling up the low ground, levelling down the higher ground and smoothing out the surface. What is the Lord calling His own of this age to do? For His return in glory His people, or a faithful remnant of His people, have a vital responsibility, which is, to make ready the way for the Lord's glorious return to this earth.

'Preparing the way of the Lord' is not on the agenda of most churches. How indeed could it be? How can those with their own agendas give first priority to His? Only as He is recognized as the builder of His one church, according to His plan and purpose, will preparation for His return be possible.

'Make a straight....road....Straighten out the curves'. The shortest distance between two points is a straight line. Endless deviations on matters of doctrine will take our eyes away from Jesus and cause ever increasing division. Unity in the Spirit alone can provide a straight road. The disunity and division existing among the many Christian denominations leads great numbers of unbelievers to reject outright the gospel of the kingdom that the Lord Jesus desires be offered to all mankind everywhere.

Shortly before Jesus was crucified He prayed to the Father for those who would be His, *"I do not ask on behalf of these alone, but for those also who believe in Me through their word; that they may all be one...."* John 17:20-21. To make His path straight, we must live according to this prayer of the Lord Jesus – *'that they may all be one'*. We must rid ourselves of all Christian affiliations that include some and exclude others. All denominational associations and divisive dogmas are a denial of the unity to be found alone in Jesus Christ. *'Make a straight....road'!*

'Fill the valleys and level the hills'. In Matthew 23:5-12 we read of Jesus exposing some of the hypocrisies of the Pharisees and Sadducees: *'they do all their deeds to be noticed by men...."They love the place of honour at banquets and the chief seats in the synagogues....and being called Rabbi by men'*. Then He pointed out to them the attitude they should adopt. *"But do not be called Rabbi; for One is your Teacher, and you are all brothers. "Do not call anyone on earth your father; for One is your Father, He who is in heaven. "Do not be called leaders; for One is your Leader, that is, Christ. "But the greatest among you shall be your servant. "Whoever exalts himself shall be humbled; and whoever humbles himself shall be exalted."*

The way of the Lord must be both straight and level. In most Christian communities today there are those exalted above, even far above, the common believers - those who are thereby abased. There are the rulers and there are the acquiescing followers. The valleys can only be filled up when those seemingly less gifted are permitted and encouraged to exercise their individual gifts given by the Holy Spirit. 1 Corinthians 12:7 *'....to each one* (member of the one body) *is given the manifestation of the Spirit for the common good'*. See also 1 Corinthians 14:26, 31. Conversely, those who are exalted in the eyes of others (and maybe in their own eyes also) must function less, to allow balance between their contribution and that of others less gifted, so that *'the proper working of each individual part will cause the growth of the body for the building up of itself in love'*. Ephesians 4:16.

To those who would rule over other members of the body there is a stern warning in Revelation 2:15-17 against *'some who....hold the teaching of the Nicolaitans.....I will make war against them with the sword of My mouth'*. (Nicolaitan means 'dominating the common members'.) In the Church of Jesus Christ, those who accept titles and assume power over others are an abomination to the Lord. *"Do not be called leaders; for One is your Leader, that is, Christ. "But the greatest among you shall be your servant."*

'Smooth off the rough spots'. Not only must the way be straight and level, it must also be smooth. The rough places must be made

smooth. When the apostle Paul wrote his first letter to Corinth he admonished the believers, *'there is jealousy and strife among you.... are you not walking like mere men?'* Envy and strife make for a rough road. Also in Revelation 12:10 we read, *'the accuser of our brethren has been thrown down, he who accuses them before our God day and night'*. When brother accuses brother, who is being served? Satan! Matthew 18:15-17. We must never permit unfounded and unproven accusations to be made against or between brothers. This is a shame to the Name above all names.

'....and all people will see the salvation of God'. Those who *'Make a straight, smooth road through the desert for our God'* by living in unity with each other; who meet together with Jesus supreme in their midst as Leader and Teacher; who simply accept the name and role of brothers; who work out problems that arise among them as the Spirit leads: These will bear the true testimony of Jesus before fellow believers and before those also who are still stuck in the wilderness (the world). They will be the example that is spoken of in Psalm 133:1: *'Behold, how good and how pleasant it is for brothers to dwell together in unity!'* The body of Christ is a living organism in which all the members perform their role on behalf of the body *'to the building up of itself in love'*. Ephesians 4:15-16.

The promised coming of the Lord in glory appears to have taken a very long time, yet it is worth remembering the words of Jesus that would portend His return: *"This gospel of the kingdom shall be preached in the whole world as a testimony to all the nations, and then the end will come."* Surely, *'all the nations'* will only have been reached with *'this gospel of the kingdom'* quite recently.

The dire predictions given in 2 Peter 3 which relate to the last days have not yet come to pass. *'But the day of the Lord will come like a thief, in which the heavens will pass away with a roar and the elements will be destroyed with intense heat, and the earth and its works will be burned up. Since all these things are to be destroyed in this way, what sort of people ought you to be in holy conduct and godliness, looking for and hastening the coming of the day of God'.* Those who look for the coming of the day of the Lord may hasten His coming by preparing the way before Him.

Ahead of us lie unimaginably distressing events for all inhabitants of the earth. Jesus warned His disciples, *"For then there will be a great tribulation, such as has not occurred since the beginning of the world until now, nor ever will. "Unless those days had been cut short, no life would have been saved...."* Matthew 24:21-22.

Before the imminent coming darkness of the tribulation creeps across the world, may we who hear what the Spirit is telling us, give ourselves utterly to the Lord Jesus to be His testimony, united in His love, and thus draw down upon us the blessing commanded by the Lord in the closing words of Psalm 133, *'....for there the Lord commanded the blessing – life forever'*. May we be the light of the world, the city set on a hill, that all may *'see the glory of God'* among His people. May we joyfully join hands with all those who will devote themselves to *'prepare the way of the Lord'* before Him.

Then the glory of God will be displayed before all the peoples of the earth through the Lord Jesus and through those who are with Him at His coming. *'Behold, He is coming with the clouds, and every eye will see Him, even those who pierced Him; and all the tribes of the earth will mourn over Him. So it is to be. Amen'*. Revelation 1:7.

We must not leave this topic without reference to many hidden ones, not only of this age but also throughout all of history, many of whom are known only to the Lord. Theirs is what might be described as an ecumenism of the heart:

- They have maintained transparent openness with all whom they have met who also love the Lord
- They have been humble in heart to encourage those less advanced in faith to express their God-given gift, while giving place to those more advanced along the heavenly way at whose feet they willingly learn
- They have, above all, been the *'peacemakers'* referred to by the Lord in Matthew 5:9 whom He assures us are blessed by Him to be *'sons of God'*.

May the writer and each one who reads these words be joined with others who will also play their part, that together we may *'prepare the way of the Lord'*.

CHAPTER 16
THIS GOSPEL OF THE KINGDOM

Scripture references: Matthew 24:14, Matthew 3:1-2, Matthew 4:17, Matthew 10:5-8, Galatians 6:7-8, Romans 8:11, 1 Thessalonians 1:1, Revelation 1:5-6, Ephesians 4:3-6.

In the New Testament the terms *'kingdom of heaven'* and *'kingdom of God'* are used interchangeably. One way or the other, the kingdom is referred to many times. In Matthew's Gospel alone the *'kingdom of heaven'* is mentioned thirty two times; the *'kingdom of God'* on two occasions. In the remaining three Gospels the *'kingdom of God'* is mentioned forty eight times and in the rest of the New Testament it is mentioned a further twenty times. Before the coming of the Lord Jesus in glory *'this gospel of the kingdom shall be preached in the whole world as a testimony to all the nations, and then the end will come"*. Matthew 24:14.

When the Lord Jesus came to earth He became the door that all the faithful ones, from under the law and under grace, must pass through to enter the kingdom of heaven. While Jesus was in this world the kingdom of heaven was *'at hand'*. Matthew 3:2. At Pentecost the kingdom of heaven became established on earth as the body of Christ, His church. From that auspicious day onwards all who have believed unto salvation through faith have been granted entrance into the kingdom. Since this kingdom cannot be divided there can only be one church, one body of Christ. Division is a tool of the devil. It comes from partaking of the fruit of the tree of the knowledge of good and evil.

The kingdom of heaven was embodied in the Lord Jesus when He, *'Son of God'*, was incarnated and became also *'Son of Man'*. From that time, although He is fully Son of God, He will forever be fully Son of Man. We who have received Him into us through repentance and faith are His increase. We have eternally been made members of His body. As such, that which is transformed in us into His likeness is also a living and eternal part of the kingdom of heaven. His intention is that we, who are fully sons of men, may also be made fully sons of God. Then His bride, who will incorporate all the perfected ones in Christ Jesus, both New and Old Testament saints, will be of the very essence and substance of her Bridegroom.

The old fallen flesh can have no part in the kingdom of heaven. Only that which has been transformed into His likeness can participate in His kingdom. The gospel of salvation provides entrance into the kingdom when the Holy Spirit enters a believer's spirit. *'.... that which is born of the Spirit is spirit'*. John 3:6. The Spirit is given as the pledge or down payment of the full perfection that shall be ours. Ephesians 1:14. From the instant of the new birth it is incumbent upon each believer to surrender all to Jesus so that, by walking daily in the Spirit, transformation into the perfect likeness of Jesus may be fully accomplished. This is the goal of salvation.

John the Baptist was the first to proclaim the message, *'repent for the kingdom of heaven is at hand'*. Matthew 3:2. The Amplified Version puts it this way: *'Repent (think differently; change your mind, regretting your sins and changing your conduct), for the kingdom of heaven is at hand'*. Shortly after commencing His ministry, *'Jesus began to preach and say, "Repent for the kingdom of heaven is at hand."* Matthew 4:17. Yet some while later Jesus sent forth His twelve disciples to *'preach, saying, "The kingdom of heaven is at hand."'* Matthew 10:7. The Lord could not send His disciples to tell others to repent, before they themselves had repented. It was not until after they had forsaken the Lord Jesus and had completely failed Him that they repented. It was only when they had come to the end of their natural strength that they were ready to receive the Holy Spirit and be clothed with power as His ambassadors to preach the gospel of the kingdom with His authority to all the nations.

Until Jesus rose from death *'the Holy Spirit was not yet, because Jesus was not yet glorified'*. John 7:39. (The word 'given' is not in the original Greek text.) Before the Holy Spirit could be *'the Spirit of Jesus'* (Acts 16:7) He must include the death and resurrection of Jesus and all the experiences that Jesus would go through in order to be glorified. *'But if the Spirit of Him who raised Jesus from the dead dwells in you, He who raised Christ Jesus from the dead will also give life to your mortal bodies through His Spirit who dwells in you'.* Romans 8:11.

"This gospel of the kingdom shall be preached in the whole world as a testimony to all the nations...." The gospel of salvation is widely acknowledged and proclaimed throughout Christendom, yet the gospel of the kingdom is almost universally misunderstood.

Why is this? It is because those who live in a state of disunity and division cannot proclaim the gospel of the kingdom, the holy and indivisible realm in which God makes His dwelling place. When Israel came out of Egypt and the tabernacle was constructed in the wilderness, the holy of holies became God's dwelling place on earth in the midst of His people Israel; likewise much later in the temple. The holy of holies was a type of the new Jerusalem which will be the eternal dwelling place of God and the Lamb. In this present age, all the perfected ones in Christ are being built together with all the believers of all the ages to compose the new Jerusalem.

What then is the kingdom? The kingdom is the realm over which God has absolute sovereignty. What is *'this gospel of the kingdom?'* The gospel of the kingdom is that through transformation into the likeness of Jesus all who believe unto salvation may participate in the *'bride, the wife of the Lamb'*.

Our entrance into the kingdom is by the new birth, in which the Holy Spirit joins with our human spirit. He, as the pledge of our inheritance, makes our ultimate destiny certain. However, the extent and willingness of our obedience to the Spirit will determine the progress we make towards perfection. *'Do not be deceived, God is not mocked; for whatever a man sows, this he will also reap. For the one who sows to his own flesh will from the flesh reap corruption, but the one who sows to the Spirit will from the Spirit reap eternal life'.* Galatians 6:7-8.

1 Thessalonians 1:1 uniquely expresses the heavenly position of the church while its members are situated here on earth. *'Paul and Silvanus and Timothy, to the church of the Thessalonians in God the Father and the Lord Jesus Christ: Grace to you and peace'.* The members of the church may be assembling physically on earth yet

the sphere of their assembling together and operation is *'in God the Father and the Lord Jesus Christ'*.

From the time of Pentecost it was God's plan and intention that His people should experience the fullness of the kingdom as priests unto Him. *'To Him who loves us and released us from our sins by His blood - and He has made us to be a kingdom, priests to His God and Father - to Him be the glory and the dominion forever and ever. Amen'*. Revelation 1:5-6. *'And coming to Him as to a living stone which has been rejected by men, but is choice and precious in the sight of God, you also, as living stones, are being built up as a spiritual house for a holy priesthood, to offer up spiritual sacrifices acceptable to God through Jesus Christ'*. 1 Peter 2:4-5.

The new Jerusalem, God's eternal dwelling place, is a spiritual house for a holy priesthood being built up with living stones. Those who have come to Him are both the living stones for the building and also the functioning priests who serve in it. We must always keep in mind that all who believe are functioning priests, not just a chosen few.

By whom then can *'this gospel of the kingdom....be preached in the whole world as a testimony to all the nations'*? It can be preached only by those who take a position of unity with all who belong to the Lord Jesus. Why? Because, if we preach to others that which we ourselves are not practicing, this is hypocrisy, and the anointing of the Holy Spirit will not be upon us. *"And to the angel of the church in Philadelphia write: He who is holy, who is true, who has the key of David, who opens and no one will shut, and who shuts and no one opens, says this: 'I know your deeds. Behold, I have put before you an open door which no one can shut, because you have a little power, and have kept My word, and have not denied My name'.* (Revelation 3:7-13). Only those who take the position of the church in Philadelphia, and they alone, are qualified to present this all important message of the kingdom to the nations.

We may be able to affirm that the gospel of salvation has been preached in the whole world as a testimony to all nations, but only the Lord can know whether *'this gospel of the kingdom'* has yet reached every nation.

Those who would be His true ambassadors must refuse division of any kind. In their individual walk and in their meeting together they must take the position of Philadelphia, *'being diligent to preserve the unity of the Spirit in the bond of peace. For there is one body and one Spirit, just as also you were called in one hope of your calling; one Lord, one faith, one baptism, one God and Father of all who is over all and through all and in all'*. Ephesians 4:3-6.

CHAPTER 17
I WILL COME AGAIN

Scripture references: Revelation 21:4, Revelation 12:1-12, Genesis 37:9-11, Revelation 3:21, 2 Thessalonians 2:7, John 14:3, 1 Thessalonians 4:15-17, Revelation 3:7-13, Luke 21:36.

The promise of Jesus, *'I will come again and receive you to Myself'*, John 14:3, expresses the living hope implanted by the Holy Spirit in all who have come to Jesus for grace and salvation. In the early church the word 'Maranatha' was often used as a greeting between believers. Maranatha means 'the Lord is coming' or 'Come, O Lord'. We who believe look forward to the Lord's promised return, when at last *"He will wipe away every tear from* (our) *eyes; and there will no longer be any death; there will no longer be any mourning, or crying, or pain; the first things have passed away."* Revelation 21:4.

Many references to the Lord's return and to the catching away of believers mention *'the trumpet of God'* or *'in the clouds'*. For example, *'....the Lord Himself will descend from heaven with a shout, with the voice of the archangel and with the trumpet of God, and the dead in Christ will rise first. Then we who are alive and remain will be caught up together with them in the clouds to meet the Lord in the air, and so we shall always be with the Lord'.* 1 Thessalonians 4:16-17. Other Scriptures such as 1 Corinthians 15:51-52, Daniel 7:13-14, Matthew 24:29-31, Revelation 1:7, 10:5-7 and 11:15 all refer to this same occasion. From these Scriptures it is clear that the ultimate fulfilment of Jesus' words, *'I will come again and receive you to Myself'* will occur right at the close of the age when *'The kingdom of the world has become the kingdom of our Lord and of His Christ; and He will reign forever and ever."* Revelation 11:15.

Teaching is widespread that Christians will not go through the tribulation, regardless of their readiness to meet the Lord; the erroneous doctrine of a pre-tribulation 'rapture'. We must take note and pay heed to the words of the Lord Jesus, *'you also must be ready; for the Son of Man is coming at an hour when you do not think He will'*. Matthew 24:44. A careful study of Scripture will show that only those who meet the Lord's definition of readiness will be caught away before the Lord's return. While salvation is *'not as a result of works, so that no one may boast'*, transformation into the likeness of Jesus will only be accomplished through utter surrender to Him and in moment by moment obedience to His will. These are *'the good works that God planned beforehand that we should walk in them'*. Ephesians 2:10.

In Revelation 12:1-12 we read of a male child about to be born from a woman. Before her is a great red dragon waiting to devour her child. However, as soon as the male child is born he is *'caught up to God and to His throne'*. This woman is *'clothed with the sun, and the moon under her feet, and on her head a crown of twelve stars'*. The sun which clothes the woman is Jesus through whom is the only way of salvation. The moon represents the law. Although *'until heaven and earth pass away, not the smallest letter or stroke shall pass from the Law until all is accomplished'*, yet the law under the woman's feet signifies that, in Christ, the woman has fully met the requirements of the law.

In Genesis 37:9 we read of Joseph's dream in which the sun and moon and eleven stars bowed down to him; Joseph himself being a twelfth star. The patriarchs, those who lived under the law, and those who have believed during the age of grace are all included in this woman. She represents the full complement of all those who have lived by faith, from Adam until the time of the events unveiled in this vision.

While he is in the woman the male child is part of her. He is her hidden and strongest part. After he is born he represents her before the throne of God in opposing the great red dragon, Satan. In the Garden of Eden, Satan was the serpent who stood before the woman and tempted her to sin. Now, this woman's offspring, the male child, who is to rule all the nations with a rod of iron, stands before the throne of God to petition that Satan, who has now become the great red dragon and *'the accuser of our brethren'*, be cast forever out of heaven. This male child carries the full authority of God which Adam forfeited through disobedience.

'He who overcomes, I will grant to him to sit down with Me on My throne, as I also overcame and sat down with My Father on His throne'. Revelation 3:21. Jesus Himself is the first overcomer, and all who overcome do so in Him. The male child is composed of many overcomers in Christ.

How did this male child overcome Satan? *'....they overcame him because of the blood of the Lamb and because of the word of their testimony, and they did not love their life even when faced with death'.* Those who overcome Satan know with certainty the power of the blood to cleanse from all sin. They bear the testimony of Jesus, for they display in their lives not themselves, but Him. Their lives are also utterly in His hands to do with as He will. They are willing to give their life's blood for their Beloved. *'For the mystery of lawlessness is already at work; only he* (the male child) *who now restrains will do so until he is taken out of the way'.* 2 Thessalonians 2:7. At this time in which we are living all Hell is about to break loose on the earth.

'And there was war in heaven, Michael and his angels waging war with the dragon. The dragon and his angels waged war, and they were not strong enough, and there was no longer a place found for them in heaven'. Since the beginning of time Satan has appeared before God as *'the accuser of our brethren'*. *'Now there was a day when the sons of God came to present themselves before the Lord, and Satan also came among them'.* Job 1:6. Finally, Satan will be cast out of heaven, thrown down to the earth, and his accusations before God will have been stopped.

"Woe to the earth and the sea, because the devil has come down to you, having great wrath, knowing that he has only a short time." How short a time? After *'her child was caught up to God and to His throne....the woman fled into the wilderness where she had a place prepared by God, so that there she would be nourished for one thousand two hundred and sixty days'.* One thousand two hundred and sixty days is forty two lunar months or three and a half years. The tribulation, according to the prophecy of the seventy weeks given to Daniel, will last seven years, so three and a half years represent the second half of the tribulation. Therefore we can say

with confidence that the birth of the male child and his being caught up to God will occur just before the commencement of the great tribulation.

"And to the angel of the church in Philadelphia write....". Although the church in Philadelphia existed among the churches at the time that the Revelation was unveiled to the apostle John, its inclusion here is also prophetic for the future. Philadelphia means 'brotherly love' (love for the brothers). This is the characteristic of the church in Philadelphia. If someone is a brother he is welcome, no other qualification is necessary. All may attend the gatherings of the saints and all may participate as the Spirit shall lead.

The Lord commends them with these words, *"I know your deeds. Behold, I have put before you an open door which no one can shut...."* People, or principalities and powers, may try to oppose these Philadelphians but the Lord has put before them *'an open door which no one can shut'*.

Why has the Lord put before them an open door? *"....because you have a little power, and have kept My word, and have not denied My name."* Paul said *'....I am well content with weaknesses, with insults, with distresses, with persecutions, with difficulties, for Christ's sake; for when I am weak, then I am strong'*. 2 Corinthians 12:10. Those of Philadelphia know they have but a little strength yet, if the Lord is in a matter, they know whatever they do will prosper.

To deny the Lord's name is to adopt another name. We note that *'the disciples were first called Christians in Antioch'*. When asked about our faith we may respond that we are a Christian. However, if we are meeting with others as members of an assembly which bears a name which distinguishes and sets it apart from other gatherings of believers, we are denying that the church, God's ekklesia, is one and indivisible. *"My beloved responded and said to me, 'Arise, my darling, my beautiful one, And come along."* Song of Solomon 2:10. Our Bridegroom is calling His bride-to-be to come to Him, leaving all else.

'Because you have kept the word of My perseverance, I also will keep you from the hour of testing, that hour which is about to come upon the whole world, to test those who dwell on the earth'. Those who meet the Lord's requirements as Philadelphians will also be caught up to the heavens before this worldwide hour of testing. This hour of testing will be the great tribulation. The Lord assures those of Philadelphia that they already have the crown. Their danger is that they may lose it.

Why would the Lord Jesus give so great a reward to those of Philadelphia? Jesus died that *'He might also gather together into one the children of God who are scattered abroad'*. John 11:22. *'But now in Christ Jesus you who formerly were far off have been brought near by the blood of Christ. For He Himself is our peace, who made both groups into one and broke down the barrier of the dividing wall....'* Ephesians 2:13-14. The blood of Christ not only dealt with the dividing wall that existed between Jew and Gentile but created peace and unity forever between all who would follow Him thereafter. All divisions among God's people are a denial of what Jesus accomplished through His sacrificial death on the cross.

Since these two companies of overcomers, those who comprise the male child and the ones who take the position of Philadelphia, are taken mid-way through the tribulation we must assume that those who do not qualify as overcomers will not be caught away until they do qualify or, as we have noted, at the time of Jesus' return.

May we maintain the unity of the Spirit in the bond of peace with all who love our Lord Jesus Christ. May we *'accept one another, just as Christ also accepted us to the glory of God'*. Romans 15:7. May we, too, be given grace that we may be among the overcoming ones who stand fast in Christ to face Satan. *"But keep on the alert at all times, praying that you may have strength to escape all these things that are about to take place, and to stand before the Son of Man."* Luke 21:36.

CHAPTER 18
YOUR WILL BE DONE

Scripture references: Luke 11:1-4, Matthew 6:9-10, Matthew 25:1-30, Galatians 6:7-8,. Revelation 18:4-5, John 17:20-23.

'Lord, teach us to pray', the disciples asked Jesus. Luke 11:1-4. In reply He gave them a simple yet profound prayer. This prayer is not only familiar to all believers, but is widely known to others who do not share our faith. *"Your will be done"* means first of all, your will be done in me. This means giving up my right to myself to Jesus that I may follow Him and become His disciple.

"Your will be done, on earth as it is in heaven" Matthew 6:10. This is the central theme within this prayer. It is God's intention that this be achieved through His people here on earth. God wants a clear and unwavering testimony before mankind.

Identifying and overcoming the failures to do God's will and to meet God's standards has been the subject of the first seventeen chapters of this book. As these shortcomings are faced and as all is brought back to God's standard, the heart of our Father in heaven will be satisfied and this prayer that the Lord gave us will be fulfilled.

Following the birth of the church at Pentecost and for quite a while afterwards, God's testimony was being displayed through His people *'on earth'*. Heaven ruled in the power of the Spirit through a united people. It was said of Paul and his companions, *"These men who have upset the world have come here also."* Acts 17:6. Wherever the Lord's will is being done, worldly ones will be stirred up by Satan to oppose the faithful ones who are performing His will.

Something that is noteworthy throughout the Scriptures is that God never takes shortcuts in attaining His goals, nor does He permit His people to do so. Although all power has been given to Jesus in heaven and on earth, when He gives authority to His people to act in some way He will not step in and take over the assignment Himself. All that is accomplished in His Name will be measured in accordance with His standards, whether concerning His people individually or collectively.

Take heed 'foolish virgins'! Your unwillingness to pay the price for transformation will cost you *'the marriage supper of the Lamb'*. Then you must pay the full price for the oil you ought to have purchased during your lifetime. Take heed 'wicked and lazy slaves'! You bury your talent in the ground. Your restoration will be in outer darkness where there is *'weeping and gnashing of teeth'*. This is a most serious matter. Matthew 25:1-30.

'Do not be deceived, God is not mocked; for whatever a man sows, this he will also reap. For the one who sows to his own flesh will from the flesh reap corruption, but the one who sows to the Spirit will from the Spirit reap eternal life'. Galatians 6:7-8. At the new birth the Spirit sows Himself into us as eternal life. His life in us will increase as we permit Him to do His work. Sowing to the Spirit is the means by which we increase the oil or multiply the talent we have received. This is how we are transformed and made ready to receive *'the prize of the upward call of God in Christ Jesus'*.

Take heed those who usurp the authority of the Holy Spirit! You hinder and suppress the functioning of His people. How can His body, the church, be built up unless all the gifts are permitted to play their part? God hates *'the deeds of the Nicolaitans'*. Nicolaitans are those who usurp the Lord's authority over the common believers.

Almost all the failures and shortcomings of the church on earth today occur because Jesus is not Lord among His gathered people. *'I heard another voice from heaven, saying, "Come out of her, my people, so that you will not participate in her sins and receive of her plagues; for her sins have piled up as high as heaven, and God has remembered her iniquities."* Revelation 18:4-5.

If we would be among those true and faithful ones, the Lord's overcomers, we cannot wait. We must come out now and, in the power of the Spirit, be part of a separated people in our locality whose sole aim is *"Your will be done, on earth as it is in heaven."*

Jesus prayed to the Father shortly before His atoning death, *"The glory which You have given Me I have given to them, that they may be one, just as We are one....so that the world may know that You sent Me."* John 17:22-23. At the core of this prayer are the words, *'so that the world may know that You sent Me'*.

There can be no doubt that this prayer of the Lord Jesus will be answered by the Father. There will be a remnant who will bear His testimony of unity that the world can no longer deny. Then all who are confronted by this *'testimony of Jesus'* will have no choice but to acknowledge that the Father has indeed sent His Son, Jesus, into the world. Those who respond to the gospel will be saved. Those who reject so great a salvation will be eternally lost. There will no longer be any excuse.

It is impossible to meet God's standard except in the power of the Spirit. His will and His eternal purpose can only be accomplished through those who trust in the Lord with all their heart. Those who trust the Lord fully will join together with others of like mind and will dedicate themselves to meet God's standard at whatever cost.

The writer of these words prays that the contents of the preceding seventeen chapters will offer guidance to all whose heart longs that 'God's will be done on earth as it is in heaven'.

God's divine authority expressed among His people will have these characteristics:

- The 'so great salvation' offered at such a cost to the Lord will be sought with all their heart
- Their aim will be to allow the Holy Spirit's work to be completed unto perfection
- They will walk step by step with Jesus, yoked to Him and in absolute dependence upon Him
- Their fellowship together with others will always be devoted to the building up of His one body in love
- Wherever two or three meet in His name, His presence and His authority will be evident
- He will be the sole and undisputed Lord of His body, the church
- He will be regularly remembered with gratitude in the bread and the wine

- All will recognize that every moment of their earthly life belongs to the Lord, that His will may be done
- Prophets will be raised up and will function within the daily corporate life
- What the Lord desires from His people will be the focus of all events and choices of action
- Every member will be a consecrated channel through whom the word of God may come
- All will hold their possessions, even their spiritual gifts, as not theirs but His
- There will be one Head, and all believers will be welcomed as brothers
- Members will freely use their gifts, as the Spirit leads, for the common good
- Through humble obedience they will in mutuality prepare the way of the Lord
- All will function as messengers and ambassadors of the kingdom of heaven
- In their united stand in opposing Satan they will hasten the Lord's coming

May the Lord Jesus provide a clear vision of the calamitous days that lie immediately ahead of us. May we respond and act accordingly that we may, in truth, be the true testimony of Jesus *'known and read by all men'*. May heaven rule in these days through a called out people, in the mighty power of the Spirit. Maranatha. *'Amen. Come, Lord Jesus'*.

CHAPTER 19
THE TESTIMONY OF JESUS

Scripture references: John 14:8-10, John 10:8-10, John 1:14, John 17:22-23, 1 Peter 2:9-10, John 9:5, Matthew 5:14-16, 2 Corinthians 2:14-17,.

In order to bear testimony to someone or to something surely we must portray the unmistakable image or quality of who or what we portray. As a simple illustration, a video or a biography may bear testimony to an exceptional human life. Although these examples can only provide a window through which we may gain a glimpse of a noteworthy individual yet, if what is portrayed reveals qualities that we would wish to emulate, then we may choose to make this individual our role-model.

Many who have come to salvation through faith did so because they received a glimpse of Jesus through a believer or directly through the word of God. Even though limited and seemingly small, this glimpse drew them to Him. Although they may not have been aware of it, each one who had this experience will have encountered the testimony of Jesus. What had previously been hidden from them of the Person of Jesus was all at once displayed.

In John 14:8-10 we have a wonderful example of one who is bearing the testimony of another. Jesus disciple Philip requested of Jesus, *"Lord show us the Father and it is enough for us."* Jesus replied *"He who has seen me has seen the Father; how do you say, 'Show us the Father'?* In other words, Jesus told Philip, "I am the testimony of My Father." When you look at Me you are beholding the image of My Father. Jesus is the exact image of the invisible God. Colossians 1:15.

Jesus continued, *"Do you not believe that I am in the Father, and the Father is in Me? The words that I say to you I do not speak on My own initiative, but the Father abiding in Me does His works."* When you hear the words that I speak, it is the Father Himself speaking through Me. When you see the deeds I do, you are watching the Father working through Me

In John 1:14 we are given a wonderful description of Jesus as the testimony of His Father, *'....we beheld His glory, glory as of the only begotten of the Father, full of grace and truth'*. Also in 2 Corinthians 4:6 *For God, who said, "Light shall shine out of darkness," is the One who has shone in our hearts to give the Light of the knowledge of the glory of God in the face of Christ.*

Contained within the prayer of Jesus to His Father recorded in John 17:22-23 are these words *'....the glory which You have given to Me I have given to them'*. The glory that He has given to His own will shine the glorious light of His testimony through them. The purpose of this glory is *'that they may be one, just as We are one'*. God's desire and plan is that His people might in perfect unity display His glory.

From this it must be obvious that Christendom, or any of its countless divisions, cannot bear or display the testimony of Jesus. The testimony of Jesus will always be expressed in perfect unity that will demand the attention of those before whom it is displayed.

The words of 1 Peter 2:9-10 describe the testimony of Jesus upon His people in a slightly different way. *'....you are a chosen race, a royal priesthood, a holy nation, a people for God's own possession, so that you may proclaim the excellencies of Him who has called you out of darkness into His marvelous light'*. Surely as the excellencies of Him are being proclaimed through the words, works and behaviour of His own they will bear His image and display His testimony.

"While I am in the world, I am the Light of the world." John 9:5. Just as the Lord Jesus was the light of the world throughout His earthly life, so His light is given to His people that He may shine through them. *"You are the light of the world. A city set on a hill cannot be hidden; nor does anyone light a lamp and put it under a basket, but on the lampstand, and it gives light to all who are in the house."* Matthew 5:14-16. This is a reminder that His people are to be a lampstand shining forth His glory to all those within His house; that is, to the members of His church on earth, as well as to all inhabitants of the earth.

'But thanks be to God, who always leads us in triumph in Christ, and manifests through us the sweet aroma of the knowledge of Him in every place. For we are a fragrance of Christ to God among those who are being saved and among those who are perishing....' 2 Corinthians 2:14-15. As individuals and as a company of believers, if we will truly be a fragrance of Christ to God and to the saved and unsaved ones, then what will be a more compelling testimony of Jesus than that?

We have alluded several times in these chapters to the deep significance of His people bearing the testimony of Jesus. Now may we humbly conclude Part One of this treatise with a description of what being the testimony of Jesus really means in practice.

- Others when they look at us will see Him, even though they may not be aware Whom they are seeing and even though we are unaware that we are displaying Him
- It will be His voice and His message they will hear, even though the words are expressed through our mouth, in our manner of speaking
- It will be His nature and ways they will observe, even though the behaviour and actions they are observing are expressed through us

The Holy Spirit was given to every individual believer to transform each one into the perfect likeness of Jesus. The Holy Spirit was given that every gathering of God's people might exalt the Lord Jesus as central and supreme in their midst and that full attention of all present might be focused upon Him.

That *'we are a fragrance of Christ to God among those who are being saved and among those who are perishing'* will be the evidence that we are indeed the living individual and collective testimony of Jesus. Amen! So be it Lord.

PART TWO
WALKING IN THE TRUTH

Introduction to Part Two

Poem: 'Behold the Holy City'

Chapter 20 – Right to the Tree of Life 96

Chapter 21 – Receive the Holy Spirit 102

Chapter 22 – All with One Mind 107

Chapter 23 – According to the Pattern 113

Chapter 24 – Clothed with Power...................117

Chapter 25 – Preach the Gospel...................123

Chapter 26 – The Kingdom of Heaven...................127

Chapter 27 – Assembling Together 133

Chapter 28 – Filled with Joy and with the Holy Spirit 138

Chapter 29 – You May All Prophesy 142

Chapter 30 – Building Up the Body of Christ 147

Chapter 31 – The Word has Sounded Forth 151

Chapter 32 – In Much Tribulation 156

Chapter 33 – The Church in God 161

Chapter 34 – He Himself is Our Peace 166

Chapter 35 – His Wife has Made Herself Ready 171

Chapter 36 – The Marriage Supper of the Lamb 177

Chapter 37 – The Dwelling Place of God 182

Chapter 38 – The Spirit and the Bride 186

Introduction to Part Two

This second part – 'Walking in the Truth' has been written especially for those who have a deep desire to meet God's standards; to follow the Lord Jesus fully; to live the victorious life in Christ.

Its focus is upon the New Testament era unto the dawn of eternity and the unveiling of *'the bride, the wife of the Lamb'*. It is within this time span that we who have believed unto salvation find ourselves that we may play the part determined for us by the Lord. *'....For we are His masterpiece, created in Christ Jesus for good works, which God prepared beforehand in order that we would walk in them'*. Ephesians 2:10, Recovery Version.

Since each one of us as individuals and together as a company of His own, have this foreordained purpose laid upon us, let us pursue it with loving devotion; for the sake of *'Him who loves us and released us from our sins by His blood - and He has made us to be a kingdom, priests to His God and Father - to Him be the glory and the dominion forever and ever. Amen.* Revelation 1:5-6.

Jesus made it quite clear to His disciples, as to us today, that *"many are called, but few are chosen."* Matthew 22:14. In order to be chosen we must be wholly and devotedly available to Him, as those did in His parable of the labourers in the vineyard. Matthew 20:1-16. How could they be chosen to work in the master's vineyard if they had not made themselves available to Him in the marketplace.

The Lord's great plan, within which all who believe have been given a vital part, is much more than a matter of our individual walk. Its ultimate outcome will be the new Jerusalem as the eternal dwelling place of God and the Lamb, which is even now being built up of countless saved and glorified saints, all of whom have been constituted as precious stones through the work of the divine Spirit.

Thomas H. Walker
August 2017

BEHOLD THE HOLY CITY

In Eden's fairest garden God's tree of life was found,
There He located Adam to tend and till the ground;
Knowledge of good and evil, a rival tree beguiles
Eve and her husband Adam, deceived by Satan's wiles.

A seed through Eve was promised to bruise the serpent's head,
His heel would suffer also, yet He'd rise from the dead;
Destroyed the works of Satan, a new creation comes,
A righteous, holy nation, her priests are God's own sons.

At Pentecost descended the Spirit of the Lord
On all of those devoted to pray in one accord,
To clothe them with His power and make them bold to send
The gospel of the kingdom to earth's remotest end.

In unity she started, the church of God's own choice,
All members of His body spoke with a single voice;
All sold their homes, possessions, and gave the money paid
To share among all members as any needed aid.

Yet after such beginnings the church began decline,
One church in every city had been the Lord's design;
Now monster church took over, it claimed the truth to hold,
Then multiplied divisions sprang up as hearts grew cold.

Yet through it all a remnant who walked the way of truth,
God kept His hand upon them as they His path pursued;
They've faced much persecution; they've shared their Master's pain;
Their cross they've boldly taken; for Him there's been great gain.

For such the marriage supper, then reign a thousand years,
From those who've suffered with Him He'll wipe away all tears;
These precious overcomers, the meek, the earth will own,
While those who scorned their talent in outer darkness groan.

Behold the Holy City, the dwelling place of God,
Descending out of heaven, bride for the Lamb adorned,
With precious stones her substance, with costly pearls her gates,
From every tribe and nation her Bridegroom she awaits.

God's dwelling place forever, her lamp the precious Lamb
The temple deep within her, home of the Great I Am;
Displayed before new heavens the bride in beauty lies,
All galaxies behold her whose glory fills the skies.

Thomas Walker
September 2016

CHAPTER 20
RIGHT TO THE TREE OF LIFE

Scripture references: Genesis 2:7-9, Genesis 2:15-17, Ezekiel 28:11-15, Genesis 3:22-24, Revelation 2:1-7, 1 Corinthians 14:26, Revelation 22:14.

Then the Lord God formed man of dust from the ground, and breathed into his nostrils the breath of life; and man became a living being. Genesis 2:7. Through a creative act of the Lord God, Adam was formed of the common elements of which the earth consists. He was given the breath of life that he might become a living soul. God also formed in Adam a spirit; *Thus declares the Lord who stretches out the heavens, lays the foundation of the earth, and forms the spirit of man within him....* Zechariah 12:1. However, Adam's spirit was not yet spiritually alive. In order that his spirit might be enlivened, he needed the Holy Spirit to come and indwell his spirit so that he might share in the divine life of God. *'That which is born of the Spirit is spirit'* John 3:6. Had Adam and his wife Eve chosen to eat of the fruit of the tree of life they would immediately have entered upon eternal life. There would have been no need for redemption.

In the genealogy of Mary, the mother of Jesus, in the closing verses of Luke 3 we read, *'....the son of Enosh, the son of Seth, the son of Adam, the son of God'*. As God's unique creation, Adam is stated to be *'the son of God'*. All who have ever been born upon this earth since the beginning have come from one – Adam. *'....and He made from one man every nation of mankind to live on all the face of the earth'*. Acts 17:26. God's eternal purpose and plan started with one man and it will be completed in one glorious bride for the Lord Jesus Christ, composed of countless individual members; all the redeemed and transformed ones down through the ages.

'The Lord God planted a garden toward the east, in Eden; and there He placed the man whom He had formed'. Within this wonderfully endowed earth God chose a special place to plant a garden. This was a perfect garden in which *'the Lord God caused to grow every tree that is pleasing to the sight and good for food'*.

We might assume from the description of the order of things that God did not plant this garden until after Adam had been created, yet in Ezekiel 28:13-15 we read that God Himself placed Lucifer *'the anointed cherub who covers'* in *'Eden, the garden of God'*, before he rebelled and became Satan. He is described thus; *"You were blameless in your ways from the day you were created until unrighteousness was found in you."* When Eve and Adam encountered Satan as the serpent in the garden, he embodied all unrighteousness.

The Garden of Eden was unique. In the midst of this garden were two trees, *'the tree of life'* and *'the tree of the knowledge of good and evil'*. These two trees that the Lord God caused to grow *'out of the ground'* represented two kingdoms. The tree of life represented *'the kingdom of God'*. This tree represented dependence on God, enjoyment of His presence, partaking of His divine life, and acting in accordance with His purpose in perfect harmony with Him. The tree of the knowledge of good and evil represented *'the kingdom of this world'*, which is the domain of Satan. It offers a life of independence from God in which there is constant exposure to the suggestions and insinuations of the evil one. It offered independence to choose to obey or to override the conscience.

Before Eve was taken out from Adam and fashioned into a woman to become his wife, the Lord God had *'commanded the man, saying, "From any tree of the garden you may eat freely* (including the tree of life)*; but from the tree of the knowledge of good and evil you shall not eat, for in the day that you eat from it you will surely die."'* Genesis 2:16-17. Thus these two trees offered a choice to Adam and to his wife Eve. If they partook of the fruit of the tree of life they would receive the divine life into them and would live forever in perfect harmony with God's will and purpose. If, however, they chose to disobey God's command and eat the fruit of the tree of the knowledge of good and evil, they would be condemned to enter Satan's domain of death, disharmony and destruction. Alas, we know the choice they made.

Adam had led a privileged existence while he was alone and later together with his wife Eve. The Lord God had bestowed on them

His authority to rule over all created things and over every living thing that moves on the earth, including the serpent. Yet, although they knew the penalty for disobeying God, they chose to lay aside His authority and to listen to Satan.

Previously it had been customary for the Lord God to visit the garden to walk and to talk with Adam and his wife. Now we read that *'they heard the sound of the Lord God walking in the garden in the cool of the day'*. Genesis 3:8. They had come to recognize the sound of His footsteps as He walked in the garden on His way to commune with them. How they must have looked forward to these wonderful times of fellowship. However, on this occasion, they were both overwhelmed with guilt because of what they had done, so they hid themselves.

We pause to note that the Lord God, whose fellowship they enjoyed in the garden, must have been Jesus, for *'God made man in His own image'*. Genesis 1:27. And we know that Jesus is *'the image of the invisible God....'* Colossians 1:15.

We might suppose that, if we ourselves had enjoyed such visitations and fellowship with Jesus, we would surely never have fallen for Satan's lies. However this would be to deny the persuasive powers of the evil one to influence the unregenerate heart. The choice that first Eve, who came forth from Adam, and that he himself chose to make, not only affected them, but through their *'transgression there resulted condemnation to all men'*. Romans 5:18.

When the Lord God issued His verdict upon Satan, then upon Eve, and lastly upon Adam, he promised that a seed would come through the woman that would bruise the head of Satan under that seed's bruised heel. Many centuries later Jesus, the promised seed of Eve, was incarnated. He *'appeared for this purpose, to destroy the works of the devil'*. 1 John 3:8.

Having disobeyed God and suffered the consequences, the Lord God had no alternative but to expel the disobedient pair from the Garden of Eden and *'He stationed the cherubim and the flaming sword which turned every direction to guard the way to the tree of life'*. Thus they, and all their descendants, lost the right to eat of the tree of life.

However, the right to eat of the fruit of the tree of life has been restored again to all those who believe unto salvation through the sacrificial death of the promised seed, our Lord Jesus Christ. Before He died He had told His disciples *'I am the living bread that came down out of heaven'* He also told them, *'so he who eats Me, he also will live because of Me'*. John 6:51,57.

Right here we need to pause and make something quite clear: It is God's intention and provision for those who come to the Lord Jesus in repentance and faith, that they not only partake of the fruit of the tree of life (that is *'the living bread'*), but that they sustain themselves with no other spiritual food.

In the long forty year wandering of the Israelites in the wilderness of Sinai, God daily supplied His people with food from the heavens. They gave it the name manna, meaning 'What is it?' All they had to do was to collect it each morning. It was the complete food. All they needed besides manna was water to quench their thirst.

Revelation 2:1-7 records the Lord's message to the church in Ephesus. This church is commended for many of its attributes and actions. *'I know your deeds and your toil and perseverance.... you have perseverance and have endured for My name's sake, and have not grown weary'*. The message continues however, *'But I have this against you, that you have left your first love'*. This word *'first'* can also mean 'best'. The love the members of this assembly had displayed for the Lord at the beginning had begun to grow cold. The message ended with a promise to those who maintained that first passionate love for the Lord Jesus; *'He who has an ear, let him hear what the Spirit says to the churches. To him who overcomes, I will grant to eat of the tree of life which is in the Paradise of God.'*

Can we perhaps recall the fervour that was ours following our coming to Jesus in repentance and faith? Our life, our whole future had taken a fresh and exciting new direction.

We must ask ourselves "Is this mighty flow of love that *'has been poured out within our hearts through the Holy Spirit'* that is spoken about in Romans 5:5 still being poured out from us back to the Giver as it was in those former days?" *We love, because He first loved us.* 1 John 4:19.

The freshness and intensity of our love for Jesus will determine our appetite for the real and transforming spiritual food; that which is only to be found in Him.

How very serious a matter this is for, if we have left our first and best love, we will lose our appetite for the fruit of the tree of life and we will no longer desire it. We may look to the world to fill the void with its empty distractions. Above all else we shall lose the awareness and constancy of His presence accompanying us along life's journey. What a great loss!

1 Corinthians 14:26 *What is the outcome then, brethren? When you assemble, each one has a psalm, has a teaching, has a revelation, has a tongue, has an interpretation. Let all things be done for edification.* It is the Lord's intention that when His people come together to meet with Him, whether they are many or few, each one has something to contribute out of the divine life that indwells them.

May daily enjoyment of the heavenly manna of the Scriptures in communion with the Lord Jesus become our invariable practice, that we may always be ready and able to supply His divine life to others.

John 21:15,17. *"Feed My lambs"...."Feed My sheep".* If we would feed and encourage His lambs and His sheep then, surely, we must first be fully fed ourselves.

Likewise, if we would become qualified to spread the *'gospel of the kingdom'* to others, or out into the world that so greatly needs to hear it, then must we not first receive into us and experience in our personal walk with the Lord Jesus that which we have been called upon to proclaim? Yet the word cautions us that we may not go forth to preach unless we are sent by the Spirit of God? *How will they preach unless they are sent?'* Romans 10:15. Only the Holy Spirit can prepare us and send us out into the harvest.

Deuteronomy 6:5, *"You shall love the Lord your God with all your heart and with all your soul and with all your might."* This was given as the great commandment to the people of Israel through God's servant Moses. No one could keep it. Yet, as we press on to enter into the fullness of life in the Spirit we shall find that our love for the Lord Jesus will grow in our heart until it becomes our constant joy and experience. Then, *'we may have the right to the tree of life, and may enter by the gates into the city'*, Revelation 22:14.

May the transmitter of these words, and those who read them, be granted grace to enter into this ever deepening love relationship with the Lord Jesus; the love possessed by the wife of the Lamb who, because of her love for Him, has chosen to make herself ready for her marriage. *'To him who overcomes* (maintains his first/best love), *I will grant to eat of the tree of life which is in the Paradise of God.'* *'....so he who eats Me, he also will live because of Me'*.

CHAPTER 21
RECEIVE THE HOLY SPIRIT

Scripture references: John 1:1-5, Genesis 1:3, Psalms 33:8-9, Mark 4:37-41, Luke 5:12-13, Genesis 2:7, 1 Corinthians 15:45-46, John 14:16-18, John 20:19-22 Darby, Ephesians 1:13-14 AMP.

'In the beginning was the Word, and the Word was with God, and the Word was God'. Like a clarion call, these few initial words of the Gospel of John announce to all who will read and receive them, that the Lord Jesus is the great Creator of all that exists in the heavens and on earth, including God's highest creation of the man Adam. We are left with no doubt that the Word is Jesus and that Jesus Himself is God. *'All things came into being through Him, and apart from Him nothing came into being that has come into being'*.

Then God said, "Let there be light"; and there was light. Genesis 1:3. *For He spoke, and it was done; He commanded, and it stood fast.* Psalm 33:9. God's speaking and acting are one. Not only was this true in the events of creation but it is true on any and every occasion when He exercises His authority in any situation. However, freedom to choose whether to obey God's ordinances and commandments has been given to mankind. We are free to choose His will or ours.

During His life on earth Jesus lived in perfect obedience to the Father's will. What the Father instructed Jesus to do He carried out perfectly. In fact He said and did nothing that He was not instructed to say or to do. John 5:19-21. *"Truly, truly, I say to you, the Son can do nothing of Himself, unless it is something He sees the Father doing; for whatever the Father does, these things the Son also does in like manner. "For the Father loves the Son, and shows Him all things that He Himself is doing; and the Father will show Him greater works than these, so that you will marvel. "For just as the Father raises the dead and gives them life, even so the Son also gives life to whom He wishes."*

A wonderful example of this last statement is the raising of Lazarus from the dead. John 11:41-44 *'So they removed the stone. Then Jesus raised His eyes, and said, "Father, I thank You that You have heard Me. "I knew that You always hear Me; but because of the people standing around I said it, so that they may believe that You sent Me." When He had said these things, He cried out with a loud voice, "Lazarus, come forth." The man who had died came forth, bound hand and foot with wrappings, and his face was wrapped around with a cloth. Jesus said to them, "Unbind him, and let him go."*

Throughout His ministry there are numerous examples of Jesus speaking the word, immediately followed by the effect. For instance in Mark 4:38-41. *Jesus Himself was in the stern, asleep on the cushion; and they woke Him and said to Him, "Teacher, do You not care that we are perishing?" And He got up and rebuked the wind and said to the sea, "Hush, be still." And the wind died down and it became perfectly calm.* The wondering disciples responded to this event, *"Who then is this, that even the wind and the sea obey Him?"*

Prior to His sacrificial death, Jesus gathered His disciples to inform them of His departure to the Father and His provision for them of *'another Helper, that He may be with you forever; that is the Spirit of truth, whom the world cannot receive, because it does not see Him or know Him, but you know Him because He abides with you and will be in you'*. *"I will not leave you as orphans; I will come to you'*. John 14:16-18. Although they did not fully understand it at the time, Jesus was telling them that He would come to them as the *'life-giving Spirit'* who would come into them and dwell in them. *'So also it is written, "The first man, Adam, became a living soul." The last Adam became a life-giving spirit.* 1 Corinthians 15:45-46.

It was through His death and resurrection that Jesus became *'a life-giving spirit'*. All the experiences of Jesus' earthly life, His death and resurrection, were also entered into by the Holy Spirit.

This brings us to the central point of this chapter which is how and when did the disciples receive the Holy Spirit?

On the evening of His resurrection Jesus appeared among His disciples who were gathered in an upper room. He passed into the room through the closed door. Not surprisingly we are informed that *'they were startled and frightened'*, Luke 24:37. Jesus calmed them with the words, *"Peace [be] to you." And having said this, he shewed to them his hands and his side. The disciples rejoiced therefore, having seen the Lord. [Jesus] said therefore again to them, Peace [be] to you: as the Father sent me forth, I also send you.* But it is what happened next that is key to this appearance of the Lord Jesus. *And having said this, he breathed into [them], and says to them, Receive [the] Holy Spirit:* John 20:19-22, Darby Version. Jesus spoke the word, then He breathed into them. Right then and there all those who were present in that upper room were born again of the Spirit of God and became sent ones commissioned by the Lord. As we noted earlier, God speaks and it is done.

There will have been others in that upper room, as well as the apostles, who received the Holy Spirit, how many we cannot know. We do know that Thomas was not present. Before the Lord could impart the Holy Spirit into Thomas and commission him also, he must be brought to believe that God had raised Jesus from the dead, for Thomas had expressed doubt that Jesus had been resurrected.

It was eight days later that Thomas, after being invited by Jesus to put his finger into the nail holes in His hands and to reach out his hand and put it into His side, confessed *"My Lord and my God"* and he was likewise born of the *'life-giving Spirit'* and commissioned to go forth.

Shortly thereafter, at Pentecost, all who were in that upper room were *'clothed with power from on high'* by the same Holy Spirit that they might go forth to fulfil their part of the great commission to preach the gospel of the kingdom to all nations.

All the descendants of the man Adam who would enter this journey of faith must be born of this *'life-giving Spirit'*. For, *'if anyone does not have the Spirit of Christ, he does not belong to Him'*. Romans 8:9.

Ephesians 1:13, *In Him, you also, after listening to the message of truth, the gospel of your salvation - having also believed, you were sealed in Him with the Holy Spirit of promise....*Seals provide evidence that a decision has been taken, or something has been approved, by someone in authority. In days gone by, hot wax was applied at a joining point of a folded document and a unique stamp was imprinted into the soft wax. When the Lord sets His seal on us it means that He claims us as His own forever. 1 Corinthians 6:19-

20. *Or do you not know that your body is a temple of the Holy Spirit who is in you, whom you have from God, and that you are not your own? For you have been bought with a price: therefore glorify God in your body.* This is the Lord's authoritative word. He has paid the full price for us. We are no longer our own. We who believe unto salvation have no rights independent of Him.

Ephesians 1:14, '*....the Holy Spirit....is given as a pledge of our inheritance, with a view to the redemption of God's own possession'*. Throughout history, right down to the present day, money, or something of value, may be given as a guarantee that, within agreed terms, the full amount will be paid or fulfilled. Such is the intention here. Redemption is the act of buying back, or rescuing from loss, something that needs to be returned to its rightful owner, or be restored to its original condition.

On the cross the Lord Jesus paid the full price for our redemption. Our responsibility is to surrender to the one who bought us for Himself, so that His full restorative work may be done in us. The ones who have received the Holy Spirit have an absolute obligation laid on them to allow Him freedom to transform them into the perfect likeness of Jesus.

In every transaction there are two aspects; that of the giver and that of the receiver. We who are believers in Jesus are no longer *'our own'*. Yet we must realize that what the Lord has given to us is of unsurpassed value. We were sinners; now we are saints. We were paupers; now we are possessors of all things. We were outcasts; now we are destined to participate in the flawless and eternal bride of Christ, the eternal dwelling place of God. That ultimate goal and purpose of God is captured in 1 Corinthians 12:13, '*....by one Spirit have we all been baptized into one body'*.

The perfecting of the members of this one body that it may become *'the bride, the wife of the Lamb'* is the objective of the Holy Spirit whom we receive. The achievement of this perfection is confirmed in Revelation 22:17: *The Spirit and the bride say "Come"*. After the work of the Holy Spirit has been fully completed, in her transformed perfection, the bride and the Spirit speak with one voice.

Revelation 21:2, '*And I saw the holy city, new Jerusalem, coming down out of heaven from God, made ready as a bride adorned for her husband*'. The vision of the holy city, new Jerusalem, as the apostle John saw it, may have been far more amazing than anything our hearts or minds can imagine. Yet, if we keep before us and treasure this vision of our ultimate destiny, then surely we shall live each moment in obedience to the Holy Spirit of God. *'Receive the Holy Spirit'* is not simply an event; it must be a moment by moment experience and a consistent way of life for all who truly love Jesus.

CHAPTER 22
ALL WITH ONE MIND

Scripture references: Acts 1:8,14, Acts 2:1-2,37-39,44-47, John 17:21, Ephesians 4:3-6, Romans 12:16, Romans 15:5-7, Philippians 2:2-3, Hebrews 9:2, Hebrews 11:4.

In the previous chapter we described how, on the evening of His resurrection, Jesus appeared among His disciples who were gathered in an upper room. How He *'breathed into them'* that they might receive the Holy Spirit and be born again. One week later Thomas confessed to Jesus, *"My Lord and my God"* and he also was born again.

Those in the upper room had endured very troubling and testing times during the very recent past. Many of them had dismally failed their Lord and Master. Some had forsaken Him. One had three times denied Him. A number of women among them had gone to an empty tomb to anoint His body and had been informed by angels, *"He is not here, for He has risen, just as He said."* Matthew 28:6. All who were gathered in that upper room had learned no longer to rely upon their own fleshly strength.

Forty days following His resurrection they had watched their beloved Lord ascend into the heavens and had received the promise of angels that *'This Jesus, who has been taken up from you into heaven, will come in just the same way as you have watched Him go into heaven.'* Acts 1:11.

Jesus had commanded them to remain in Jerusalem until they were *'clothed with power from on high'* and here, in an upper room, *'These all with one mind were continually devoting themselves to prayer, along with the women, and Mary the mother of Jesus, and with His brothers'*. Acts 1:14.

In a few more days *'When the day of Pentecost had come, they were all together in one place'*. And suddenly there came from heaven a noise like a violent rushing wind, and it filled the whole house where they were sitting. Acts 2:1-2. By the indwelling Holy Spirit they were not only *'all with one mind'* but they were *'all together in one place'*.

All were in a state of God-given agreement together and they were all *'by one Spirit....baptized into one body.... and....were all made to drink of one Spirit'*, 1 Corinthians 12:13. Thus the church, Christ's one body received the power and authority of God and all was set in motion to fulfil the eternal plan and purpose of God that Jesus would one day receive a bride and that she, as the new Jerusalem, would become the eternal dwelling place of God.

The unity that was manifested that day by the Holy Spirit had never been evident on this earth before. On this great day of Pentecost was displayed the testimony of Jesus for all who participated in it or witnessed it. Around three thousand pierced hearts not only took account of it but they cried out in response to Peter's words, *"Brethren, what shall we do?" Peter said to them, "Repent, and each of you be baptized in the name of Jesus Christ for the forgiveness of your sins; and you will receive the gift of the Holy Spirit. "For the promise is for you and your children and for all who are far off, as many as the Lord our God will call to Himself."* Acts 2:37-39.

In response to their obedience to repent and be baptized in the name of Jesus this whole company of three thousand were forgiven for their sins and received the gift of the Holy Spirit as is spoken of in Ephesians 1:13-14, *'In Him, you also, after listening to the message of truth, the gospel of your salvation - having also believed, you were sealed in Him with the Holy Spirit of promise'*.

We should pause to note that the events describing the clothing with power of around one hundred and twenty at the beginning of Acts chapter 2 was of a different nature to the gathering in of new believers into the church recounted later in the same chapter. Of the three thousand who repented and were born again on that day there is no mention that they were baptized in the Holy Spirit or that they spoke in tongues at that time.

However, the company of around one hundred and twenty upon whom the Spirit fell, together with the three thousand new believers, had that day become one body in Christ.

'And all those who had believed were together and had all things in common; and they began selling their property and possessions and

were sharing them with all, as anyone might have need. Day by day continuing with one mind in the temple, and breaking bread from house to house, they were taking their meals together with gladness and sincerity of heart, praising God and having favor with all the people. And the Lord was adding to their number day by day those who were being saved. Acts 2:44-47. What an amazing demonstration this was of total commitment to the Lord Jesus and of love and unity among these new believers. *'....all those who had believed were together and had all things in common'*. That very large community was not only united in faith and in love but all they owned was made available for the common good.

Surely in these days, as the clouds of worldwide distress of nations are growing ever darker, all who love the Lord Jesus should heed the Spirit's call to come together in this manner and be ready to share their possessions, *'as anyone might have need'*.

'....breaking bread from house to house, they were taking their meals together with gladness and sincerity of heart'. These words leave little doubt that they remembered daily, as they gathered in homes for meals, *'the Lord's death until He comes'*.

Immediately before the Lord Jesus ascended to heaven His final words to His disciples had been, *"you will receive power when the Holy Spirit has come upon you; and you shall be My witnesses both in Jerusalem, and in all Judea and Samaria, and even to the remotest part of the earth."* Acts 1:8. On the day of Pentecost the church, composed as yet of Jews only, was manifest as being the mighty power of God on this earth. Its commission to preach the gospel of the kingdom had begun and *'the Lord was adding to their number day by day those who were being saved'*. Acts 2:47.

The Son of God made Son of Man had become, through the cross, *'a life-giving Spirit'*. This Spirit had now come to indwell more than three thousand souls who would soon grow to be much more than five thousand in number for we are informed that the five thousand mentioned were men. The Father, through the Son, by the Holy Spirit had launched an unstoppable mission which would ultimately lead to *'this gospel of the kingdom'* being preached in the whole world and *'the bride, the wife of the Lamb'* being made ready to be displayed as the centrepiece of the new heavens and new earth at the dawn of eternity.

We may have absolute confidence that what was initiated in the unity of the Spirit at Pentecost and which will end in the perfection of the new Jerusalem, will be performed and completed in the unity of the same Spirit. Jesus made this clear when He said to His disciples *"Abide in Me, and I in you. As the branch cannot bear fruit of itself unless it abides in the vine, so neither can you unless you abide in Me. "I am the vine, you are the branches; he who abides in Me and I in him, he bears much fruit, for apart from Me you can do nothing."* John 15:4-5. To be in the vine is to be in Christ in whom all the branches are together. Abiding in Him there will be much fruit; Severed from Him there will be nothing.

Many years after Pentecost, Saul, who was also called Paul, was sent forth from the church assembly in Antioch by the Spirit, with Barnabas as his companion. On subsequent journeys Paul's companion was to be Silas. In each case they preached to both Jews and Gentiles and gathered together those who believed that they might be the testimony of the Lord in the location where they lived. One church was established in each city. Paul's prayer in his letter to the Ephesian assembly was that its members be *'diligent to preserve the unity of the Spirit in the bond of peace. There is one body and one Spirit, just as also you were called in one hope of your calling; one Lord, one faith, one baptism, one God and Father of all who is over all and through all and in all'*. Ephesians 4:3-6. The assembly in Ephesus had been established in the unity of the Spirit and diligence was needed to preserve that unity.

Paul was well aware of the natural tendency of human beings to classify people as greater or lesser; as more important or less important. Thus he admonished the believers in Rome *'Be of the same mind toward one another; do not be haughty in mind, but associate with the lowly. Do not be wise in your own estimation'*. Romans 12:16. Unity in the Spirit recognizes that Jesus is our Master and that we are all brothers of equal standing before Him.

Later in the same letter Paul states, *'Now may the God who gives perseverance and encouragement grant you to be of the same mind with one another according to Christ Jesus, so that with one accord you may with one voice glorify the God and Father of our Lord Jesus Christ. Therefore, accept one another, just as Christ also accepted us to the glory of God'.* Romans 15:5-7. In accepting other believers as we ourselves would wish to be accepted we will provide conditions for that unity in the Spirit which blends all voices together into one expression of praise. To all who have experienced this *'one voice'* it is a unique and unforgettable joy.

To the assembly in Philippi Paul wrote, *'make my joy complete by being of the same mind, maintaining the same love, united in spirit, intent on one purpose. Do nothing from selfishness or empty conceit, but with humility of mind regard one another as more important than yourselves'.* Philippians 2:2-3. Here Paul is emphasizing that they all show humility toward one another in putting the interests of others ahead of their own, as he leads up to his unique and wonderful description of the humility of Christ Jesus in verses 5 to 11.

From the moment when Eve, and then Adam, disobeyed the command of God, and thereby deliberately chose to follow the dictates of Satan, disunity came upon mankind. Cain offered a sacrifice to God from the fruit of his own labours. *'Abel, on his part also brought of the firstlings of his flock and of their fat portions'.* Genesis 4:4.

The Lord had shown Adam and Eve what He required when He slew an animal to provide its hide for a covering for their nakedness, for *'....without shedding of blood there is no forgiveness'.* Hebrews 9:22. Cain murdered his brother Abel out of jealousy. *'By faith Abel offered to God a better sacrifice than Cain, through which he obtained the testimony that he was righteous, God testifying about his gifts, and through faith, though he is dead, he still speaks'.* Hebrews 11:4.

The Christian churches that should be representing the Lord in the world today are largely in a state of unimaginable disunity, yet somewhere on this earth the Lord surely has companies of the faithful who are displaying His testimony in perhaps largely unknown locations. Small in numbers they may be, yet known to Him, blessed by Him and kept precious unto Himself. *"For the eyes of the Lord move to and fro throughout the earth that He may strongly support those whose heart is completely His."* 2 Chronicles 16:9.

CHAPTER 23
ACCORDING TO THE PATTERN

Scripture references: Genesis 2:20-24, 1 Corinthians 15:20-50, Ephesians 2:1-10, Hebrews 8:5, Hebrews 3:1-6, Hebrews 11:9-10, Revelation 21:1-2.

From the Genesis record we understand that all living creatures, apart from man, were created by the Lord God as male and female, or with the capacity to reproduce their kind. Man was the sole exception, for the word specifically states *'but for Adam was not found a helper suitable for him'*, thus implying that all the other creatures were provided with the means of reproduction.

And the Lord God caused a deep sleep to fall upon Adam; and while he slept, He took one of his ribs or a part of his side and closed up the [place with] *flesh. And the rib or part of his side which the Lord God had taken from the man He built up and made into a woman, and He brought her to the man.* Genesis 2:21-22 AMP. Eve's fashioning by the Lord from a *'rib or part of the side'* of Adam was unique in creation and most significant in purpose.

In verse 15 of that incomparable first chapter of Colossians we are informed that Jesus *'is the image of the invisible God'*. When the Triune God created Adam, He created him in the image of Jesus for we read in Luke 3:38: *'Seth, the son of Adam, the son of God'*.

The earthy Adam and the heavenly Adam, the Lord Jesus, are contrasted in 1 Corinthians 15:22, 45 and 47. *For as in Adam all die, so also in Christ all will be made alive...."The first man, Adam, became a living soul." The last Adam became a life-giving spirit....The first man is from the earth, earthy; the second man is from heaven.*

However, Adam the type and Jesus the reality have one thing in common; from each of them was taken that which was to be *'built up and made into a woman'* to be a wife. Adam was put into a deep sleep by God. Eve was fashioned from a part of him and she was brought to him to be his wife. Out from Jesus through the cross was taken that which is being formed by the Holy Spirit to one day be presented to Jesus as His wife.

In the case of Adam we note that the Lord God took one of Adam's *'ribs or a part of his side and closed up the* [place with] *flesh'*. Because pain and suffering only came about as the result of Eve's and Adam's sin, we may rightly judge that, in taking *'one of his ribs or a part of his side'* to make into a woman there was no pain or suffering involved and there would be no scars remaining. Although a deep sleep came upon Adam there is no inference that his sleep was a prolonged one during which the *'Lord God fashioned into a woman the rib which He had taken from the man, and brought her to the man'*. Genesis 2:22.

On the other hand, the Lord Jesus suffered unimaginable pain on the cross in order that His counterpart might come forth from His body to be presented to Him one day as *'the bride, the wife of the Lamb'*. In Adam's case the Lord God *'closed up the* [place with] *flesh'*, but in the case of Jesus the 'place' was not closed up with flesh for we read that, when Jesus appeared to Thomas, He invited him to *'reach here your hand and put it into My side'*. John 20:27.

In eternity past, the Triune God, 'Elohim', communed in counsel and decided that Jesus would have a bride. How or why this plan was formed is hidden from us. Suffice it to say that the plan was made in every detail to be achieved in completeness and perfection. All contingencies were considered. Nothing would thwart this plan. In the foreknowledge of God the sin of man was already taken into account. *'The Son of God appeared for this purpose, to destroy the works of the devil'*. 1 John 3:8. When all the negative things had been dealt with through His Son's death on the cross, God's new beginning could be put into motion.

'For we are His masterpiece, created in Christ Jesus for good works, which God prepared beforehand in order that we would walk in them'. Ephesians 2:10, Recovery Version. The bride, the wife of the Lamb, has been created in Christ Jesus entirely of His essence and substance to be God's masterpiece. The good works that God pre-ordained for those who love Him that they would perform will add stitch by stitch to the wedding garment mentioned in Revelation 19:8. These pre-ordained works are referred to in that verse as *'the righteous acts of the saints'*. In eternity past the exact design and

pattern of the bride of Jesus Christ was formulated in the mind and councils of the Triune God.

The Lord's precision has been evident in all that He has done. What He plans He executes perfectly. Consider the exact description and plan that the Lord gave Moses on the mountain for the construction of the tabernacle and its furniture. The materials to be used and all the measurements were precisely given by God to Moses. *"See," He says, "that you make all things according to the pattern which was shown you on the mountain."* Hebrews 8:5.

God showed Moses His exact design for all He wanted made that He, Almighty God, might have a dwelling place among His people. Through the great skills of Bezalel and Oholiab and a host of other contributors Moses was faithful to make everything exactly in accordance with God's design, for we read, *'Now Moses was faithful in all His house as a servant, for a testimony of those things which were to be spoken later; but Christ was faithful as a Son over His house - whose house we are, if we hold fast our confidence and the boast of our hope firm until the end.* Hebrews 3:5-6. Just as the Lord had His pattern for the design of the tabernacle in the wilderness, so He has a pattern for that which shall be the bride for His Son, our Lord Jesus Christ.

The more intricate and complex is a project, the greater the care that must be taken to do everything based upon a pattern or upon a number of inter-related patterns. By carefully following these guidelines, those who perform the huge variety of tasks will accomplish them in perfect coordination to achieve the desired result.

We read in Hebrews 11:9-10 that Abraham *'lived as an alien in the land of promise, as in a foreign land, dwelling in tents with Isaac and Jacob, fellow heirs of the same promise; for he was looking for the city which has foundations, whose architect and builder is God'*. This city that Abraham looked for, the apostle John saw and described in detail.

Just as God gave the exact design for the tabernacle to Moses and for the temple to King David, so His Son Jesus has from eternity past known the exact design and He has been given absolute authority over God's perfect plan. *'Then I saw a new heaven and a new earth; for the first heaven and the first earth passed away, and there is no longer any sea. I saw the holy city, new Jerusalem, coming down out of heaven from God, made ready as a bride adorned for her husband'.* Revelation 21:1-2.

CHAPTER 24
CLOTHED WITH POWER

Scripture references: Luke 24:29, 1 Corinthians 15:3-9, Acts 2:1-37, Matthew 28:18-20, Acts 3:1-26, John 14:12, Acts 4:7-8, Acts 4:31, Acts 10:34-35,44, Matthew 16:19.

The kingdom of heaven came to earth in the person of the Lord Jesus. *'And the Word became flesh, and did tabernacle among us, and we beheld his glory, glory as of an only begotten of a father, full of grace and truth'.* John 1:14 Young's Literal Translation. The message of John the Baptist had been *"Repent for the kingdom of heaven has drawn nigh."* Precisely the same expression was employed by our Lord when He entered His ministry. Some while later Jesus sent forth His disciples to proclaim, *"The kingdom of heaven has drawn nigh".* During His time on earth Jesus was the dwelling place of God among mankind. In Him the kingdom of heaven had drawn nigh.

On the evening of His resurrection Jesus entered the upper room where the twelve and others of His disciples were gathered for fear of the Jews. He breathed into them and said, *"Receive the Holy Spirit."* They had all received His life into them and thereby entered the kingdom, but they did not yet bear His authority. Thus He spoke to them, *"And behold, I am sending forth the promise of My Father upon you; but you are to stay in the city until you are clothed with power from on high."* Luke 24:29.

The church, which is the body of Christ, came into being as soon as those first ones received the Holy Spirit. Embodied in the Holy Spirit is the kingdom of heaven. The kingdom of heaven grows within each member of the church, the body of Christ, through daily obedience to the Holy Spirit. Thus will our simple acts of submission to His will increase in us the kingdom of heaven and they will also transform us into the likeness of Jesus.

There were, in fact, many more than those in the upper room on the resurrection evening who had received the Holy Spirit before Jesus' ascension, because we read in 1 Corinthians 15:6 that Jesus *'appeared to more than five hundred brethren at one time'* prior to His ascension into heaven.

Those gathered in that upper room before Pentecost were now true representatives of Christ's body the church for they *'with one mind were continually devoting themselves to prayer'*. Such unity and devotion can only come about through the sovereign work of the Holy Spirit.

This brings us to the main point of this chapter which is the manifestation of the church on earth, having upon her God's authority, to be His testimony before all nations. Adam had forfeited his God-given authority to Satan, who is *'the god of this world'*, and so had brought defeat and death upon his descendants, but absolute victory was assured through the promised seed, Jesus *'the last Adam'*, to be carried out by *'the church, which is His body'*.

Following Pentecost, the love and the unity of purpose existing within that greatly enlarged company of more than three thousand was abundantly in evidence. No longer fearful of the Jews, these disciples were equipped to become a force on earth, to perform His will and carry out the great commission that Jesus had given them *"Go therefore and make disciples of all the nations, baptizing them in the name of the Father and the Son and the Holy Spirit, teaching them to observe all that I commanded you...."* Matthew 28:19-20.

Pentecost was about much more than receiving power. It was about sending forth a Spirit-filled contingent of what would become a mighty workforce to build up the body of Christ. All must be done in accordance with the pattern designed by God before time began. As was the case in that mighty early move of God following Pentecost, only those meeting today in the freedom of the Spirit and under the supreme and undisputed headship of the Lord Jesus may be His builders. The pattern of church life after Pentecost and thereafter in the New Testament Scriptures is no mystery. It is there for all to see.

In Acts chapters 3 and 4 we find an account of a notable miracle of healing of a man who had been lame from his mother's womb. This mighty act of God through His servant Peter gave opportunity for the first thrust of the gospel to the people of Jerusalem and to the Jewish leaders.

To the lame man begging alms at the gate called Beautiful Peter said, *"I do not possess silver and gold, but what I do have I give to you: In the name of Jesus Christ the Nazarene - walk!" And seizing him by the right hand, he raised him up; and immediately his feet and his ankles were strengthened.* Acts 3:6-7.

Had we been close observers, we would have watched with awe the sinews, muscles and tissue of the legs and feet of this man transforming into normal contours and strength as Peter reached out his hand and propelled the man to his feet. Glory be to God that nothing shall be impossible with Him! The Lord Jesus had promised, *"Truly, truly, I say to you, he who believes in Me, the works that I do, he will do also; and greater works than these he will do; because I go to the Father."* John 14:12.

This man was so completely restored to normal function that he went walking and leaping and praising God as he headed into the temple. A large crowd quickly gathered following this miracle, for all the temple worshippers knew of his previous condition.

With great power Peter proclaimed the crucified and risen Jesus to the crowd, giving all the glory to Him and announcing His power to heal and to save. His message was uncompromising concerning their part in delivering Jesus up to be crucified, though done *'in ignorance, just as your rulers did also'*. His invitation to them is the same as ours must be to people today, *"Therefore repent and return, so that your sins may be wiped away, in order that times of refreshing may come from the presence of the Lord; and that He may send Jesus, the Christ appointed for you...."* Acts 3:19-20.

In verse 4 of the next chapter we read, *'But many of those who had heard the message believed; and the number of the men came to be about five thousand'*. This freshly garnered Jewish community of the church had just greatly increased because the five thousand mentioned here were the male members only. What a harvest! What a mighty demonstration of the power of God. The response of the Jewish leaders was swift and predictable. They arrested Peter and John and put them in jail until the following day.

On the next day Peter and John were arraigned before the chief priests and the Jewish Council to examine them concerning their message to the crowd and the healing of the lame man. *'When they had placed them in the centre, they began to inquire, "By what power, or in what name, have you done this?" Then Peter, filled with the Holy Spirit, said....'* Acts 4:7-8. The word for 'filled' in the Greek here is 'pletho', the very same Greek word used in Acts 2:4 when all those in the upper room were 'filled' with the Holy Spirit. This establishes that being imbued with power by the Holy Spirit is not a single event, but is God's provision whenever He requires His power and authority to be exercised.

The content of Peter's response to the questions of the Council was bold and uncompromising. It is to be supposed that each of his first three recorded messages were delivered with mighty power in the Spirit the like of which few today will ever have witnessed or experienced. Peter was now a fully surrendered soul who had been at the forefront of the mightiest example of unity ever to be displayed on earth.

If we today would speak, act and behave as Peter and John did, then we must also do so in the same complete unity in the Spirit that they exhibited. Nothing will be achieved for the eternal purpose of God which, in word and action, does not stand in the certainty that the body is one, even though of many members. *For even as the body is one and yet has many members, and all the members of the body, though they are many, are one body, so also is Christ. For by one Spirit we were all baptized into one body, whether Jews or Greeks, whether slaves or free, and we were all made to drink of one Spirit.* 1 Corinthians 12:12-13.

On the return of the two apostles to the company of believers, there occurred a meeting of great joy and praise to God, at the close of which *'the place where they had gathered together was shaken, and they were all filled with the Holy Spirit and began to speak the word of God with boldness.* Acts 4:31. It is significant to note, in this case also, that the Greek word for 'filled' is 'pletho'. In this great power, poured out yet again, these *'all began to speak the word with boldness';* Yes, *'all began to speak'*, not only the apostles.

How tempting it is to read this account and to reflect in our heart, 'that was then – this is now'. In His actions and in His standards the

Lord never compromises or changes His mind. If we desire to be vessels for God's eternal purpose, then the unity of heart and purpose which was demonstrated among those at Pentecost will be required of us also. The power with which the church was clothed at the beginning has never been rescinded or revoked. It simply will not find expression if the heart is not fully surrendered to the Lord and in a state of unity with those who are His own.

Just as Peter was chosen and used of God to open the door of the kingdom to the Jews, so he was also used to open it to the Gentiles. To the Jews, the Gentile nations were outside the realm of God's grace. They were unclean and irredeemable. They were sinners without hope. So it was that the Lord prepared Peter through a vision of a great sheet let down by the four corners from heaven. This great sheet contained some creatures that were not even to be touched by God's chosen people. Peter received the words, *"Get up, Peter, kill and eat!"* Peter remonstrated with the Lord and had to be told that what God had cleansed he, Peter, was no longer to consider unclean.

At this very time, messengers from a centurion named Cornelius arrived at the door of the house where Peter was staying and he went with them to Cornelius' home where many Gentiles were gathered awaiting his arrival.

Peter's first words to the large company of people in Cornelius' house were significant, *"I most certainly understand now that God is not one to show partiality, but in every nation the man who fears Him and does what is right is welcome to Him."* Acts 10:34-35. He did not speak to them for long for, while he *'was still speaking these words, the Holy Spirit fell upon all those who were listening to the message'*.

On Peter's return to Jerusalem he faced opposition from those who had not yet entered fully into the freedom that is to be found alone in Christ. Jesus had told Peter long before, *"I will give you the keys of the kingdom of heaven; and whatever you bind on earth shall have been bound in heaven, and whatever you loose on earth shall have been loosed in heaven."* Matthew 16:19. Peter had been used of God to open the door of the kingdom of heaven to the Jews at

Pentecost. Now he had been used to open the door of the kingdom to the Gentiles. The same manifestations of the Spirit were apparent in the home of Cornelius as had been experienced at Pentecost. The church, the body of Christ, had been launched at Pentecost. Now by the same Holy Spirit it would be participated in by all mankind.

Many years later, in his letter to the church in Ephesus, Paul triumphantly proclaimed, *'But now in Christ Jesus you who formerly were far off* [the Gentiles] *have been brought near by the blood of Christ. For He Himself is our peace, who made both groups* [Jews and Gentiles] *into one and broke down the barrier of the dividing wall, by abolishing in His flesh the enmity, which is the Law of commandments contained in ordinances, so that in Himself He might make the two into one new man, thus establishing peace, and might reconcile them both in one body to God through the cross, by it having put to death the enmity'*. Ephesians 2:13-16.

'For by one Spirit we were all baptized into one body, whether Jews or Greeks, whether slaves or free, and we were all made to drink of one Spirit'. 1 Corinthians 12:13. To be baptized by the one Spirit into one body is the portion given to all believers when they come in simple faith to Jesus. However, the outward filling or clothing, 'pletho', of the power of the Spirit is provided in circumstances and occasions of the Lord's choosing, on those who stand united in His one body and in utter dependence upon Him.

CHAPTER 25
PREACH THE GOSPEL

Scripture references: John 1:1-8, Malachi 3:1, Matthew 3:1-2, Matthew 4:17, John 18:36, Acts 2:22-36, Luke 12:32, Matthew 24:14.

In the beginning was the Word, and the Word was with God, and the Word was God. He was in the beginning with God. All things came into being through Him, and apart from Him nothing came into being that has come into being. In Him was life, and the life was the Light of men. The Light shines in the darkness, and the darkness did not comprehend it. John 1:1-5. With some of the most amazing words ever conceived, given by the Spirit of God to the apostle John, is introduced to us the person of Jesus as the Word, the creator of all things and the giver of light and life. He is the 'Logos' of God. Without His speaking nothing came into being and nothing of lasting value will ever be said or done. *'Thy will be done'* is accomplished by the utterance of the Logos. From the beginning He has spoken into man and through man to convey the message of God's eternal will and purpose.

"Behold, I am going to send My messenger, and he will clear the way before Me. And the Lord, whom you seek, will suddenly come to His temple." Malachi 3:1. As had been foretold by the prophet Malachi, John the Baptist came as the forerunner to Jesus. *'There came a man sent from God, whose name was John. He came as a witness, to testify about the Light....'* John 1:6. The Light that John testified to was Jesus. He is *'the Light of the world'*. Through the cross, Jesus has been made available to all who will repent and believe the gospel that they, in turn, may become *'the light of the world. A city set on a hill cannot be hidden'*. Matthew 5:14.

Now in those days John the Baptist came, preaching in the wilderness of Judea, saying, "Repent, for the kingdom of heaven is at hand." Matthew 3:1-2. John the Baptist was sent by God to proclaim to the Jewish nation, *"Repent, for the kingdom of heaven is at hand."* This message that all must turn their hearts back to God in repentance has been the call of all the prophets in every historical period, from Enoch and onwards. Alas John the Baptist had all too little time to proclaim this message before he was imprisoned and beheaded by Herod.

However, after John was imprisoned, *'From that time Jesus began to preach and say, "Repent, for the kingdom of heaven is at hand."* Matthew 4:17. John had been *'a voice crying in the wilderness'*, *"Repent, for the kingdom"* and *'prepare the way of the Lord'*. Now, the Lord, who had been fully launched into His ministry was bearing the same message.

When, some while later, Jesus gathered His twelve disciples together and sent them out two by two, He instructed them *"And as you go, preach, saying, 'The kingdom of heaven is at hand.'"* He could not yet send them out with the message of repentance for they themselves had not yet repented.

This message of repentance that was being proclaimed at that time was accompanied by baptism. This baptism of repentance came to be referred to as the baptism of John. For we read in Acts 19 of twelve men of Ephesus who had received the baptism of John, yet had never heard *'that there is a Holy Spirit'*. After Paul had preached Jesus to them, *'they were baptized in the name of the Lord Jesus. And when Paul had laid his hands upon them, the Holy Spirit came on them, and they began speaking with tongues and prophesying'*. Acts 19:5-6.

During His earthly ministry the main theme of the Lord Jesus was *'the kingdom of heaven'* (often alternatively referred to as *'the kingdom of God'*). In many of His parables Jesus used the phrase *'the kingdom of heaven is like....'* Probably the best known example is the parable of the sower. In this parable Jesus describes the outcome of the preaching of the word. The sower is Jesus, the seed is the word, the various conditions into which the seed is sown represent the condition of the human heart and the birds are emissaries of Satan.

As we shall see in a later chapter, the message that Jesus sent His disciples forth to preach in the whole world was *'this gospel of the kingdom'*. In order to fulfil this great commission, all those who were His disciples then and those who have since become His followers, must be commissioned by the Holy Spirit and clothed with His power.

The kingdom life is a heavenly life, a life that is not of this world. Jesus told the Roman governor Pontius Pilate *"My kingdom is not of this world."* John 18:36.

Soon after the major turning point of world history in the death, resurrection and ascension of Jesus, the church sprang forth on that great day of Pentecost. Peter delivered the first message of the *'gospel of the kingdom'* to the huge crowd that gathered in response to the manifestations of the Spirit. The main points of his message were:

- *"Jesus the Nazarene a man attested to you by God with miracles and wonders and signs which God performed through Him.* Jesus was validated to be both 'Lord and Christ' through the 'miracles and wonders and signs which God performed through Him'.
- *"....this Man, delivered over by the predetermined plan and foreknowledge of God, you nailed to a cross by the hands of godless men and put Him to death."* What had been foretold and promised in the Garden of Eden was fulfilled through the crucifixion of Christ. The Jewish people unknowingly, in godless hatred, became God's agents in ensuring that this happened.
- *"But God raised Him up again, putting an end to the agony of death, since it was impossible for Him to be held in its power."* Jesus was God's perfect sacrifice, having lived a sinless life of complete dependence on the Father. Death could not hold Him in the grave.
- *"This Jesus God raised up again, to which we are all witnesses."* Peter, and those with Him in that upper room, had seen and experienced the presence of the resurrected Lord.
- *"Therefore having been exalted to the right hand of God, and having received from the Father the promise of the Holy Spirit, He has poured forth this which you both see and hear.* On this God-ordained day, that which the Father's Son had

wrought for all mankind was given mighty expression in this outpouring of the Holy Spirit on those who were of one mind.

- *"Repent, and each of you be baptized in the name of Jesus Christ for the forgiveness of your sins; and you will receive the gift of the Holy Spirit. For the promise is for you and your children and for all who are far off, as many as the Lord our God will call to Himself."* For these first believers, and for all since who believe in Jesus, a true turning of the heart in repentance and faith must be followed by baptism that we may be forgiven for our sins and that we may receive the promised gift of the Holy Spirit.

In response to Peter's powerful appeal, *'those who had received his word were baptized; and that day there were added about three thousand souls'*. Acts 2:42.

The step which the three thousand took by faith on that great day of Pentecost had ushered them into the kingdom of heaven. Now it was God's intention for them to enter into the fullness of their inheritance on the basis of their faith. Their inheritance, and also ours who believe, is to live constantly in the full enjoyment of *'the kingdom of heaven'*.

May we, whose heart is stirred by these words, recall and be encouraged by a special assurance given by the Lord Jesus to His disciples, *"Do not be afraid, little flock, for your Father has chosen gladly to give you the kingdom."* Luke 12:32.

Lastly we shall look briefly at the statement of Jesus, which is often referred to as 'the great commission', in which He summarized the work of God that His own would carry out before His coming again. *"This gospel of the kingdom shall be preached in the whole world as a testimony to all the nations, and then the end will come."* Matthew 24:14. These words of Jesus are perfectly clear and understandable. They raise the question, has this been completed yet? Many might say "Surely, yes." But let us examine again what Jesus really said. What was to be preached in the whole world? *'This gospel of the kingdom'*. This raises a very important question. What is the kingdom?

CHAPTER 26
THE KINGDOM OF HEAVEN

Scripture references: John 3:1-21, Colossians 1:1-22, 1 Peter 2:9, 1 John 1:7, John 10:1-16, 1 Peter 5:1-4, Acts 2:42-45

The title of this chapter might just as well be *'The Kingdom of God'* for the terms 'kingdom of heaven' and 'kingdom of God' are synonymous. In parallel texts in the other gospels the term is always *'the kingdom of God'*; only in Matthew is the term *'the kingdom of heaven'* used, where it is found thirty two times.

The account of Nicodemus coming by night to see Jesus is a very familiar story, not only to believers, but many who have grown up in Christian families or settings. Yet, while multitudes have found their way to living faith through the wonderful truths found in this third chapter of John, there may perhaps be only a small number who probe deeper into an understanding of Jesus' words.

'....a man of the Pharisees, named Nicodemus, a ruler of the Jews....came to Jesus by night and said to Him, "Rabbi, we know that You have come from God as a teacher; for no one can do these signs that You do unless God is with him."' Surely, this is a statement, not a question, yet Jesus perceived exactly what was really on Nicodemus' mind and that is why He *'answered and said to him, "Truly, truly, I say to you, unless one is born again he cannot see the kingdom of God."'* Nicodemus, your issue is not intellectual, but spiritual. It is not of the flesh, but of the Spirit. You must be born again before you will have your spiritual eyes opened. If you truly *'see the kingdom of God'* you will come to know who I am.

In answer to Nicodemus mistaken understanding of what it means to be born anew, Jesus responded *"Truly, truly, I say to you, unless one is born of water and the Spirit he cannot enter into the kingdom of God."* In order to enter the kingdom of God you must be born of water; that is, you must *'repent and be baptized for the forgiveness of your sins'* and be born anew of the Spirit. *"That which is born of the flesh is flesh, and that which is born of the Spirit is spirit."* Nicodemus, you were born in the natural way in the flesh but, in order for you to be born anew you must be born of the Spirit, by the

Holy Spirit entering your human spirit. 1 Corinthians 6:17 ....*he who is joined to the Lord is one spirit with Him.* NKJV

"The wind blows where it wishes and you hear the sound of it, but do not know where it comes from and where it is going; so is everyone who is born of the Spirit." The coming of the Holy Spirit is quite mysterious. Like the wind you know it has reached you and has passed on, yet the visitation is quite apparent. Some know the time and date when the Spirit came, others become aware that He has come, yet do not know exactly when.

Jesus continued, *"No one has ascended into heaven, but He who descended from heaven: the Son of Man. "As Moses lifted up the serpent in the wilderness, even so must the Son of Man be lifted up; so that whoever believes will in Him have eternal life. "For God so loved the world, that He gave His only begotten Son, that whoever believes in Him shall not perish, but have eternal life."* Finally, Jesus revealed to Nicodemus who He is, and what had been the purpose of His descending out of heaven as the Son of Man; that he might, through being lifted up on the cross for all to see, demonstrate the limitless extent of the love of God for mankind and for all He had created; that He might become God's perfect sacrifice for sin, that the grace of eternal forgiveness might be made available to all who would believe.

So many who have come to Jesus and have gloriously received His great salvation from sin, do not understand the life that God intended that they should enter upon, or what they should expect following this great experience, nor do they know how to enjoy their inheritance, *'the kingdom of heaven'*.

In the glorious first chapter of Paul's letter to the assembly in Colossae is an unveiling of the incomparable Christ and what He has provided through the cross for those faithful ones who have believed in Him. This whole chapter is so rich yet, in relation to our topic, verses 13 and 14 capture the very essence of what the Lord has brought to those who receive Him, *'....He rescued us from the domain of darkness, and transferred us to the kingdom of His beloved Son, in whom we have redemption, the forgiveness of sins'*. We have been brought from a kingdom that is devoid of hope into a kingdom of endless joy. In one aspect we may say that everything this kingdom offers is in His beloved Son. In Him is redemption, in Him is forgiveness of sins and in Him also is everything we shall need to live this life abundantly and in victory. All we require in order to face all challenges He is and He will always prove to be.

But you are a chosen race, a royal priesthood, a holy nation, a people for God's own possession, so that you may proclaim the excellencies of Him who has called you out of darkness into His marvelous light; 1 Peter 2:9. To be brought out of darkness into the kingdom of His beloved Son is to be brought into *'His marvelous light'*. This is the kingdom. This is the inheritance of all who have come to put their trust in Jesus through repentance and faith in His finished work on the cross.

Now that we have come *'into His marvelous light'* we must live our life, moment by moment in the light, for *'if we walk in the Light as He Himself is in the Light, we have fellowship with one another, and the blood of Jesus His Son cleanses us from all sin'*. 1 John 1:7. All of our inheritance is found, entered into and enjoyed as we walk in the Light.

Jesus is the door of the sheepfold. The sheepfold is the kingdom. Yes! There is but one door into one sheepfold. *"Truly, truly, I say to you, I am the door of the sheep."*

"When he puts forth all his own, he goes ahead of them, and the sheep follow him because they know his voice, "A stranger they simply will not follow, but will flee from him, because they do not know the voice of strangers.... He, the Good Shepherd, leads His sheep in and out to find pasture. *'They know His voice'* and *'they do not know the voice of strangers'*. The kingdom life is lived in the presence of the Good Shepherd, listening to His voice and following Him.

"The thief comes only to steal and kill and destroy; I came that they may have life, and have it abundantly." I am the good shepherd; the good shepherd lays down His life for the sheep." The thief, who is the devil and Satan, is the real enemy of the Good Shepherd and of His sheep. Satan is the one who leads them astray into division, disillusionment and destruction. Jesus, as the Good Shepherd, lays

down His life for the sheep and He leads His sheep *'in and out to find pasture'*.

"I have other sheep, which are not of this fold; I must bring them also, and they will hear My voice; and they will become one flock with one shepherd." In His death on the cross our Good Shepherd *'broke down the barrier of the dividing wall'* between Jew and Gentile so that, through faith in Him, they might *'become one flock with one shepherd'*.

What then does this figure of speech that Jesus gave to His disciples show us about the kingdom of God? Jesus is the one door into one fold. The one fold is the kingdom of heaven into which all who have believed unto salvation have entered. He, the Good Shepherd, is the only one who can lead His own in and out to find their spiritual food and supply their every need.

A hired hand is one who receives payments to care for the sheep. If he is not paid he will not do the work. There is a world of difference between such a hired hand and one who is appointed by God to shepherd the flock of God. Jesus had told Peter *"feed My sheep"* and *"feed My lambs"*. Consider the exhortation Peter gives to elders. *'Therefore, I exhort the elders among you, as your fellow elder and witness of the sufferings of Christ, and a partaker also of the glory that is to be revealed, shepherd the flock of God among you, exercising oversight not under compulsion, but voluntarily, according to the will of God; and not for sordid gain, but with eagerness; nor yet as lording it over those allotted to your charge, but proving to be examples to the flock. And when the Chief Shepherd appears, you will receive the unfading crown of glory'*. 1 Peter 5:1-4.

Finally, let us recall the great day of Pentecost and the events that immediately followed. Around three thousand had obeyed the word proclaimed to them. They had repented, had been baptized and had received the gift of the Holy Spirit. Their strict obedience to Peter's instructions brought them entry into a completely new life; life in the kingdom of heaven.

'They were continually devoting themselves to the apostles' teaching and to fellowship, to the breaking of bread and to prayer....' Acts

2:42. They were continually and devotedly receiving the living word of God; sharing their faith with other believers under the anointing of the Holy Spirit; remembering the Lord's death in the bread and the wine; praying.

'And all those who had believed were together and had all things in common; and they began selling their property and possessions and were sharing them with all, as anyone might have need'. Acts 2:44-45. By selling all and sharing the proceeds with the whole company, these new believers gave a living demonstration of brotherly love and of the equal value to the Lord of each member of the new community, the body of Christ. From the birth of the church and throughout the Book of Acts is portrayed the individual and community life of believers who found, who came into, and who enjoyed the kingdom of heaven.

Sadly, what we read about their assembling together, their conduct in the meetings and their daily life is, for the most part, in woeful contrast with the practices of what is known as the Church on earth today. In the coming chapters a number of characteristics of the kingdom life will be described from the perspective of the New Testament account.

No brief description of the kingdom of heaven can adequately describe the wonder of our inheritance in Christ. Outwardly, it is the true testimony of Jesus before *'the spiritual forces of wickedness in the heavenly places'* and before an unbelieving world. However, it also displays the testimony of Jesus before believers held captive within religious Babylon. Inwardly, it is the true and real experience of community life in the Spirit, in which the many members are of one heart and one mind in their obedient performance of the will and purpose of God.

In contrast, religion is that which builds around concepts of God, human methods and systems, human organization and human institutions and programs. This is religious Babylon.

Much of Christendom today is sunk in religion yet, due to a multitude of devoted believers who are largely hidden away within this vast system, there are glimpses of better things.

Luke 12:32. *'Do not be afraid, little flock, for your Father has chosen gladly to give you the kingdom'*. The new Jerusalem will be the ultimate expression of the kingdom of heaven. The new Jerusalem, the *'bride, the wife of the Lamb'*, will forever display the glory of God to the new earth and to the far reaches of the new heavens in which righteousness will reign forever.

CHAPTER 27
ASSEMBLED TOGETHER

Scripture references: Acts 2:41-42, 1 Corinthians 11:23-26, Colossians 3:12-17, 1 Corinthians 12:4-14, 1 Corinthians 14:23-33,

As soon as the church of Jesus Christ was brought into being by the Holy Spirit, the life of it was infused from four sources. We read that this great company of new believers were *'continually devoting themselves to the apostles' teaching and to fellowship, to the breaking of bread and to prayer'*. Acts 2:42.

While the Scriptures we now know as the Old Testament were readily available to these early believers, the apostles were the only ones who had first-hand experience and knowledge of the life and ministry of the Lord Jesus. On the evening of His resurrection, He came where they were gathered and *'He opened their minds to understand the Scriptures'*. Luke 24:45. So it was to the apostles as the main source of enlightenment that the new believers turned. Yet there were others in that upper room, who had also received understanding and who had significant exposure to Jesus daily life. These were, no doubt, also a valued source of spiritual wisdom.

Fellowship is the flow of the divine life among and between believers. It involves the sharing of experience and testimony, of spiritual insight and wisdom, of praise and worship and many other expressions of spiritual value under the anointing of the Holy Spirit. The objective of fellowship in the Spirit is that all may be encouraged and built up together as the visible and active body of Christ.

Within each living member at that time long ago was a God-given desire and eagerness to function for the benefit of the other members; to be a life-giving contributor to the whole. This was and is the reality of fellowship.

Before His death on the cross *'the Lord Jesus in the night in which He was betrayed took bread; and when He had given thanks, He broke it and said, "This is My body, which is for you; do this in remembrance of Me." In the same way He took the cup also after supper, saying, "This cup is the new covenant in My blood; do this, as often as you drink it, in remembrance of Me." For as often as you eat this bread and drink the cup, you proclaim the Lord's death until He comes.* 1 Corinthians 11:23-26. This sacrament was being proclaimed as a testimony to the Lord's death by all the new believers in their homes. They were *'breaking bread from house to house'*. To remember with gratitude and devotion the fact and efficacy of the *'Lord's death until He comes'* was one of the four main elements of the life of this so recently formed community of believers. Today, we who truly love the Lord Jesus must surely recover this sacrament with thankfulness and joy in remembrance of Him.

In the original Greek it is not *'to prayer'* but *'to the prayers'* that they were devoting themselves. This was no once a week prayer meeting attended by a very few, but was a universally participated in joyful practice of common desire and purpose, that moved the very throne of heaven to perform on earth that which was the will of God in heaven. How evocative of the prayer given by Jesus to His disciples. *Pray, then, in this way: 'Our Father who is in heaven, Hallowed be Your name. 'Your kingdom come. Your will be done, On earth as it is in heaven'.* Matthew 6:9-10.

In summarizing these four main elements of life in the early church, let it be noted that the words *'continually devoting'* were applied to all of them. Thus was vitality and effectiveness maintained within the body of Christ, His church, in its ministry and acts of worship in those early days.

The Lord ordained that it should be *'beginning from Jerusalem'* that the gospel of the kingdom should spread throughout the Roman world and to the ends of the earth. We have records of how this gospel went forth and expanded, especially through the ministry entrusted to Paul and his companions, from the letters he wrote to assemblies in major cities such as Rome, Corinth, Ephesus, Philippi, Colossae and Thessalonica.

In Colossians 3:12-17 is a brief yet informative description of how the believers conducted their meetings together. While much of Paul's counsel concerns their behaviour, verse 16 focuses on the functioning of members in their gatherings together. *'Let the word of Christ richly dwell within you, with all wisdom teaching and admonishing one another with psalms and hymns and spiritual songs, singing with thankfulness in your hearts to God'*. This instruction was written to all the members of the assembly in Colossae, not simply to those especially gifted. *'Let the word of Christ richly dwell within you'* reminds us of Paul's encouragement to Timothy *'Be diligent to present yourself approved to God as a workman who does not need to be ashamed, accurately handling the word of truth'*. 2 Timothy 2:15.

'....with all wisdom teaching and admonishing one another with psalms and hymns and spiritual songs, singing with thankfulness in your hearts to God'. These words may be few but there is a wealth of meaning and importance contained within them. This is a very significant requirement, *'....with all wisdom'*. Only the blessed person of the Holy Spirit possesses all wisdom; thus He must be Lord over every word spoken in the assembling together of God's people. *'....teaching and admonishing one another'*. This is the right and duty of all the members of the body, not the right and duty of a privileged individual or a few. *'....with psalms and hymns and spiritual songs'*. The Psalms are Scripture, but the hymns and songs spoken about here must also be written and sung under the anointing of the Holy Spirit. *'....singing with thankfulness in your hearts to God'*. How vital is a heart of gratitude to God for all He has done and above all, who He is.

In his first letter to the assembly in Corinth, Paul devotes significant attention to the conduct of their meetings and the employment of spiritual gifts in their gatherings together.

Now there are varieties of gifts, ministries and effects, yet it is *'the same God who works all things in all persons. But to each one is given the manifestation of the Spirit for the common good'*. 1 Corinthians 12:4-7. Every single member of the whole body is gifted by the Spirit *'for the common good'*. What is described here is clearly a meeting in mutuality in which all are free to exercise their gifts as the Holy Spirit shall lead. One thing is certain; the conduct of their meetings was in accordance with the leading of the Holy Spirit; nothing was pre-planned by man.

'But one and the same Spirit works all these things, distributing to each one individually just as He wills'. Some of these gifts are noted; the word of wisdom, the word of knowledge, faith, gifts of healing, effecting of miracles, prophecy, various kinds of tongues, interpretation of tongues.

Unity in the Spirit negates all exercise of the fleshly mind. *'For even as the body is one and yet has many members, and all the members of the body, though they are many, are one body, so also is Christ'*. The original Greek reads *'so also is the Christ'*. Just as our head directs all the members of our human body, so also does the Head of His body, Christ, direct those who are unitedly His own. *'The Christ'* means the full Christ. The Head joined with the completed and perfected body.

'For by one Spirit we were all baptized into one body, whether Jews or Greeks, whether slaves or free, and we were all made to drink of one Spirit'. When we received the Holy Spirit into us and we were born again, each one of us was also baptized by the same Spirit into the body of Christ. What a wonderful and unalterable truth!

'For the body is not one member, but many'. There is great emphasis on the fact that the body of *'the Christ'*, the full expression of Christ, is one; yet there is equal emphasis that the body is composed of many members.

'What is the outcome then, brethren? When you assemble, each one has a psalm, has a teaching, has a revelation, has a tongue, has an interpretation. Let all things be done for edification'. 1 Corinthians 14:26. What is the outcome when you meet together? Each member has something to offer to the other members from their Spirit-given gift, for the building up of the body of Christ. The word edification literally means *'building up'*.

In the account of the creation of Eve we read *'And Jehovah God causeth a deep sleep to fall upon the man, and he sleepeth, and He taketh one of his ribs, and closeth up flesh in its stead. And Jehovah God buildeth up the rib which He hath taken out of the man into a woman, and bringeth her in unto the man....'* Young's Literal Translation. The picture here is of Jehovah God building a woman from *'a rib or part of his side'* of Adam and bringing her unto the man. Surely this is a type of what God has been doing through the members of His 'ekklesia' from Pentecost until she, as His wife, will be presented to her Bridegroom. *"Let us rejoice and exult, and give him glory; for the marriage of the Lamb is come, and his wife has made herself ready.* Revelation 19:7, Darby.

Through the anointed activity of each and every member of His body, the fixed purpose and intention of the Lord Jesus, as *'the life giving Spirit'*, is to build a woman, His wife, that at the dawn of eternity, *'He might present to Himself the church in all her glory, having no spot or wrinkle or any such thing; but that she would be holy and blameless'*. Ephesians 5:27.

CHAPTER 28
FILLED WITH JOY AND WITH THE HOLY SPIRIT

Scripture references: Acts 13:52, Acts 4:18-31, Acts 16:22-33, Luke 14:26-35, John 17:13-14, Hebrews 12:3, Ephesians 5:18-20, Jude 24-25.

'And the disciples were continually filled with joy and with the Holy Spirit'. This statement, which closes Acts chapter 13, is spoken about the assembly that was raised up by the Lord, through Paul and Barnabas in Pisidian Antioch, a wild place noted for robbery and rebellion. An unlikely environment, one might think, for a noteworthy response to the gospel, yet can any more stirring expression of a young church be found in the New Testament Scriptures?

The members of this assembly were not simply believers or new converts, they are described as disciples. They were filled with joy and they were filled with the Holy Spirit and their fullness of joy and of the Holy Spirit was continual.

Surely this is a landmark description of any assembly in any age of the Christian church. Would that it might be said of assemblies raised up by God in every place, for this is what our Lord Jesus desires in our time, right now throughout the whole earth. The words of the Lord Jesus ring in our ears: *"You are the light of the world. A city set on a hill cannot be hidden; nor does anyone light a lamp and put it under a basket, but on the lampstand, and it gives light to all who are in the house. "Let your light shine before men in such a way that they may see your good works, and glorify your Father who is in heaven."* Matthew 5:14-16.

In Acts 4:18-31 is described an example of what we have been speaking about. Peter and John had been brought before the Jewish council which had *'commanded them not to speak or teach at all in the name of Jesus....When they had been released, they went to their own companions and reported all that the chief priests and the elders had said to them'*. There followed a memorable meeting of praise, worship and thanksgiving, *'And when they had prayed, the place where they had gathered together was shaken, and they were all filled with the Holy Spirit and began to speak the word of God with boldness'.*

A second example may be drawn from Acts 16:22-24. Paul and Silas had been unjustly accused, beaten and imprisoned. We read that *'The crowd rose up together against them, and the chief magistrates tore their robes off them and proceeded to order them to be beaten with rods. When they had struck them with many blows, they threw them into prison, commanding the jailer to guard them securely; and he, having received such a command, threw them into the inner prison and fastened their feet in the stocks'.* Then the account continues. *'But about midnight Paul and Silas were praying and singing hymns of praise to God, and the prisoners were listening to them; and suddenly there came a great earthquake, so that the foundations of the prison house were shaken....'*

The mighty power of God will surely be expressed through those in every era and in every situation who are entirely His; such ones will be *'continually filled with joy and with the Holy Spirit'.*

Jesus was very specific concerning the standard of becoming His disciple, and that standard has never varied or changed. It applied back then, and it applies right now. First of all, those who would be His disciples must come to Him and follow Him. This is the first essential.

Even the most used of human vessels must follow and focus alone on Christ, for we must be disciples of no other. Just as the Lord Jesus lived wholly by faith in His Father so also those who would be Jesus' disciples must live by faith in Him alone.

Jesus spoke much about the requirements and conditions for becoming His disciple. The following are some of these. *"If anyone comes to Me, and does not hate his own father and mother and wife and children and brothers and sisters, yes, and even his own life, he cannot be My disciple."* Luke 14:26. The appeal of family with its desires and demands must never be permitted to interfere with the call of God, or compete with His demands.

"Whoever does not carry his own cross and come after Me cannot be My disciple." To carry our cross is ongoing and constant. It must

be a way of life to deny what we want, in order to do what Jesus wants. Paul puts this in a very positive statement, *'Therefore we also have as our ambition, whether at home or absent, to be pleasing to Him'*. Many believers attempt to go through periods of severe self-denial, yet come out of these experiences hard and even proud of their achievement. This is not what Jesus means by carrying our cross. However, if obedience to the Lord Jesus comes from a deep love for Him it will bring pleasure to His heart and great reward to those who follow Him.

In the next few verses of this passage in Luke, Jesus emphasises the need to count the cost of discipleship. His final condition is very exacting for anyone, especially if they are rich in material things. *"So then, none of you can be My disciple who does not give up all his own possessions."* This certainly describes the actions the newly established church took immediately after Pentecost. The believers sold their properties and possessions and the money raised was applied for the benefit of the whole community, as any had need.

We might reasonably ask, what did Jesus intend when He said that His disciple must *'give up all his own possessions'*? Every individual who surrenders their all to Jesus will be made aware of what this means. No law can be written to define this vital step. The evidence of a surrendered life will always be a transparently Christ-like character.

The words of Jesus provide a fitting conclusion to this topic. *"A disciple is not above his teacher, nor a slave above his master. "It is enough for the disciple that he become like his teacher, and the slave like his master."* Matthew 10:24-25.

The joy that Jesus knew lay beyond the unspeakable agony of Calvary. In Hebrews 12:3 we are exhorted to fix *'our eyes on Jesus, the author and perfecter of faith, who for the joy set before Him endured the cross, despising the shame, and has sat down at the right hand of the throne of God'*. The fullness of the joy of Jesus that was experienced by those disciples in Pisidian Antioch, has been gifted by the Lord Jesus to us also if we will take up our cross to follow Him.

Ephesians 5:18, '....*And do not get drunk with wine, for that is dissipation, but be filled with the Spirit, speaking to one another in psalms and hymns and spiritual songs, singing and making melody with your heart to the Lord; always giving thanks for all things in the name of our Lord Jesus Christ to God, even the Father'*. The Greek verb used in the phrase *'be filled with the Spirit'* is in the present tense continuous, 'be being filled with the Spirit'.

May we, who are moved to ever deeper devotion to the Lord Jesus so come together as a fully surrendered people, gathered unto Him, that it may be said of us also, that we are *'continually filled with joy and with the Holy Spirit'*.

It seems fitting to close this chapter with the wonderful benediction from Jude 24-25. *"Now to Him who is able to keep you from stumbling, and to make you stand in the presence of His glory blameless with great joy, to the only God our Savior, through Jesus Christ our Lord, be glory, majesty, dominion and authority, before all time and now and forever. Amen."*

CHAPTER 29
YOU MAY ALL PROPHESY

Scripture references: Hebrews 1:1-2, 2 Chronicles 20:14-17, John 14:10-11, John 12:49-50, Acts 2:17-18, 2 Peter 2:19-21, 1 Corinthians 14:29-33.

'God, after He spoke long ago to the fathers in the prophets in many portions and in many ways....' Hebrews 1:1. Prophetic utterances come in many forms and convey a variety of intentions. We read in the Old Testament of numerous occasions when the Spirit of the Lord came upon someone to speak forth a special message on God's behalf, to warn, admonish or encourage. Sometimes this special word applied to circumstances at that time and sometimes it had to do with the future, even the very distant future. Many Old Testament prophecies have yet to be fulfilled.

2 Chronicles 20:14-17 provides an excellent example of a prophecy which was immediate, instructional and greatly encouraging. *'Then in the midst of the assembly the Spirit of the Lord came upon Jahaziel the son of Zechariah, the son of Benaiah, the son of Jeiel, the son of Mattaniah, the Levite of the sons of Asaph; and he said, "Listen, all Judah and the inhabitants of Jerusalem and King Jehoshaphat: thus says the Lord to you, 'Do not fear or be dismayed because of this great multitude, for the battle is not yours but God's. 'Tomorrow go down against them. Behold, they will come up by the ascent of Ziz, and you will find them at the end of the valley in front of the wilderness of Jeruel. 'You need not fight in this battle; station yourselves, stand and see the salvation of the Lord on your behalf, O Judah and Jerusalem.' Do not fear or be dismayed; tomorrow go out to face them, for the Lord is with you."* In the very centre of this prophecy is a message of encouragement that is as important today as it was then, *'Do not fear or be dismayed....for the battle is not yours but God's'*.

Hebrews 1:2. God, *'....in these last days has spoken to us in His Son, whom He appointed heir of all things, through whom also He made the world'*. Jesus came as the Word. Embodied in Him was, and is, and ever shall be, the content and summary of all God's speaking. He is the great Creator made flesh. His offering of

Himself in death spoke forth the redemption of all things back to God in just three words that echoed through the hallways of heaven, *"It is finished!"* These three words, echoing still, will be our constant reminder that Satan has nothing against *'those who are in Christ Jesus'*. Romans 8:1.

The 'Word' came as a wee babe who grew up and *'being about thirty years of age'*, having been baptized and clothed with power by the Spirit, was launched by the Father into His earthly ministry. Every word He spoke was given Him by the Father. Every deed He performed He saw the Father doing and He performed it in perfect obedience and co-ordination with Him. Every word He spoke during His mission on earth was prophetic, for every word delivered His Father's message to mankind. *"Believe Me that I am in the Father and the Father is in Me; otherwise believe because of the works themselves.* John 14:11. *"For I did not speak on My own initiative, but the Father Himself who sent Me has given Me a commandment as to what to say and what to speak. "I know that His commandment is eternal life; therefore the things I speak, I speak just as the Father has told Me."* John 12:49-50.

For the church of Jesus Christ, its mission and ministry began at Pentecost when those in that *'house where they were sitting'* were clothed with power from on high. Peter spoke with great power to the immense crowd that gathered. Can anyone doubt that every word he spoke came forth in the full power of the Holy Spirit? The harvest that resulted that day surely speaks for itself.

Quoting from the prophet Joel, Peter affirmed that *'it shall be in the last days,'* God says, *'that I will pour forth of My Spirit on all mankind; and your sons and your daughters shall prophesy, and your young men shall see visions, and your old men shall dream dreams; even on My bond slaves, both men and women, I will in those days pour forth of My Spirit And they shall prophesy'*. Acts 2:17-18. These words testify that *'Your sons and your daughters....My bond slaves, both men and women....shall prophesy'* by means of and under the anointing of the poured out Holy Spirit. So, throughout the centuries since, every word Jesus has spoken and still speaks today through His own, as the life-giving Spirit, is prophetic. It is as though Jesus Himself is speaking. The words may be stumbling, or the voice may quaver due to old age, but the message shall be as though from the Lord Himself.

Peter, in 2 Peter 1:19-21, enlightens us concerning the substance of prophecy. *'So we have the prophetic word made more sure, to which you do well to pay attention as to a lamp shining in a dark place....'* Peter recalls the message from the heavens when he, James and John were with Jesus on the Mount of transfiguration. *"This is My beloved Son, with whom I am well-pleased; listen to Him!"* Matthew 17:5. This word is shown to have been made more sure in the words of Peter on the day of Pentecost *"Therefore let all the house of Israel know for certain that God has made Him both Lord and Christ - this Jesus whom you crucified."* Acts 2:36.

'....until the day dawns and the morning star arises in your hearts'. This may seem a very mysterious statement. If we pay attention to the prophetic word by listening closely to Jesus then the time will come when a new day will dawn and He, as the morning star, will arise in our hearts. The writer believes that this dawn will be a deep personal disclosure of the person of Jesus to us accompanied by the birth of a passionate love for Him. As He, the morning star, arises in our heart, so our love for Him will grow and increase until it burns like an all-consuming fire inside us. Proverbs 4:18 *But the path of the righteous is like the light of dawn, That shines brighter and brighter until the full day.*

Surely this is the state to which God desires to bring us. *'For God, who said, "Light shall shine out of darkness," is the One who has shone in our hearts to give the Light of the knowledge of the glory of God in the face of Christ'.*

But know this first of all, that no prophecy of Scripture is a matter of one's own interpretation, for no prophecy was ever made by an act of human will, but men moved by the Holy Spirit spoke from God'. 2 Peter 1:19-21. The essence of *'prophecy'* and *'the prophetic word'* is summed up in the last statement *'....men moved by the Holy Spirit spoke from God'.*

At this point we must make a distinction between those who have been raised up to be prophets and contrast this with the freedom to prophesy bestowed upon every member of the body of Christ. Prophets communicate messages from the very throne of God in specific circumstances and times whereas all the members of His church, as prompted by the Holy Spirit, may speak for the common good of the hearers at the time and in the manner that He leads. In either case, prophecy is the speaking of every word in accordance with the anointing of the Holy Spirit.

The account of the selection of Barnabas and Saul to be sent forth as apostles provides a perfect example of the prophetic function in action. *'Now there were at Antioch, in the church that was there, prophets and teachers: Barnabas, and Simeon who was called Niger, and Lucius of Cyrene, and Manaen who had been brought up with Herod the tetrarch, and Saul'.* Acts 13:1. These five were themselves dual gifts to the church in Antioch. They were both prophets and teachers. However, there is no indication that they were acting in a leadership role; to the contrary in fact. Saul had by now been a believer for around thirteen years, Barnabas for longer, for he is mentioned as having sold a piece of land soon after the launch of the church at Pentecost. After a large number of Gentiles had believed and swelled the numbers of the church in Antioch, Barnabas had been sent there from Jerusalem. He first went to Tarsus to find Saul and bring him with him to Antioch, where the two of them taught in this assembly for a year.

'While they were ministering to the Lord and fasting, the Holy Spirit said, "Set apart for Me Barnabas and Saul for the work to which I have called them."' The whole assembly in Antioch was *'ministering to the Lord and fasting'* and the Holy Spirit spoke a very precise message through one of those present. No man was leading this meeting. It is not indicated that the Holy Spirit spoke this command; *"Set apart for Me Barnabas and Saul for the work to which I have called them"* through any of the five prophets named, although He almost certainly did.

'Then, when they had fasted and prayed and laid their hands on them, they sent them away'. Who fasted and prayed? Who laid their hands on them? Who sent them away? The whole assembly did. The

Holy Spirit was Lord over everything. Every member discerned that this was indeed a directive from God.

1 Corinthians 14:29 NIV makes clear that there are two aspects to prophesy. There is the speaking forth of an anointed word and there is the need for spiritual discernment on the part of the hearers. *'Two or three prophets should speak, and the others should weigh carefully what is said'.*

'So, being sent out by the Holy Spirit, they went down to Seleucia and from there they sailed to Cyprus'. Saul and Barnabas were sent out together by the Holy Spirit to many cities across the Roman Empire. They spread the gospel of the kingdom and gathered the believers together so that, in the power of the Holy Spirit, they might be the Lord's testimony in each location.

There are those who are raised up as one of the greater gifts; the gift of prophet. *'And He gave some....prophets'.* Ephesians 4:11. But, applying to every member, Paul writes *'For you can all prophesy one by one, so that all may learn and all may be exhorted; and the spirits of prophets are subject to prophets; for God is not a God of confusion but of peace, as in all the churches of the saints'.* 1 Corinthians 14:31-33.

These and other Scriptures provide instruction for the gatherings of the church unto Jesus. Worship, prayer and teaching are to be in mutuality as the Spirit shall direct. Words of testimony, exhortation, admonition, instruction, comfort, support for the weak, direction, action must be in accordance with the leading of the Holy Spirit.

Every member of the body of Christ has ultimate control over releasing their anointed contribution. Sometimes the prompting of the Holy Spirit will be to release a word immediately and at other times it will be to hold back the given word to coincide with the contribution of another. The leading of the Spirit and sensitivity of the members to the Spirit will bring perfect harmony as God's people meet together. *'What is the outcome then, brethren? When you assemble, each one has a psalm, has a teaching, has a revelation, has a tongue, has an interpretation. Let all things be done for edification'.* 1 Corinthians 14:26. Edification means building up, which will lead us directly into the next chapter.

CHAPTER 30
BUILDING UP THE BODY OF CHRIST

Scripture references: Genesis 2:18-23, Ephesians 4:11-16, Revelation 19:5-9, Matthew 16:15-18, John 17:22-23, 1 Corinthians 14:26.

In an earlier chapter the subject of 'building up the body of Christ' was introduced. In this current chapter we will lean on the Lord's grace and mercy to take this topic further, that he who writes and those who read may receive true revelation of the part He has given us to play in bringing to perfection the eternal purpose of Almighty God.

In the account of the beginnings of mankind in Genesis 2 is described the creation of Eve as a bride for Adam. *'Then the Lord God said, "It is not good for the man to be alone; I will make him a helper suitable for him."* How portentous are those words, for Adam is the type of God's *'one and only Son'*, and Adam's bride Eve is the type of *'the bride, the wife of the Lamb'*. Just as it was not good for Adam to be alone so, in the counsels of the Godhead, the decision was made that 'a helper suitable for Him' would be provided to Jesus.

'And Jehovah God caused a deep sleep to fall upon the man, and he slept; and He took one of his ribs and closed up the flesh in its place. And Jehovah God built the rib, which He had taken from the man, into a woman and brought her to the man'. Genesis 2:21-22 Recovery Version. Likewise Elohim, the Triune God in council together, determined that Jesus should endure the sleep of death, for we read that He is *'the Lamb that was slain from the creation of the world'*, Revelation 13:8 NIV, that from His very essence and substance might be taken that which would be built into His bride, to be brought to her Bridegroom at the end of time.

'The man said, "This is now bone of my bones, And flesh of my flesh; She shall be called Woman, Because she was taken out of Man." Genesis 2:23. It seems that more than a rib was taken from Adam; the inference being that it was part of his side; for Adam declares *"This is now bone of my bones, And flesh of my flesh...."* Be that as it may, Adam now had a bride who would be his counterpart

to complete him. In what way, we may ask, is it possible that Jesus might benefit from a counterpart to complete Him? We cannot know the answer to that question. Yet in God's sovereign plan and provision it is so.

God completed His task of building Eve while Adam was still in *'a deep sleep'*. Adam was unaware of the building work of God that became Eve and took no part in it. However, it is significant to note that, although the Lord Jesus accomplished all that was required to obtain His bride in and though His death on the cross, yet the working out of the process is dependent on members of His body willingly giving themselves to be His co-workers in this building process which is still in progress.

The *'good works, which God prepared beforehand so that we would walk in them'* spoken of in Ephesians 2:10 are expressed in the righteous acts mentioned in Revelation 19:7-8: *"Let us be glad and rejoice and give Him glory, for the marriage of the Lamb has come, and His wife has made herself ready." And to her it was granted to be arrayed in fine linen, clean and bright, for the fine linen is the righteous acts of the saints.* NKJV

In the case of Eve it was God who fully accomplished the task. In the case of His wife, Jesus will accomplish this task in and through those who unreservedly give themselves to Him. Thus there is a major call for action on the part of His own, as the day draws near when He *'will appear a second time for salvation without reference to sin, to those who eagerly await Him'*. Hebrews 9:28.

The Lord Jesus had told Peter and His other disciples, *"I will build My church."* Matthew 16:18. The means and methods which the Lord has chosen to use will be the subject of the rest of this chapter.

"The glory which You have given Me I have given to them, that they may be one, just as We are one; I in them and You in Me, that they may be perfected in unity, so that the world may know that You sent Me, and loved them, even as You have loved Me." John 17:22-23. The glory of God has been given to His own, that they may be one, just as the Triune God is one.

Many believers in Jesus discuss the importance of unity even if they are not experiencing it in their own fellowships. Yet the real question remains: What is the real significance of unity? It surely is this, that if we are walking in unity we will enjoy the glory of God which has been given to us for this very purpose?

The holy city, new Jerusalem, is not only the perfection of beauty, it is the ultimate expression of unity. Thus, only those who walk in unity, as God defines it in John 17, may be engaged upon *'building up the body of Christ'*.

'I heard another voice from heaven, saying, "Come out of her, my people, so that you will not participate in her sins and receive of her plagues'. Revelation 18:4. We must not leave it to the last second to come out of the confusion and disunity which characterizes religious Babylon. Right now the Lord is calling all those who have ears to hear, *"Come out of her, my people."* In every village, town or city the Lord desires to establish a community of believers in Jesus that will welcome all others within whom is the Holy Spirit of God that, together, they may co-operate with Him in *'building up the body of Christ'*.

Having said this, we must recognize that there will continue to be countless numbers who faithfully display the Lord's testimony within Christian affiliations who, for various reasons, remain in far less than ideal circumstances. Church history is replete with such ones who, in dark places, have let their *'light shine before men'* and their deeds are *'manifested as having been wrought in God'*.

'....speaking the truth in love, we are to grow up in all aspects into Him who is the head, even Christ, from whom the whole body, being fitted and held together by what every joint supplies, according to the proper working of each individual part, causes the growth of the body for the building up of itself in love'. Ephesians 4:15-16. It is not only in unity that we must gather, but we must gather unto *'Jesus, the author and perfecter of faith'*. If every joint of supply and every individual member of the body, *'speaking the truth in love'*, performs their role *'according to the proper working of each individual part'*, then the body will be built up in love.

On the one hand Jesus is the one who is building His church, His body, His bride; on the other hand He is achieving His building work through those who *'preserve the unity of the Spirit in the bond of peace'*; those who gather unto Him as their supreme Head, and who freely exercise their proper function.

'What then, brothers? Whenever you come together, each one has a psalm, has a teaching, has a revelation, has a tongue, has an interpretation. Let all things be done for building up'. 1 Corinthians 14:26. Recovery Version. What is the outcome when you meet together? Each member has something to supply, from their individual Spirit-given gift, for building up the body of Christ. May the Lord lead us into a community of His own that follows this pattern:

- They meet together, accepting in love and in unity all in whom is the divine Spirit
- Their gathering together is around the Head, Christ, as their supreme and only Leader
- All members present are free to exercise their gift as the Spirit shall lead

Thus may we prove to be *'fellow workers for the kingdom of God'* and builders up of the body of Christ.

CHAPTER 31
THE WORD HAS SOUNDED FORTH

Scripture references: Mark 4:26-29, John 4:35-38, Luke 10:1-21, Acts 4:5-31, Acts 8:1-4, Acts 11:19-24, 1 Thessalonians 1:6-8.

"The kingdom of God is like a man who casts seed upon the soil; and he goes to bed at night and gets up by day, and the seed sprouts and grows - how, he himself does not know. "The soil produces crops by itself; first the blade, then the head, then the mature grain in the head. "But when the crop permits, he immediately puts in the sickle, because the harvest has come." Mark 4:26-29. At the time of the creation, God ordained that the plant life will have seed in itself, so that when the seed is sown in the soil, over a period of time it will produce a harvest. So it is in the kingdom of God. As the word of the kingdom is sown, so *'the soil produces crops by itself; first the blade, then the head, then the mature grain in the head'*. In due course the soil will produce a crop that may be harvested. The farmer's task is to sow the seed, to watch over it and to reap the harvest that comes from the seed.

When the seed of the gospel of the kingdom is sown and responded to in the hearts of hearers, the Holy Spirit enters into the human spirit. John 3:6, *'....that which is born of the Spirit is spirit'*. How growth takes place in the individual is a mystery, just as the sower in the above verses *'does not know'* how the seed sprouts and grows.

It has been God's intention that, just as one seed is multiplied to become many seeds, so the gospel of the kingdom may sound forth until it has reached the entire inhabited earth. The promise of the Lord Jesus is that *"This gospel of the kingdom shall be preached in the whole world as a testimony to all the nations, and then the end will come."* Matthew 24:14. When this task has been accomplished then He, as King of kings and Lord of lords, will return to reign forever and ever. Revelation 11:15.

'Behold, I say to you, lift up your eyes and look on the fields, that they are white for harvest...."I sent you to reap that for which you have not labored; others have labored and you have entered into their labor." John 4:35,38. Jesus words to His disciples are equally

true today. The seed that has been sown throughout the kingdom age by other labourers is now fully ripe and ready to be harvested.

'And He was saying to them, "The harvest indeed is great, but the workers are few. Pray therefore the Lord of the harvest to thrust out laborers into His harvest'. Luke 10:2 Wuest. Jesus is not asking that we plead with Him to send more labourers into His harvest. He will always select from the labourers available to Him those whom He approves. What the Lord is urging His own to pray for is *'to thrust out laborers into His harvest'*. Anyone who has themselves used a scythe to harvest barley or wheat knows that the implement is swung with vigour. It is this wide sweeping thrusting motion that slices through much with each stroke.

Very soon after that great day of Pentecost, when those gathered in an upper room had been clothed with power from on high, there is an example of labourers being *'thrust out'* into His harvest. On their way into the temple Peter with John had been used of the Lord to raise up and restore to full function a lame man sitting at the gate called Beautiful. The Jewish council was informed of the ensuing commotion, as great numbers of people had been observers at this great miracle of healing. They imprisoned Peter and John and the next day they brought them before their rulers. After questioning them they severely warned them against speaking any more in the name of Jesus.

'When they had been released, they went to their own companions and reported all that the chief priests and the elders had said to them. And when they heard this, they lifted their voices to God with one accord and said...."And now, Lord, take note of their threats, and grant that Your bond-servants may speak Your word with all confidence, while You extend Your hand to heal, and signs and wonders take place through the name of Your holy servant Jesus." Acts 4:23-24, 29-31. The entire company *'lifted their voices to God with one accord'*. Here was an instance of the company of believers in one mind, with one voice, petitioning God 'that they, His bond-servants, might speak His word with all confidence'.

What was the response from the throne of heaven to this mighty, united outpouring of praise, worship and petition to God? *'And when they had prayed, the place where they had gathered together was shaken, and they were all filled with the Holy Spirit and began to speak the word of God with boldness'.* The place where they had gathered together was shaken and the power of God descended upon them all as it had at Pentecost, for the Greek word employed for 'filled' is 'pletho', the same word used when those at Pentecost were clothed with power.

The outcome of this second visitation was that *'they were all filled with the Holy Spirit and began to speak the word of God with boldness'.* Not just a few, but all began to speak the word of God with boldness. Surely this is what Jesus meant when He urged His own to pray, *"Pray therefore the Lord of the harvest to thrust out laborers into His harvest."* All are given the task of harvesting, and all need to be thrust out in the mighty power of the Spirit. May the writer of these words and those who read them be granted the Lord's favour that the locations in which we gather may be so shaken.

There follows an example in which the thrust of the gospel went forth in great power and resulted in large numbers turning to the Lord. This great thrust of the gospel came about as a result of severe persecution and those who were thrust forth are largely unnamed.

Stephen had just been stoned *'and Saul was in hearty agreement with putting him to death. And on that day a great persecution began against the church in Jerusalem, and they were all scattered throughout the regions of Judea and Samaria, except the apostles....'Therefore, those who had been scattered went about preaching the word'.* Acts 8:1-4. Presumably, having previously sold their property and possessions, these scattered ones left Jerusalem with little or nothing than the clothes they were wearing.

We are reminded of the word of the Lord Jesus to the seventy whom He sent forth. He had sent them in pairs with these instructions. *"Go; behold, I send you out as lambs in the midst of wolves. "Carry no money belt, no bag, no shoes; and greet no one on the way. "Whatever house you enter, first say, 'Peace be to this house.' "If a man of peace is there, your peace will rest on him; but if not, it will return to you. "Stay in that house, eating and drinking what they give you; for the laborer is worthy of his wages. Do not keep moving from house to house. "Whatever city you enter and they receive you, eat what is set before you; and heal those in it who are sick, and say to them, ' The kingdom of God has come near to you.' "But whatever city you enter and they do not receive you, go out into its streets and say, 'Even the dust of your city which clings to our feet we wipe off in protest against you; yet be sure of this, that the kingdom of God has come near.'* Luke 10:3-11.

As these believers who had been dispersed from Jerusalem went forth, no doubt these words of the Lord were proven abundantly true in their case, for a great harvest resulted. *'So then those who were scattered because of the persecution that occurred in connection with Stephen made their way to Phoenicia and Cyprus and Antioch, speaking the word to no one except to Jews alone. But there were some of them, men of Cyprus and Cyrene, who came to Antioch and began speaking to the Greeks also, preaching the Lord Jesus. And the hand of the Lord was with them, and a large number who believed turned to the Lord'.* Acts 11:19-21. Here is described a dual thrust of the gospel of the kingdom, on the one hand to the Jews only and on the other hand *'men of Cyprus and Cyrene, who came to Antioch and began speaking to the Greeks also, preaching the Lord Jesus'*. In the latter case the foundation of what became a tremendously influential assembly in Antioch was established.

'....and the news about them reached the ears of the church at Jerusalem, and they sent Barnabas off to Antioch. Then when he arrived and witnessed the grace of God, he rejoiced and began to encourage them all with resolute heart to remain true to the Lord; for he was a good man, and full of the Holy Spirit and of faith. And considerable numbers were brought to the Lord'. Acts 11:22-24. We note that considerable numbers were brought to the Lord and that Barnabas became a part of that great assembly. It is also worth mentioning that his first move was to fetch Saul from Tarsus and bring him to Antioch. We note that the two of them *'for an entire year met with the church, and taught considerable numbers'*.

Several years later, after Paul and Barnabas had preached in Thessalonica and had established an assembly there, Paul wrote to these Thessalonian believers. His letters were very complimentary. At one point he writes, *'You also became imitators of us and of the Lord, having received the word in much tribulation with the joy of the Holy Spirit, so that you became an example to all the believers in Macedonia and in Achaia. For the word of the Lord has sounded forth from you, not only in Macedonia and Achaia, but also in every place your faith toward God has gone forth, so that we have no need to say anything'.* We note first of all that they themselves *'received the word in much tribulation with the joy of the Holy Spirit'.* Just as had happened to those who were scattered because of persecution in Jerusalem, so these Thessalonian believers had endured much tribulation. Yet we read, *'the word of the Lord has sounded forth from you, not only in Macedonia and Achaia, but also in every place your faith toward God has gone forth, so that we have no need to say anything'.*

From Pentecost and onwards the immeasurable power of the Holy Spirit has been available to those of His people who are willing to follow the Lord with their whole heart. Persecution and suffering has often been their lot. It has always been to a remnant that this power has been given, that the gospel of the kingdom might 'sound forth' to all the nations.

CHAPTER 32
IN MUCH TRIBULATION

Scripture references: Matthew 5:10, John 16:33, James 5:10-11, Jeremiah 25:1-12, Daniel 6:1-23, Acts 7:51-60, 1 Thessalonians 1:6-7, 1 Peter 4:12-14, Colossians 1:24, Romans 8:35-39.

Among the best known discourses of Jesus is what has widely become known as 'the sermon on the mount'. This occupies three chapters in the book of Matthew. Right at the beginning of His message are those sayings that have become popularly known as 'the beatitudes', Matthew 5:1-12. Recorded as verse 10, Jesus said, *"Blessed are those who have been persecuted for the sake of righteousness, for theirs is the kingdom of heaven."* These words are of great comfort to those He calls upon to undergo suffering. Jesus says that they are *'blessed'*. Yet what a wonderful promise is theirs, in the here and now, who uphold righteousness at the cost of misunderstanding and ridicule, *'for theirs is the kingdom of heaven'*. Jesus also told His disciples, *"In the world you have tribulation, but take courage; I have overcome the world."* John 16:33.

The two verse parable of Jesus found in Matthew 7:13-14 is about a narrow gate which few find and fewer enter. Why is this? All that a believer holds dear to himself must be renounced and counted as loss for Jesus' sake. The constricted gate may only be entered through Jesus and the one seeking to enter must enter in Him, with empty hands. As it was with the great apostle Paul, those who would go through this narrow gate must affirm that *'I count all things to be loss in view of the surpassing value of knowing Christ Jesus my Lord, for whom I have suffered the loss of all things, and count them but rubbish so that I may gain Christ'*. Philippians 3:8.

In contrast, how available is the wide gate and how easy the broad way that the vast majority of those who profess to follow Jesus take as their choice. The epitaph of those who stroll in great numbers down this broad way are found in Matthew 13:22: *'the worry of the world and the deceitfulness of wealth choke the word, and it becomes unfruitful'*.

As an introduction to two examples of godly suffering from the Old Testament, we will quote from James 5:10-11. James says, *'As an example, brethren, of suffering and patience, take the prophets who spoke in the name of the Lord. We count those blessed who endured....'* How much we admire the faith of such as Jeremiah and Daniel and honour their willingness to face death for the sake of Jehovah.

The prophet Jeremiah is perhaps best known for his prophecy that Judah would be captive in Babylon for seventy years. Jeremiah 25:1-12. Jeremiah had been warning his people to turn back to the Lord from their wickedness and idolatry for twenty three years, yet without effect. With the Babylonian army besieging the walls of Jerusalem, Jeremiah gave the Lord's word to the men of Judah that they should surrender to the king of Babylon. In their pride and obstinacy some evil men took him captive and lowered him into a well, empty of water, where he sank into the mud. Jeremiah most certainly would have perished without food or water in this dreadful state were it not for an Ethiopian eunuch named Ebed-melech, who went to King Zedekiah and gained permission to rescue him with the help of some men. Yes! *'We count those blessed who endured....'*

Consider also the faithfulness of Daniel. A more upright man can scarcely be found in all of Scripture. There was a fragrance of Jesus about Daniel. He had been a wise counsellor to King Nebuchadnezzar and was now the highly valued advisor to King Darius.

Others of influence in Babylon were envious of Daniel and sought to destroy him. Their plot made use of the irrevocable law of the Medes and Persians that, once signed by the king, no edict could be amended or set aside. They persuaded Darius that he alone should receive all petitions for the next thirty days. The King in his pride signed the decree. These men were well aware of Daniel's practice of praying to Yahweh from his upper windows three times each day, as he gazed towards Jerusalem. Daniel continued his practice without wavering and was reported to the king. With great reluctance Darius had Daniel cast into the den of lions.

After a sleepless night, Darius came at daybreak to the mouth of the den and cried out, *"Daniel, servant of the living God, has your God, whom you constantly serve, been able to deliver you from the lions?" Then Daniel spoke to the king, "O king, live forever! "My God sent His angel and shut the lions' mouths and they have not harmed me, inasmuch as I was found innocent before Him; and also toward you, O king, I have committed no crime." Then the king was very pleased and gave orders for Daniel to be taken up out of the den. So Daniel was taken up out of the den and no injury whatever was found on him, because he had trusted in his God'.* Daniel 6:20-23.

It is noteworthy that the Aramaic word for His *'angel'* is the same word used by Nebuchadnezzar of the One who walked with Hananiah, Mishael and Azariah in the fiery furnace. Did the pre-incarnation Jesus descend into the lion's den with Daniel? If so, it is not surprising that the lions were quiet and peaceful.

In the New Testament era one outstanding example out of many will suffice. In the early days of the church there was one who faced death, for whom there would be no rescue, Christ's first martyr, Stephen. His path to glory is noteworthy, for he came as a shining star into the firmament of the kingdom of heaven, after being one of seven chosen to oversee food distribution to the Greek widows. That task completed, he was found preaching with such conviction that fierce opposition ensued. He was brought before the Jewish council. *'And fixing their gaze on him, all who were sitting in the Council saw his face like the face of an angel'.* Acts 6:15.

False witnesses had spoken against him before Stephen was permitted to speak. He regaled his audience with a powerfully delivered historic record of God's grace upon the nation of Israel. Starting with Abraham and proceeding with Moses and the frequent rebellions and opposition on the part of the desert wanderers, he moved on to David and finally to Jesus. All was well until he drew a parallel between the rebellious opposition of the children of Israel and the recent hostile part the ones he was addressing had played in the death of Jesus, *'the Righteous One, whose betrayers and murderers'* they had now become. As one, they gnashed their teeth at him and dragged him off to stone him.

'But being full of the Holy Spirit, he gazed intently into heaven and saw the glory of God, and Jesus standing at the right hand of God; and he said, "Behold, I see the heavens opened up and the Son of Man standing at the right hand of God." But they cried out with a loud voice, and covered their ears and rushed at him with one impulse'. As His servant Stephen was about to be stoned, Jesus arose from His throne and stood. What greater commendation could there be than that?

Before Stephen passed forever into the presence of his beloved Master *'he called on the Lord and said, "Lord Jesus, receive my spirit!" Then falling on his knees, he cried out with a loud voice, "Lord, do not hold this sin against them!" Having said this, he fell asleep'.*

On his second apostolic journey Paul, with Silas as his companion, visited Thessalonica where a number of Jews and many Gentiles received the word of the gospel and believed. They founded a church in that city which, according to Paul's two letters to the believers, became a thriving Christian community. We read, *'You also became imitators of us and of the Lord, having received the word in much tribulation with the joy of the Holy Spirit, so that you became an example to all the believers in Macedonia and in Achaia'.* 1 Thessalonians 1:6-7. At the heart of what Paul was commending them for are these words that carry much significance: *'in much tribulation with the joy of the Holy Spirit'.*

'Beloved, do not be surprised at the fiery ordeal among you, which comes upon you for your testing, as though some strange thing were happening to you; but to the degree that you share the sufferings of Christ, keep on rejoicing, so that also at the revelation of His glory you may rejoice with exultation. If you are reviled for the name of Christ, you are blessed, because the Spirit of glory and of God rests on you'. 1 Peter 4:12-14. In these latter days it is quite evident that the Lord is completing His bride. She is being perfected through suffering, that she may enter into a deeper appreciation and identification with the heart of her coming Bridegroom. As He was reviled and rejected, so will this be the portion of His own. Yet *'the Spirit of glory and of God'*, who has been charged with preparing

the bride, rests upon all who place themselves unreservedly in His hands.

'Now I rejoice in my sufferings for your sake, and in my flesh I do my share on behalf of His body, which is the church, in filling up what is lacking in Christ's afflictions'. Colossians 1:24. As with Paul, a small but significant minority are willing to share in the afflictions of Christ *'on behalf of His body, which is the church'*, who will one day be His wife who *'has made herself ready'*. May we choose the pathway of suffering and be counted among these blessed ones.

As these lines are being written, a kind of darkness is creeping across the whole world, a darkness that can be felt by all who know the workings of Satan. History is moving swiftly towards its inevitable conclusion. The tribulation years are almost upon us. This will be a time of the deepest darkness, followed by a dawn whose brilliance will never end.

'Who will separate us from the love of Christ? Will tribulation, or distress, or persecution, or famine, or nakedness, or peril, or sword? Just as it is written, "for your sake we are being put to death all day long; we were considered as sheep to be slaughtered." But in all these things we overwhelmingly conquer through Him who loved us. For I am convinced that neither death, nor life, nor angels, nor principalities, nor things present, nor things to come, nor powers, nor height, nor depth, nor any other created thing, will be able to separate us from the love of God, which is in Christ Jesus our Lord'. Romans 8:35-39.

CHAPTER 33
THE CHURCH IN GOD

Scripture references: 1 Corinthians 2:9-13, 1 Thessalonians 1:1, 2 Thessalonians 1:1-2, Psalms 46:4-5, Matthew 18:20, Ephesians 1:3-4, Hebrews 12:1-2, Psalm 16:11.

"Things which eye has not seen and ear has not heard, and which have not entered the heart of man, all that God has prepared for those who love Him." For to us God revealed them through the Spirit; for the Spirit searches all things, even the depths of God. For who among men knows the thoughts of a man except the spirit of the man which is in him? Even so the thoughts of God no one knows except the Spirit of God. Now we have received, not the spirit of the world, but the Spirit who is from God, so that we may know the things freely given to us by God, which things we also speak, not in words taught by human wisdom, but in those taught by the Spirit, combining spiritual thoughts with spiritual words. 1 Corinthians 2:9-13. As believers unto salvation through faith in the Lord Jesus, we beseech Him that we may receive understanding of *'all that God has prepared for those who love Him'*. Our human imagination cannot begin to grasp the extent of what God has given us in Christ. May the blessed person of the Holy Spirit open our eyes that we may see significantly more.

As we read these memorable verses, we may feel they apply only to the life hereafter and not to our life here and now. So many, even among the truly redeemed, feel that they must struggle through their earthly sojourn, to arrive one day in a vaguely perceived heaven, where all will be bliss forever. Many find themselves living in a sort of twilight zone with barely enough spiritual sustenance to keep them going. The intention of this chapter is to reveal some of the *'all that God has prepared for those who love Him'*. May the Lord be gracious to us.

In fact, God has provided an Eden of delights in the here and now, *'for those who love Him'*, every source of sustenance for complete spiritual growth and well-being. In the centre of this garden is the tree of life. There is also the river of life which issues from the very throne of God. The name that Jesus gives this garden is 'the kingdom of heaven'. It is the Father's intention that all His own be gathered together unto His beloved Son that they may enter fully into its delights.

'For who among men knows the thoughts of a man except the spirit of the man which is in him? Even so the thoughts of God no one knows except the Spirit of God'. Just as our thoughts are hidden from all but ourselves, so the thoughts of God are unknown except to the Spirit of God.

'Now we have received, not the spirit of the world, but the Spirit who is from God'. The Holy Spirit, who is a party to the full counsel of the Triune God, has been given to us *'so that we may know the things freely given to us by God'.* It is God's desire that those who love Him shall know with absolute confidence and certainty the things that He has for them. The fountainhead of God's revealed wisdom is the Holy Spirit. As we welcome Him to take His rightful place as Lord of our lives, surely we shall know and enter into the fullness of what the Lord Jesus gave His life to provide for us.

'....which things we also speak, not in words taught by human wisdom, but in those taught by the Spirit, combining spiritual thoughts with spiritual words'. Our daily enjoyment of the presence of Jesus and what the Holy Spirit reveals to us will provide much that we may share, as we meet together in ones and twos, or assembled together as a company of God's people. The glory of our meetings together with Jesus as our supreme Head, and as anointed by the blessed Holy Spirit, cannot be measured. As each one speaks forth that which the Holy Spirit gives them to speak, it will combine the spiritual thoughts into spiritual words that will rejoice the heart of our Father in heaven and will transport us into the heavenly places with Him. We shall indeed have met on holy ground. It is in this Eden of the kingdom of heaven that God desires His loved ones to meet and to live out their lives, in exaltation of His Son, our Lord Jesus Christ.

Paul opens his two letters to the assembly in Thessalonica with almost identical words, *'Paul and Silvanus and Timothy, To the church of the Thessalonians in God the Father and the Lord Jesus Christ: Grace to you and peace'.* 1 Thessalonians 1:1. In 2

Thessalonians 1:1 the only change is *'in God our Father'*. Contained within these greetings is a wonderful revelation. Paul is affirming that the church in Thessalonica has its true location *'in God our Father and the Lord Jesus Christ'*. Do we comprehend this? The very life of individual believers and of a company of believers is *'in God our Father and the Lord Jesus Christ'*.

Why might we be unaware of this, our heritage and our right? Could it be that our eyes are upon a building, an organization and familiar routines, rather than upon Jesus? Jesus represents the tree of life in the middle of our Eden. He is the source of our nourishment and joy. He is the object of our worship, our praise and our thanksgiving. Jesus comforts us with these words, *"Do not be afraid, little flock, for your Father has chosen gladly to give you the kingdom."* Luke 12:32.

'There is a river whose streams make glad the city of God, The holy dwelling places of the Most High. God is in the midst of her, she will not be moved; God will help her when morning dawns'. Psalms 46:4-5. This is the river of life that flows forever in the kingdom of heaven, from which the thirsty can drink at will. As the thirsty ones drink in the water of life they will experience the freedom to express it forth in individual streams of praise, worship and adoration as they employ their spiritual gifts. These many streams of life together increase the flow of the river as it returns to make glad the city of God.

One day, perhaps quite soon, the whole world will be brought under the governance of one usurping ruler, the antichrist. The god of this world, Satan, will give his authority to this antichrist; known to heaven as 'the beast'. How soon after that event will meetings of believers have to be approved, or else banned? We cannot know. How long will it be before pastors and reverends must swear allegiance to this beast? Who can tell? Yet meetings of two or three believers *'in God our Father and the Lord Jesus Christ'* will be near impossible to prevent. *"For where two or three have gathered together in My name, I am there in their midst."* Matthew 18:20. Wherever they may gather, Jesus will be in their midst as the tree of life. Even two or three may meet in representation of Christ's church on earth, carrying His authority.

As the visible, yet closeted in heaven, church of Jesus Christ we may experience the fullness of the joy of Jesus in the forests, in outhouses or barns, on rock strewn hillsides or in underground passages, as did the persecuted believers of ancient Rome in the catacombs. *'Blessed be the God and Father of our Lord Jesus Christ, who has blessed us with every spiritual blessing in the heavenly places in Christ, just as He chose us in Him before the foundation of the world, that we would be holy and blameless before Him'*. Ephesians 1:3-4.

Perhaps we will be led into circumstances or conditions in which we feel oppressed and alone. Yet, in all such situations, Hebrews 12:1-2 will provide us with a very encouraging heavenly perspective: *'Therefore, since we have so great a cloud of witnesses surrounding us, let us also lay aside every encumbrance and the sin which so easily entangles us, and let us run with endurance the race that is set before us, fixing our eyes on Jesus, the author and perfecter of faith, who for the joy set before Him endured the cross, despising the shame, and has sat down at the right hand of the throne of God'*.

In running our individual or collective race, a great multitude of those whose race has been run are actively applauding us from the stadium in the heavens, urging us on to the finishing line. We will know that same joy that Jesus looked ahead to, as He was about to endure the cross. He encouraged His disciples with these words, *"These things I have spoken to you so that My joy may be in you, and that your joy may be made full."* John 15:11.

There can be no greater joy on earth than to meet as His people in the fullness of the divine presence. David exclaims, *'You will show me the path of life; In Your presence is fullness of joy; At Your right hand are pleasures forevermore'*. Psalm 16:11 NKJV. Surely, the pleasures that are ours as we meet *'in God our Father and the Lord Jesus Christ'* cannot be measured.

In writing this book it has been given me to see that to the degree which Jesus is truly Lord of a member of His body, or of a representative company of His people, to that degree is His blessing upon them and His irrepressible joy evident among them. May this joy become the constant experience of the writer and of all who shall read these words.

"Things which eye has not seen and ear has not heard, and which have not entered the heart of man, all that God has prepared for those who love Him." For to us God revealed them through the Spirit." 1 Corinthians 2:9-10.

CHAPTER 34
HE HIMSELF IS OUR PEACE

Scripture references: Ephesians 2:10-22, Romans 11:1-36, Ephesians 4:11-16, Revelation 3:7-13.

'For we are His masterpiece, created in Christ Jesus for good works, which God prepared beforehand in order that we would walk in them'. Ephesians 2:10, Recovery Version. The church, the body of Christ, which will one day be presented to Him as His bride, is yet a work in progress. As the Holy City, the dwelling place of God, she will be displayed as the centrepiece before all His new creation. From her conception in the heart and councils of God, surely she might be described as more than *'His workmanship'*; rightly she should be described as *'His masterpiece'*.

The bride of Christ is the unique work of God. She holds the central place within the plan and purpose of Almighty God in creation. Everything that was made and everything that was done was in support of, in conformity with, and contributory to the Father's determination that *'His one and only Son'* should be presented with a bride, she who will forever be the wife of the Lamb.

In order for God's masterpiece to be completed according to His perfect plan and purpose, the works required to be performed by those who are His own, were pre-ordained before time began. The word is clear. We have been *'created in Christ Jesus unto good works, which God prepared beforehand that we would walk in them'*. These good works have been appointed to every member of the body of Christ during their earthly life so that all believers may contribute their part to the completion unto perfection of *'the bride, the wife of the Lamb'*. Jesus told Peter, *"I will build my church"*, yet He is working through His own to accomplish this great task.

The Lord appeared to Abram when he was ninety nine years old, telling him, *"No longer shall your name be called Abram, But your name shall be Abraham; For I have made you the father of a multitude of nations. "I will make you exceedingly fruitful, and I will make nations of you, and kings will come forth from you'.* Genesis 17:5-6. God gave Abraham the sign of circumcision in his flesh, He changed his wife Sarai's name to Sarah, meaning 'princess', and He promised that she would bear him a son.

When Isaac was still a lad, God spoke to Abraham. *'He said, "Take now your son, your only son, whom you love, Isaac, and go to the land of Moriah, and offer him there as a burnt offering on one of the mountains of which I will tell you."* Genesis 22:2. Abraham obeyed God and while he had the knife in his hand, ready to slay his son, the Lord interposed and showed him a ram caught by its horns in a thicket. Because of this act of obedience, the Lord gave Abraham many wondrous promises; among them was one that gives a living hope to we who are Gentiles. *'In your seed all the nations of the earth shall be blessed, because you have obeyed My voice."* Genesis 22:18 *'All the nations'* refers to the Gentiles who, according to the grace of Almighty God, were to be included in the redemptive death of Jesus. *'But now in Christ Jesus you who were once far off have become near in the blood of Christ'.* Ephesians 2:13.

'For He Himself is our peace....' How these words need to be impressed into our memory for, as He Himself is our peace, so even the tiniest evidence of disunity must be dealt with promptly, for it is a shame to the cross of Jesus Christ. God's determined and unchangeable goal is *'one new man'*, Christ and His one body; Christ and the church; Christ and His bride, His wife. The blessing of God cannot fall upon a divided church.

'He who has made both one and has broken down the middle wall of partition, the enmity, Abolishing in His flesh the law of the commandments in ordinances, that He might create the two in Himself into one new man, so making peace, And might reconcile both in one Body to God through the cross, having slain the enmity by it'. Ephesians 2:14-16. This is a most sober word, for it makes transparently clear that *'through the cross'* what had divided the Jews and the Gentiles has been forever done away with. The blessings the Jewish people had enjoyed were now to be the portion of Gentile believers also. God's great purpose that *'He might create the two in Himself into one new man, so making peace, And might reconcile both in one Body to God through the cross, having slain the enmity by it'* has been assured. It is now an eternal fact. If we

walk in disunity, we shall flagrantly be denying that *'He Himself is our peace'* and we will thereby place ourselves under grave condemnation.

In Romans 11:17-18 Paul alludes to the fact that, in creating *'the two in Himself into one new man'*, the believing Gentiles, as members of a wild olive tree, have been grafted into the Jewish cultivated olive tree. He puts it this way, *'But if some of the branches were broken off, and you, being a wild olive, were grafted in among them and became partaker with them of the rich root of the olive tree, do not be arrogant toward the branches; but if you are arrogant, remember that it is not you who supports the root, but the root supports you'*. Revelation 22:16 reveals who is the root of the olive tree, *'Jesus....the root and the offspring of David'*. The root, Jesus, began His support of the wild olive branches in the home of Cornelius when the Gentiles were grafted into the cultivated olive tree.

We should keep in mind that Jesus our Saviour was incarnated through the Virgin Mary into the nation of Israel. *'He was in the world, and the world was made through Him, and the world did not know Him. He came to His own, and those who were His own did not receive Him. But as many as received Him* [both Jews and Gentiles] *to them He gave the right to become children of God, even to those who believe in His name, who were born, not of blood nor of the will of the flesh nor of the will of man, but of God'*. John 1:10-13.

'And coming, He announced peace as the gospel to you who were far off, and peace to those who were near, For through Him we both have access in one Spirit unto the Father'. Ephesians 2:17-18. If Jesus, who announced peace as the gospel to the far off ones, the Gentiles, and to the near ones, the Jews, and it is through Him that both Jewish and Gentile believers *'have access in one Spirit unto the Father'*, must we not lay aside all evidence of disunity if we are to be granted such access?

Through the apostle John, God gave *'the revelation of Jesus Christ'* which constitutes the last book in the Bible. In this Book of Revelation chapters 2 and 3, there are messages given by the Lord to seven churches, represented in this vision by seven lampstands. John the apostle was in the Spirit on the Lord's day and heard a loud voice saying, *"Write in a book what you see, and send it to the seven churches: to Ephesus and to Smyrna and to Pergamum and to Thyatira and to Sardis and to Philadelphia and to Laodicea." Then I turned to see the voice that was speaking with me. And having turned I saw seven golden lampstands; and in the middle of the lampstands I saw one like a son of man....'* Revelation 1:11-13. The state and characteristics of these seven churches no doubt described those churches then, yet they carry messages of great importance to believers in Jesus today.

Five of the seven churches are admonished by the Lord for shortcomings from which they must repent. Two receive no reprimands. One of these two is the suffering church in Smyrna. The other is the church of brotherly love in Philadelphia. In the Scriptures, names are significant. Philadelphia means 'brotherly love' or 'love for the brothers'. This is the characteristic of this church of which the Lord Jesus approves. All who are brothers are received and welcomed to be a part of this believing community.

We should first explain that when Jesus told His disciples *'do not be called Rabbi; for One is your Teacher, and you are all brothers'*, Matthew 23:8, He was speaking to a large crowd, no doubt composed of many women as well as men. We know, therefore that Jesus statement *'you are all brothers'* was to be applied equally to women. When we meet in the presence of our great Teacher we, male and female, do so as brothers, none greater and none lesser. Even if the Lord should make us great gifts to His church it does not place us ahead of others with lesser gifts.

'He who is holy, who is true, who has the key of David, who opens and no one will shut, and who shuts and no one opens, says this: 'I know your deeds. Behold, I have put before you an open door which no one can shut, because you have a little power, and have kept My word, and have not denied My name'. Revelation 3:7-8. He who has the key of David is the Lord Jesus. He puts before these ones who love the brothers an open door which no one can shut. They know their power is limited; they keep and obey His every word and

have not denied His name; that name is one. *'Has Christ been divided'?* asks Paul in 1 Corinthians 1:13.

'Because you have kept the word of My perseverance, I also will keep you from the hour of testing, that hour which is about to come upon the whole world, to test those who dwell on the earth'. Revelation 3:10. The reward for these ones of Philadelphia who have persevered is a very great one. *'I also will keep you from the hour of testing, that hour which is about to come upon the whole world, to test those who dwell on the earth'.* Those of Philadelphia will be caught up to be with God before the great tribulation, the period of three and a half years before the return in glory of the Lord Jesus Christ.

'I am coming quickly; hold fast what you have, so that no one will take your crown'. In these last days, as the darkness deepens across our world before the great dawn of His endless day, Almighty God is working through companies of His own devoted ones who will walk in the way of Philadelphia. To these He has already given the crown which they must be steadfast to keep, lest they lose it.

The way of the Lord is the way taken by those of Philadelphia. Not only do they love one another but they are *'diligent to preserve the unity of the Spirit in the bond of peace'*. This expression of love and unity is the testimony that the Lord Jesus greatly desires to be exhibited on the earth today by all His own.

CHAPTER 35
HIS WIFE HAS MADE HERSELF READY

Scripture references: Revelation 19:7-9 NKJV, John 1:12-13, Romans 8:16-17, John 14:1-3, Matthew 11:28-30, Matthew 24:44, Philippians 3:7-16, Matthew 25:1-13, 2 Corinthians 3:18.

In the Book of Revelation there are eight references to *'he who overcomes'* or *'to him who overcomes'*. To be one who overcomes will prove to have been a choice without regret. Overcomers are a special category of believer who have committed themselves to the Lord that they may measure up to God's standard. Great rewards for those who overcome are promised. For instance, in Revelation 2:7, we read that the overcomers who kept their first love for Jesus were granted *'the right to eat of the tree of life, which is in the Paradise of God'*.

The Lord desires 'companies' of people who will overcome, as His testimony on the earth today. Those who walk in the way of the church in Philadelphia represent such a company, in their complete openness to receive all in whom is the Spirit of God and to gather simply as brothers unto Jesus.

This condition of unity in accordance with the Lord's desire is expressed in the exhortation of the apostle Paul in Romans 15:5-7. *'Now may the God who gives perseverance and encouragement grant you to be of the same mind with one another according to Christ Jesus, so that with one accord you may with one voice glorify the God and Father of our Lord Jesus Christ. Therefore, accept one another, just as Christ also accepted us to the glory of God'.*

In God's time, all the past and present overcoming ones who have made themselves ready will receive a grand invitation to the marriage supper of the Lamb. *"Let us be glad and rejoice and give Him glory, for the marriage of the Lamb has come, and His wife has made herself ready."* Revelation 19:7, NKJV.

'And to her it was granted to be arrayed in fine linen, clean and bright, for the fine linen is the righteous acts of the saints'. Revelation 19:8, NKJV. During their time on earth these overcomers had been performing the righteous acts 'which God

prepared beforehand that they should walk in them'. These acts of righteousness have created the bridal gown, stitch by stitch, of *'fine linen, bright and clean'*, in which the wife of the Lamb will be arrayed.

'Then he said to me, "Write: 'Blessed are those who are called to the marriage supper of the Lamb!'" And he said to me, "These are the true sayings of God." Revelation 19:9, NKJV. It will be the aim and purpose of this chapter to identify steps in a Jewish marriage in Biblical times and use these, as the Lord shall lead, to assist in understanding the process that God has laid out for those who will be blessed with an invitation *'to the marriage supper of the Lamb'*.

1. The father of a would-be-bridegroom asked the father of the desired bride for her hand in marriage to his son. He might approach the father directly or send a matchmaker. If the father of the potential bride approved of the suit, he would put this offer to his daughter. She might say 'yes' or 'no'. If she agreed the two would be betrothed.

Adam is described in Luke 3:38 as *'the son of God'*. In the act of creation, Adam's father was God. However, because of the sin of Adam and his wife Eve, mankind became orphans, separated from the Father of all. But Jesus said, *"I will not leave you as orphans; I will come to you."* John 14:18. In the Comforter, the Holy Spirit, Jesus has restored our relationship with our Father. God is the Father of His Son and of all those redeemed ones, who will one day be brought together as His bride, His wife. It is our choice to receive Him. For *'as many as received Him, to them He gave the right to become children of God, even to those who believe in His name, who were born, not of blood nor of the will of the flesh nor of the will of man, but of God'*. John 1:12-13. When we receive Jesus through faith in His atoning death our relationship to God the Father is that we are His children.

'The Spirit Himself testifies with our spirit that we are children of God, and if children, heirs also, heirs of God and fellow heirs with Christ, if indeed we suffer with Him so that we may also be glorified with Him'. Romans 8:16-17. We are not only children of God, we are heirs of God and joint heirs with Christ *'if indeed we suffer with*

Him so that we may also be glorified with Him'. Surely to be glorified with Him is to be His bride glorified with her glorified Bridegroom.

The Father of Jesus is also the Father of all those who, through faith, participate in His bride. All who comprise His bride have a choice as to when or if they will be betrothed to Jesus. Those that make this their irrevocable decision are the ones who take His yoke upon them that they may learn from Him who is *'gentle and humble in heart'*. Matthew 11:28-30.

Many, however, through ignorance or neglect do not fulfil their part in the marriage contract during their lifetime. The penalty for their lack of commitment will be to be shut out from the marriage supper of the Lamb.

2. The bridegroom paid the price required in the betrothal contract. During one year both bridegroom and bride lived apart to prepare for their marriage. The bridegroom prepared a place for her that they might consummate their marriage and share their life together. The bride prepared her wedding garment and consecrated herself to her marriage so that she might be worthy of her bridegroom's love and provision for her.

The Lord Jesus paid the ultimate price for His bride. He gave His life to redeem a betraying harlot. He shed His blood to buy back her virginity. His free gift to her was eternal life. Jesus also assured His bride, *"I go to prepare a place for you. "If I go and prepare a place for you, I will come again and receive you to Myself, that where I am, there you may be also"*. John 14:2-3.

Following His ascension He has fully done His part by preparing a place for us at His side forever. Now our Bridegroom awaits a wife who has made herself ready. As soon as she was betrothed to Jesus, not one second of her time has belonged to her. All she is, all she has and all her time are His forever. That is her side of the marriage contract.

When we permit ourselves to be yoked to Jesus we shall start fulfilling our part in the marriage contract, for only in Him can we be made ready. The willingness is ours. The work is His.

'But whatever things were gain to me, those things I have counted as loss for the sake of Christ'. Philippians 3:7. The past that had been all about Paul was now all about Christ. Now it was only what the Bridegroom wanted that mattered to Paul. So it must be with all those who truly love Jesus.

'....that I may know Him and the power of His resurrection and the fellowship of His sufferings, being conformed to His death; in order that I may attain to the resurrection from the dead'. Philippians 3:10-11. It is the role of the Holy Spirit of God to reveal Jesus into us, that we may know Him and be transformed into His likeness. In the Holy Spirit is the resurrection power of Jesus that we, in Him, may overcome all the trials that will come our way, that we may be conformed to His death. His death, as referred to here, is our willingness to do our Father's will rather than our own.

Paul's whole focus was that He may attain to *'the out-resurrection from those who are dead'*. Wuest. Surely this *'out-resurrection from those who are dead'* will be composed of all those who have overcome and who have thereby made themselves ready, those who will be invited to that great marriage supper of the Lamb.

3. At a time and on a day arranged by the bridegroom's father (the exact timing being unknown to the bride) a messenger was sent to the bride's home who loudly proclaimed, "Behold the bridegroom comes." After a while, the bridegroom's entourage arrived at the bride's home where the bride would be ready for his coming and a great wedding feast would be held which might continue for up to seven days.

"For this reason you also must be ready; for the Son of Man is coming at an hour when you do not think He will." Matthew 24:44. There are evidently two categories of people that can be identified in what Jesus is saying. There are those who will have 'made themselves ready' and those who will be unprepared. For what reason must we be ready? Because He *'is coming at an hour when you do not think He will'*. Surely our readiness will determine whether we shall participate in the marriage supper of the Lamb. *"Let us rejoice and be glad and give the glory to Him, for the*

marriage of the Lamb has come and His bride has made herself ready." Revelation 19:7.

What of those who are unprepared when the Bridegroom comes? They will be *'made ready'*. The apostle John exclaims, *'And I saw the holy city, new Jerusalem, coming down out of heaven from God, made ready as a bride adorned for her husband'*. Revelation 21:2. Those that have not made themselves ready will be made ready. Apparently a bride must be *'made ready'*. The wife *'has made herself ready'*. Herein lies a vital truth that all who have come to the Lord Jesus in faith must be made aware of.

"Then the kingdom of heaven will be comparable to ten virgins, who took their lamps and went out to meet the bridegroom. "Five of them were foolish, and five were prudent." Matthew 25:1-2. In this parable of the Lord Jesus there are ten virgins who are waiting *'to meet the bridegroom'*. Each one of them has an oil lamp and each one's lamp is lit. Five virgins are described by our Lord as prudent because they *'took oil in flasks along with their lamps'* and five are described as foolish because they *'took no oil with them'*. We might say that the five prudent virgins had made themselves ready to meet the bridegroom and the five foolish ones had not.

All ten *'got drowsy and began to sleep'*. They grew old and died. At midnight (the time of the world's darkest hour – the great tribulation) there was a shout, *"Behold, the bridegroom! Come out to meet him."* All these virgins awoke from sleep. This proved to be a defining moment because when they trimmed their lamps, those of the five prudent virgins were lit and bright, while the lamps of the five foolish virgins were sputtering and going out.

The five foolish virgins said to the prudent, *"Give us some of your oil, for our lamps are going out."* But the prudent answered, *"No, there will not be enough for us and you too; go instead to the dealers and buy some for yourselves."*

The five prudent virgins who had paid the price for their oil during their lifetime were rewarded by going in with the Bridegroom into the wedding feast. The five foolish virgins were shut out from the wedding feast and were obliged to go and pay the price to purchase the precious oil. The Bridegroom disowned them, *"I never knew you."* The Bridegroom only recognizes those who bear His image.

'The spirit of man is the lamp of the Lord, searching all the innermost parts of his being'. Proverbs 20:27. Our lamp is lit when the Holy Spirit enters our spirit and we are born again. The Holy Spirit is given as a pledge or down payment. Ephesians 1:13-14. Thus each one who is born again receives a portion of the oil of the Holy Spirit to which, by constant obedience to the leading of the same Holy Spirit, the fullness of the oil must be acquired.

'But we all, with unveiled face, beholding as in a mirror the glory of the Lord, are being transformed into the same image from glory to glory, just as from the Lord, the Spirit'. 2 Corinthians 3:18. The flask that the prudent virgins had with them that was full of oil is their human soul. As we steadfastly behold the glory of the Lord, the oil of the Holy Spirit will flow into us to do His transforming work. Thus we shall be transformed into the image of Jesus as our gaze is fixed upon Him and as our life is being lived in faith and obedience to the Lord, the Spirit. This is the purpose of our earthly life. This is what Jesus paid the ultimate price for.

Those who have been transformed into His image will be like Him. They will be recognized by Him and ready for Him, their Bridegroom. This is what the word means by, *'His wife has made herself ready'*. Her reward is far beyond description. Her exceeding great reward is to receive the Lamb as her Husband forever.

CHAPTER 36
THE MARRIAGE SUPPER OF THE LAMB

Scripture references: Revelation 17 and 18, Matthew 25:1-30, Ephesians 1:13-14, Revelation 19:7-16, Revelation 20:1-6.

Revelation chapters 17 and 18 are largely devoted to the fall and destruction of Babylon the great, the mother of harlots. She is the false, the foul and the corrupted church system that has been the masquerading pretender. Satan has used her to draw seekers after truth to herself rather than to Jesus and to oppose, defame and destroy those servants of the living God who have proclaimed and lived the truth. *"And in her was found the blood of prophets and of saints and of all who have been slain on the earth."* Revelation 18:24. She is the ultimate whited sepulchre full of dead men's bones. She is a system devised by man which has operated under man's authority. She is best described in the parable of Jesus of the mustard seed which, when planted to be a nourishing herb, became instead a great tree, with countless branches in which the birds roosted and built nests.

Not long before the return of Jesus to rule and reign forever, God has determined that this spiritual Babylon's time has come to an end. In one short hour she will be destroyed. At that time she is described as having *'become a dwelling place of demons and a prison of every unclean spirit, and a prison of every unclean and hateful bird'*. Revelation 18:2.

The response of vast multitudes in heaven to great Babylon's destruction is *"Hallelujah! For the Lord our God, the Almighty, reigns. Let us rejoice and be glad and give the glory to Him, for the marriage of the Lamb has come and His 'wife' has made herself ready."* Revelation 19:6-7,

Now that the pretender has been fully and finally dealt with by God, He is ready to disclose in a private way, the true, the pure and the perfect wife of the Lamb. *'His 'wife' has made herself ready'* and the marriage supper of the Lamb can now begin. The translators have had a difficult time with the Greek word 'gune', for its correct meaning is 'woman, especially wife'. The Lamb's wife is composed of those who are overcomers. She has shared in His sufferings and has become conformed to His death. Like Paul who cried out *'That I may know Him and the power of His resurrection'*, this too has been her heart cry. A bride has still to know her bridegroom, whereas a wife already does.

In Jesus' parable, the ten virgins were awakened at midnight by the cry, *'Behold, the bridegroom! Come out to meet him'*. This was their moment of truth. What their lives had amounted to would determine whether they would prove to be ready to meet the Bridegroom and to go in with Him into the wedding feast, or be shut out. All were virgins, signifying they were washed in the blood of the Lamb and had received grace unto salvation. Those who *'took oil in flasks along with their lamps'* went into the marriage supper, while those who *'took no oil with them'* were shut out from the supper and were compelled to pay the price for the oil they had failed to pay during their earthly life.

In Ephesians 1:13-14 we read, *'In Him, you also, after listening to the message of truth, the gospel of your salvation - having also believed, you were sealed in Him with the Holy Spirit of promise, who is given as a pledge of our inheritance, with a view to the redemption of God's own possession, to the praise of His glory'*. After receiving the message of truth and believing the gospel we *'were sealed in Him with the Holy Spirit of promise, who is given as a pledge of our inheritance'*. This word 'pledge' can alternatively be translated as down-payment or deposit. When we believed, the lamp of our human spirit was lit and the oil of the Holy Spirit was poured into our lamp. God's intention is that the down-payment grows to be a full payment. Having a flask full of oil is the evidence of having made the full payment. It is God's intention that our soul, composed of our mind, emotions and will be filled with the Holy Spirit, that we be transformed into the likeness of Jesus. God's determination is to redeem His *'own possession, to the praise of His glory'*.

The outcome for the foolish virgins is far more serious than it may at first appear. It is a topic which is neglected or completely ignored in most church communities today. Yet it is also one that the writer is in fear and trembling to bring to light, for the choice to be made is the same for him and for those who will read these words as it was for those virgins.

Although the ten virgins are pictured as individuals, all those admitted to the marriage supper of the Lamb will collectively be *'His wife who has made herself ready'*. Those who compose her will display their collective readiness for the marriage in the wedding garment she will be given to be dressed in. She will be clothed in *'fine linen, bright and clean; for the fine linen is the righteous acts of the saints'*. How precious to her Bridegroom's gaze must be the evidence of what His wife has undergone for love of Him. She has done her part to fill up what was lacking of His sufferings.

Any information concerning events in the marriage supper has been hidden from us. We do not know how long this great feast with the Bridegroom will last. The honour of being invited is far more significant than the details of this celebration, for it provides access to reigning with Him for a thousand years.

Following the marriage supper, the next disclosure is of *'a white horse, and He who sat on it is called Faithful and True, and in righteousness He judges and wages war. His eyes are a flame of fire, and on His head are many diadems; and He has a name written on Him which no one knows except Himself. He is clothed with a robe dipped in blood, and His name is called The Word of God. And the armies which are in heaven, clothed in fine linen, white and clean, were following Him on white horses'.* Revelation 19:11-14. The One sat on the white horse describes without doubt the Lord Jesus, the Word of God. Those following Him on white horses, *'clothed in fine linen, white and clean'*, must surely be the ones who comprise *'the wife of the Lamb'*, those whose wedding garment of righteous acts has been exchanged for individual garments of the same material, to wage war with the beast and the kings of the earth.

'And I saw the souls of those who had been beheaded because of their testimony of Jesus and because of the word of God, and those who had not worshiped the beast or his image, and had not received the mark on their forehead and on their hand; and they came to life and reigned with Christ for a thousand years. The rest of the dead

did not come to life until the thousand years were completed. This is the first resurrection. Blessed and holy is the one who has a part in the first resurrection; over these the second death has no power, but they will be priests of God and of Christ and will reign with Him for a thousand years'. Revelation 20:4-6. This company of believers has been martyred for their refusal to obey the orders of the antichrist, the beast to whom Satan gave his authority. They were beheaded *'because of their testimony of Jesus and because of the word of God'*. These two aspects of their faith were also shared by the overcomers who were caught away just before the middle of the tribulation period. The members comprising the male child overcame Satan by *'the word of their testimony'*. The Philadelphians *'have kept My word and have not denied My name'*. This final company of overcoming saints, joined forever with those already taken up, *'came to life and reigned with Christ for a thousand years'*.

In Matthew 25:14-30 is recorded Jesus' parable of three slaves to whom He gave talents. To one he gave five talents, to another two talents and to another one talent, *'each according to his own ability; and he went on his journey'*. Matthew 25:15. The ones to whom the master of the slaves gave five and two talents put these to good use and doubled their master's gift. They proved to be overcoming saints. The slave who received one talent *'dug a hole in the ground and hid his master's money'*. On his master's return he gave back the talent without putting it to use or even making a return from depositing it in a bank. This showed serious negligence.

As with the foolish virgins, this servant had misspent the time granted to him and he was not prepared appropriately for his master's return. His fate, as with the foolish virgins, will be to pay the price that had been required of him during his time on earth. What will be his fate? It is certainly not to go to the place prepared for the devil and his angels. That is a place of unquenchable fire. The price that those wasting their Master's gift will be required to pay will be that they are cast into *'the outer darkness; in that place there will be weeping and gnashing of teeth'*.* Weeping because they have appeared with empty hands before the judgment seat of

Christ in all His glory and have seen Him face to face; gnashing their teeth in the deepest remorse for the misuse of the time and opportunity He gave them to serve and please Him during their life on earth.

The overcomers, as the wife of the Lamb who had made herself ready, will rule with Him for a thousand years. For what length of time then, will those be in outer darkness who failed to make themselves ready; that place where there is weeping and gnashing of teeth? Until they have been *'made ready'!*

May we who read and comprehend the implications of the previous paragraph take this opportunity right now, for love of Him, to dedicate or rededicate ourselves to follow the Lamb unwaveringly wherever He shall lead.

---

*See 'Addendum 'A' - Outer Darkness' at the back of the book.

CHAPTER 37
THE DWELLING PLACE OF GOD

Scripture references: Isaiah 24:1-23, Revelation 11:15-19, Revelation 20:1-15, Daniel 2:1-35, Hebrews 11:8-10, John 14:1-3, 1 Peter 2:4-5.

In the beginning God created a man in His image. *'Then the Lord God took the man and put him into the garden of Eden to cultivate it and keep it'.* Genesis 2:15. Adam was to be a steward and caretaker of Eden. Yet, following the forming of Eve, Adam joined her in disobedience to the Lord's strict command and they were driven out of the garden.

It was to Noah and his family, who were God's new beginning, that God repeated the injunction given to Adam, *'Be fruitful and multiply, and fill the earth'.* Mankind has since filled the earth, yet the state to which we have brought it is a shame and an insult to its Creator. Isaiah 24 describes a state of desecration and destruction of this earth, a condition which we are surely approaching fast.

After the angel sounded the seventh trumpet announcing Jesus return, *'there were loud voices in heaven, saying, "The kingdom of the world has become the kingdom of our Lord and of His Christ; and He will reign forever and ever."* Next we read of the twenty four elders who fall on their faces before the throne of God, *'saying, "We give You thanks, O Lord God, the Almighty, who are and who were, because You have taken Your great power and have begun to reign....and Your wrath came, and the time came for the dead to be judged, the time to reward Your bond-servants the prophets and the saints and those who fear Your name, the small and the great, and to destroy those who destroy the earth."* Revelation 11:15-18. Surely the Lord will wreak His anger upon the desecrators of this wonderful world He created for us. He will destroy them.

'Then I saw an angel coming down from heaven, holding the key of the abyss and a great chain in his hand. And he laid hold of the dragon, the serpent of old, who is the devil and Satan, and bound him for a thousand years'. Revelation 20:1-2. Before the commencement of the thousand year reign of Jesus with His overcoming saints, Satan will be laid hold of and bound. He will

have no part or influence on the dwellers on the earth during this long period of time.

Daniel chapter 2 deals in its entirety with the dream of Nebuchadnezzar. The great image, which he envisioned, describes the Gentile powers which would rule over and oppress the nation of Israel. The final annihilation of these world powers is described as follows: *"You continued looking until a stone was cut out without hands, and it struck the statue on its feet of iron and clay and crushed them. "Then the iron, the clay, the bronze, the silver and the gold were crushed all at the same time and became like chaff from the summer threshing floors; and the wind carried them away so that not a trace of them was found. But the stone that struck the statue became a great mountain and filled the whole earth."* Daniel 2:34-35.

None other than the Lord Jesus can be described as the stone cut out without hands, but who or what is the *'great mountain that filled the whole earth'*? The kingdom of our God and the authority of His Christ is the portion also of those who *'will reign with Him for a thousand years'*, His overcomers. Thus the mountain must be Christ and His enlargement, those members of His body who have been perfected. What is accomplished on the earth during the thousand years is largely hidden from us. Might it be that the damage done by thoughtless generations will be eradicated and brought back to what the Lord desires it to be? There will be countless inhabitants remaining to carry out such a work, the Lord's overcomers being their overseers.

'When the thousand years are completed, Satan will be released from his prison, and will come out to deceive the nations which are in the four corners of the earth, Gog and Magog, to gather them together for the war; the number of them is like the sand of the seashore. And they came up on the broad plain of the earth and surrounded the camp of the saints and the beloved city, and fire came down from heaven and devoured them. And the devil who deceived them was thrown into the lake of fire and brimstone, where the beast and the false prophet are also; and they will be tormented day and night forever and ever'. Revelation 20:7-10. Just as the

Lord will deal with religious Babylon before He discloses His bride, so He will close the final chapter on Satan before unveiling the holy city, new Jerusalem, before the whole new creation.

This city that will be the dwelling place of God forever was envisioned by Abraham long ago. *'By faith Abraham, when he was called, obeyed by going out to a place which he was to receive for an inheritance; and he went out, not knowing where he was going. By faith he lived as an alien in the land of promise, as in a foreign land, dwelling in tents with Isaac and Jacob, fellow heirs of the same promise; for he was looking for the city which has foundations, whose architect and builder is God'.* Hebrews 11:8-10. Designed by God, that which will be His dwelling place forever has also been built by God.

Jesus encouraged His followers, *"Do not let your heart be troubled; believe in God, believe also in Me. "In My Father's house are many dwelling places; if it were not so, I would have told you; for I go to prepare a place for you. "If I go and prepare a place for you, I will come again and receive you to Myself, that where I am, there you may be also."* John 14:1-3. In His Father's house are many dwelling places. These dwelling places which comprise together His Father's house are precious stones, foundation stones, with twelve gates that are pearls. The precious stones are believers. The foundation stones with names written on them are the twelve apostles of the Lamb. The gates of pearls are named for the twelve sons of Israel. Through Christ, the Lion of Judah, they are the entrances into the holy city.

'And coming to Him as to a living stone which has been rejected by men, but is choice and precious in the sight of God, you also, as living stones, are being built up as a spiritual house for a holy priesthood, to offer up spiritual sacrifices acceptable to God through Jesus Christ'. 1 Peter 2:4-5. The living stones for the building are also precious stones of many varieties. All these living stones from all the ages back to the beginning are being built together into a perfect bride. Following their transformation, the ones who have been perfected in the outer darkness will join the overcomers as transmitters of His glorious light. They will have

been *'made ready as a bride'*. Hallelujah! The Lord Almighty reigns.

Since that defining morning at Pentecost when the church became visible as the light of the world, she has had her dwelling place *'in God the Father and our Lord Jesus Christ'*. At the end of time the Father and our Lord Jesus Christ will make their eternal dwelling place and habitation in the church, His bride who is His wife. She will be the fullness of all His transformed ones built together to be the eternal dwelling place of God; the holy city new Jerusalem, whose glory is displayed forever before the vastness of the new creation. The new earth has no need of the sun or the moon to light her for the light of God through the Holy City illumines all. The farthest galaxies are lighted by her lamp, the Lamb who shines through her. What a glorious vision of what shall surely be!

CHAPTER 38
THE SPIRIT AND THE BRIDE SAY COME

Scripture references: Genesis 1:1-2, John 3:1-8, 1 Corinthians 12:12-14, John 7:37-39, Ephesians 2:10-22, Revelation 21:1-5, Revelation 22:17-20.

This, the final chapter of Part 2, focuses on the blessed person and work of the Holy Spirit in bringing countless fallen human beings to a glory and perfection that cannot be imagined. Salvation by grace through faith is not of ourselves, it is truly the gift of God. However, the bringing together of all the faithful of all the ages to be the holy city new Jerusalem, the dwelling place of God as His masterpiece, is beyond human comprehension. This has ever been the work and purpose of God the Holy Spirit until all is completed.

The first mention of the blessed third person of the Trinity, the Holy Spirit, is found in Genesis 1:2, *'The Spirit of God was hovering over the face of the waters'*. The Spirit awaited the command of the Word, *"Let there be light."* At the beginning the Word spoke in accordance with the will of the Father and the Holy Spirit acted, *'and there was light'*. On the third day living things were created beginning with vegetation. From the very beginning of creation, the Holy Spirit has brought light and life.

In the instant of new birth the Holy Spirit enlightens our human spirit and brings to us life forevermore. *'That which is born of the Spirit is spirit'*. John 3:6. The Holy Spirit and our spirit are joined in perfect union forever. *'....the one who joins himself to the Lord is one spirit with Him'*. 1 Corinthians 6:17.

'For by one Spirit we were all baptized into one body, whether Jews or Greeks, whether slaves or free, and we were all made to drink of one Spirit'. 1 Corinthians 12:13. At that same instant of our new birth, *'by one Spirit we were baptized into one body'*. Not only does each one who is born again receive consciousness of being rightly related to God, but also becomes aware of being mutually connected to other members of His body.

'Now on the last day, the great day of the feast, Jesus stood and cried out, saying, "If anyone is thirsty, let him come to Me and

drink. "He who believes in Me, as the Scripture said, 'From his innermost being will flow rivers of living water.'" But this He spoke of the Spirit, whom those who believed in Him were to receive; for the Spirit was not yet given, because Jesus was not yet glorified'. John 7:37-39. Until Jesus was glorified, the Holy Spirit could not be given that He might come into those who would repent and be saved through their faith. The Holy Spirit became the *'life-giving Spirit'* through the death, resurrection and ascension of Jesus, that Jesus in the Spirit might forever inhabit His own as His eternal dwelling place. John 14:16-18.

'For we are His masterpiece, created in Christ Jesus for good works, which God prepared beforehand in order that we would walk in them'. Ephesians 2:10, Recovery Version. The Holy Spirit's work is being performed in each surrendered soul in order to build together God's masterpiece, *'the bride, the wife of the Lamb'*. Since Pentecost the Spirit of truth has been leading all those who will hear and obey into all the truth that they may perform the *'good works which God prepared beforehand in order that we would walk in them'*.

The city that Abraham sought so many centuries before, the apostle John was privileged to behold in a vision. John writes, *'Then I saw a new heaven and a new earth; for the first heaven and the first earth passed away, and there is no longer any sea. And I saw the holy city, new Jerusalem, coming down out of heaven from God, made ready as a bride adorned for her husband. And I heard a loud voice from the throne, saying, "Behold, the tabernacle of God is among men, and He will dwell among them, and they shall be His people, and God Himself will be among them, and He will wipe away every tear from their eyes; and there will no longer be any death; there will no longer be any mourning, or crying, or pain; the first things have passed away." And He who sits on the throne said, "Behold, I am making all things new." And He said, "Write, for these words are faithful and true."* Revelation 21:1-5.

The Holy Spirit is executing the will of God until everything attains to His ultimate perfection and beauty. *'The Spirit and the bride say, "Come." And let the one who hears say, "Come." And let the one who is thirsty come; let the one who wishes take the water of life without cost'*. Revelation 22:17. It is evident that the Spirit and the bride are in perfect unity because they speak with one voice. Thus we know that the work of the Holy Spirit has been fully completed.

May he who writes and those who read respond to this invitation to *"Come."* '*He who testifies to these things says, "Yes, I am coming quickly."* Our grateful hearts respond, *"Amen. Come, Lord Jesus."* Revelation 22:20.

PART THREE
THE UPWARD CALL OF GOD

Introduction to Part Three

Hymn: 'Come Down O Love Divine'

Chapter 39 – He Who Loves Me 193
Chapter 40 – That I May Know Him 197
Chapter 41 – To Him Who Overcomes 203
Chapter 42 – The Upward Call of God 208
Chapter 43 – The Church in Philadelphia 212
Chapter 44 – The Male Child 217
Chapter 45 – First Fruits to God and the Lamb 222
Chapter 46 – There was War in Heaven 226
Chapter 47 – Night is Coming 230
Chapter 48 – Those Who are with Him 236
Chapter 49 – The Wife of the Lamb 241
Chapter 50 – Behold a White Horse 248
Chapter 51 – Those Who have been Beheaded 253
Chapter 52 – The Judgment Seat of Christ 258
Chapter 53 – The Stone that Struck the Statue 263
Chapter 54 – The Thousand Years 268
Chapter 55 – Satan Released from his Prison 274
Chapter 56 – The Book of Life 277
Chapter 57 – The City that has Foundations 283
Addendum 'A' – Outer Darkness 289
Addendum 'B' – Ultimate Unity 291
Communication with the Author 292

Introduction to Part Three

History provides us with a long record of the rise and fall of civilizations, empires, dynasties and of great ones who strode across the world stage and then largely faded from memory. In our world today we are frequently made aware of the rise to fame and decline of superstars and world figures. It seems that all things earthly have their day of prominence and then disappear into the mists of time.

Were we to evaluate the state of the church on earth today we might be forced to admit that her glory days are lost in the distant past. She often appears irrelevant, outdated and impotent. However, throughout her history she has faced extinction from within and without only to be renewed to life and great influence for significant periods of time.

Why is it false to consider the ebbs and flows of Christendom as being typical of the rise and fall of other endeavours? It is because there has always been a remnant among the people of God who have embodied and shone forth His true testimony to all around them. Hebrews 11 provides a sample of faithful men and women of old whose stories continue to inspire us, to which countless lives and deeds must be added from the New Testament era right down to the present day.

The tremendous sense of purpose and momentum of the early believers in Jesus is there for all to see in the book of Acts and in the letters of the apostle Paul and others. But in the book of Revelation given by God much later to the apostle John the term 'overcomer' is introduced. Overcomers are individuals who portray and represent the clear testimony of Jesus in the midst of prevailing weakness, failure and mixture.

It has surely been the loss of the vision of the risen, exalted and glorified Lord Jesus, that characterised Pentecost that has repeatedly led to spiritual decline and impotence.

Whatever the human mind may imagine; whatever the human emotions may feel; whatever conclusion the human will determines to be so; notwithstanding, Jesus is Lord of a life or of an assembly only in which He is the sole and absolute focus. His sovereignty as builder of His church must be recognized and accorded unfettered operation as He wills.

Part Three is offered to those whose heart's desire is that they *'may know Him'*, that is Jesus, and whose aim is to live a life in which His will takes precedence over our will.

It is never too late to leave what is clearly missing the mark in order to walk in the truth which is alone to be found in Jesus. The rejection of the counterfeit will make way for the ushering in of the real. If our decision of heart is to follow the Lord fully, the Holy Spirit will lead us a step at a time along the sure pathway to fulfil God's will and purpose for us so that we may please Him in our every thought, word and deed.

For the writer, the journey of compiling this book of three parts has proved to be an ever deepening experience of learning at the feet of He who is *'the author and perfecter of faith'*. May he who writes and all who will read be encouraged to *'press on toward the goal for the prize of the upward call of God in Christ Jesus'*.

Thomas H. Walker
August 2017

COME DOWN O LOVE DIVINE

Come down, O Love divine,
Seek thou this soul of mine,
And visit it with Thine own ardor glowing;
O Comforter, draw near,
Within my heart appear,
And kindle it, Thy holy flame bestowing.

O let it freely burn,
Till earthly passions turn
To dust and ashes in its heat consuming;
And let Thy glorious light
Shine ever on my sight,
And clothe me round, the while my path illuming.

Let holy charity
Mine outward vesture be,
And lowliness become mine inner clothing;
True lowliness of heart,
Which takes the humbler part,
And o'er its own shortcomings weeps with loathing.

And so the yearning strong,
With which the soul will long,
Shall far outpass the power of human telling;
For none can guess its grace,
Till he become the place
Wherein the Holy Spirit makes His dwelling.

Words: Bianco da Siena, died 1434
Translated: Richard Frederick Littledale, Jr., 1867

CHAPTER 39
HE WHO LOVES ME

Scripture references: John 13:37-38, John 21:15-19, Deuteronomy 6:4-5, Romans 5:1-5, 1 John 3:14-16, John 14:15-21.

The Bible does not shrink from describing the failures of even its most revered characters. Abraham, through fear, deceived Pharaoh in regard to his beautiful wife, stating that she was his sister. Jacob, with the help of his mother Rebecca, deceived his father Isaac by feigning to be his elder brother Esau. David looked from his rooftop and lusted for Bathsheba, committed adultery with her and had her husband murdered.

Abraham was later given the appellation of *'the friend of God'*. After God met Jacob at Bethel and wrestled with him He renamed him Israel, *'prince with God'*. David is spoken of in Acts 13 in God's estimation as *'a man after My heart, who will do all My will'*. God's mercy on those who love Him knows no limits.

It is not ours to judge the actions and behaviour of others (or indeed our own) from our fallen human perspective. If we judge ourselves, we may give credit for strengths we do not possess while we overlook or seek to justify our weaknesses. On the other hand we may feel that we can never attain to the standards expected of us by God. *"Do not judge according to appearance, but judge with righteous judgment."* John 7:24. Only the Lord sees us as we really are and what He will transform us to be. It is His assessment we need.

This tendency which is in all of us was exhibited by Peter during the Passover meal with Jesus, with all his fellow disciples also present. *'Peter said to Him, "Lord, why can I not follow You right now? I will lay down my life for You." Jesus answered, "Will you lay down your life for Me? Truly, truly, I say to you, a rooster will not crow until you deny Me three times'*. John 13:37-38. We know in stark detail what occurred.

John 21 provides an account of the third appearance of the resurrected Lord Jesus to His disciples; on this occasion He appeared to them in Galilee. He stood on the shore beside the lake.

The disciples had gone fishing and had caught nothing during the night. On the advice of Jesus they went out afresh and cast their net on the other side of the boat and enclosed a great number of fish and the net did not break. After Jesus had served them the fish and the bread that He had prepared over a charcoal fire He questioned Peter.

Jesus did not ask Peter why he had fled in the garden of Gethsemane or why he had denied Him in the judgment hall. He asked Peter three times, "Do you love Me?" To Peter's affirmations of love Jesus responded with admonitions of the role He assigned to him. *"Tend My lambs." "Shepherd My sheep." "Tend My sheep."* In other words, "Peter if you love Me, be a good shepherd of My flock."

On the cross Jesus had already dealt with Peter's sins and failures. Now He desired that Peter would demonstrate his love for Him by serving Him in whatever He assigned Peter to do.

After restoring and commissioning His disciple and apostle, Jesus informed him of *'what kind of death he would glorify God. And when He had spoken this, He said to him, "Follow Me!"* In his life and at his end Peter did indeed glorify God and demonstrated to all that he loved Jesus 'with all His heart and with all his soul and with all his might'. Deuteronomy 6:5.

To keep the great commandment in the weakness of the flesh had proved impossible to all who had been placed under the law that God had given to Moses. So it had proved with Peter also. However, in that upper room on the evening of His resurrection day Jesus had appeared among all those present and *'He breathed into them and said to them, "Receive the Holy Spirit."* John 20:22. Recovery Version.

After the gift of the Holy Spirit had been bestowed at the new birth upon Peter, and indeed upon all present in that upper room, they were enabled truly to love God and their neighbour. The same is true for us also, *'because the love of God has been poured out within our hearts through the Holy Spirit who was given to us'.* Romans 5:5.

This poured out love within us has enabled us to experience the pure selfless love of Jesus that we may express it back to Him. *'We love, because He first loved us'.* 1 John 4:19. The love *'that has been poured out within our hearts'* was bestowed upon each one personally. It has been gifted to us that we may have no doubt that He loves us with a love vastly greater than any love we have hitherto known.

We no longer need to rely on our inadequate fleshly love but on the very love of God through His Holy Spirit, with which we love Him and love all others who love Him. *'We know that we have passed out of death into life, because we love the brethren. He who does not love abides in death'.* 1 John 3:14.

Around three thousand years ago the prophet Samuel delivered a message to King Saul from God *'to obey is better than sacrifice, and to heed is better than the fat of rams'*. Saul had grievously disobeyed God at that time, but the warning given to him is an admonition that all who belong to Jesus must heed. Surrendered obedience is the pathway to God and the means of His opening to us the greatest reward possible during our life on this earth; that of knowing Him.

Paul said, *'Therefore we also have as our ambition, whether at home or absent, to be pleasing to Him'.* 2 Corinthians 5:9. To be pleasing to the Lord Jesus we must know His will for us and we must do it.

"He who has My commandments and keeps them is the one who loves Me; and he who loves Me will be loved by My Father, and I will love him and will disclose Myself to him." John 14:21. To have the Lord's commandments and to keep them is surely to know and to do the will of God; to live moment by moment in His presence and to deny our will in preference to His on a consistent basis. This is a progressive experience, because obedience in the little things will grow into obedience in the greater things, so that at last it may become obedience to the Lord in all things.

Surely the motivation to please God in all things is that we increasingly come to know Him. The more we know Him, the more we shall love Him. The more we love Him the more readily we shall obey Him and seek to do His perfect will. The more we are conformed to His will the more we shall be transformed into His image.

To discover our true identity in Jesus is His goal for our life. He is seeking to unveil the person He created us to be for His own pleasure and for the encouragement of our fellow pilgrims as we surrender to His process of transformation. As we travel with Him along the pathway laid out for us we shall have 'a holy flame of love' for Him lit within our heart that will consume and purge away the dross, leaving only the pure gold of the divine nature. Thus, in due course the unique and perfect creation He intended us to be will be portrayed as His testimony before all men. All who are given grace to find this way will experience joy beyond description.

The one who does His will is the one who truly loves Jesus. To each one who loves Him the promise is given that the Father and the Son will love him and will make their dwelling place in Him. John 14:23. Furthermore, and most marvellously He, the Lord Jesus, *'will disclose Himself to'* each obedient one whose heart cry is *'that I may know Him'*.

CHAPTER 40
THAT I MAY KNOW HIM

Scripture references: Philippians 3:10-11, Jeremiah 29:11-13, Romans 5:1-5, Ezekiel 40:1-3 and 47:1-12, Matthew 7:13-14, Colossians 3:3, Hebrews 4:9-10.

That on which we focus our greatest attention and upon which we devote the majority of our time will, at the close of life's journey prove to have been the ultimate goal we sought to achieve. In the end, only one goal among countless others that individuals choose to follow will stand out completely clear above all others; *'that I may know Him'*; that I may know Jesus. Those who have made this their all-consuming passion will have done so initially through their ready response to the call of Jesus to discipleship, *"Follow Me."*

We can only arrive at an intimate knowledge and appreciation of others to the extent of their comfort to disclose themselves to us. Their willingness to be transparently open to us will almost certainly depend on the genuineness of our approach and the degree of our openness to them. The Lord Jesus desires that each one who seeks to know Him makes it a search with absolute commitment. To these He promises *'You will seek Me and find Me when you search for Me with all your heart'*. Jeremiah 29:13.

To all of us who have received salvation by grace through faith in Jesus, *'the love of God has been poured out within our hearts through the Holy Spirit who was given to us'*. Romans 5:5. This consuming love of God has a dual purpose; to purify us and to transform us into the perfect likeness of Jesus so that we may exhibit God's totally unselfish love to Him and to others in our words, actions and behaviour.

Each seeking heart will travel along a unique path in coming to know the Lord Jesus. The process will take as long as our surrender of all to Him and our obedience to follow Him fully will permit. It is not so much the length of our journey, but the degree of our desire to know Him that will determine how long it may take to reach this goal.

Ezekiel 47:1-12 contains an account which is descriptive of the stages of progress that lie ahead of all who seek for God and search for Him with all their heart. These verses form the last part of a vision given by God to the prophet Ezekiel which commences back in Ezekiel 40:1-3, where we are introduced to a man with a measuring rod in his hand. Through all the chapters that follow and to chapter 47 and verse 12 this man is revealing to Ezekiel many significant and important facts about the design and operation of a future temple which will ultimately replace the one which King Solomon built. This temple will be constructed in accordance with the exact design given to Ezekiel, following the return of Jesus as King of kings and Lord of lords with all His overcoming saints.

'In the visions of God He brought me into the land of Israel and set me on a very high mountain, and on it to the south there was a structure like a city' Ezekiel 40:2. At the commencement of this vision God Himself brought Ezekiel into the land of Israel and set him *'on a very high mountain'*. God showed Ezekiel this *'structure like a city'* so that he could view it precisely in accordance with His design. Ezekiel was shown everything, as it were, through God's eyes.

So He brought me there; and behold, there was a man whose appearance was like the appearance of bronze, with a line of flax and a measuring rod in his hand; and he was standing in the gateway'. Ezekiel 40:3. God the Father was revealing His Son to Ezekiel in His role as judge of all things. Brass or bronze is a type of Christ's authority assigned to Him by the Father to evaluate and judge mankind and, indeed, all things. When Paul was preaching to a crowd on Mars hill in Athens he told his hearers,. *"And He ordered us to preach to the people, and solemnly to testify that this is the One who has been appointed by God as Judge of the living and the dead."* Acts 10:42.

Now that we have established who the One is *'with a line of flax and a measuring rod in his hand'* may we use this unique vision of Ezekiel 47:1-12 in the form of an analogy to describe the Lord's sure pathway for each believer whose passion of heart is *'that I may know Him'*.

Ezekiel states that the One who measured *'brought me back to the door of the house; and behold, water was flowing from under the threshold of the house toward the east, for the house faced east. And the water was flowing down from under, from the right side of the house, from south of the altar'*. Ezekiel 47:1. This description is full of significance. This man brought Ezekiel back to the door of the house. Surely, Jesus Himself is the door of the house of God for He told us *"I am the door; if anyone enters through Me, he will be saved, and will go in and out and find pasture."* John 10:9.

The threshold is the floor immediately underneath the door from below which this living water springs forth. It is mingled with the shed blood from the altar, whence it flows on the right side along the length of the temple and on eastward from there. How evocative this is of the blood and water that flowed forth from the slain body of the Lord Jesus Christ when His side was pierced by the Roman soldier. How symbolic this is of the shed blood for our redemption and the water of eternal life.

Ezekiel states that the One who measured *'brought me out by way of the north gate and led me around on the outside to the outer gate by way of the gate that faces east. And behold, water was trickling from the south side'*. Ezekiel 47:2. There is something very unusual about the river of Ezekiel's vision. It begins as a trickle and increases in its volume of flow until it flows into the sea where it becomes one with the sea and makes its waters fresh. Surely this river is the river of life that is first spoken of in Genesis 2, with its last mention in eternity future in Revelation 22:1-2.

'When the man went out toward the east with a line in his hand, he measured a thousand cubits, and he led me through the water, water reaching the ankles'. Ezekiel 47:3. To be led into just a trickle of the divine life is a great joy and it will establish an unbreakable link between each new believer and Jesus. Yet it is His will and purpose for each one of us that He lead us ever forward more fully and deeply into this divine flow of life. One thousand cubits is a significant unit of measure in the Scriptures. Now that there is *'water reaching the ankles'* the flow of life available to a believer will have become noticeably greater. We may stop along the way

and cease to proceed further through disobedience, negligence or complacency but there will be no way for us to go back.

The time it may take to be led through one thousand cubits and through each succeeding stage will depend entirely on the extent of our trust in Jesus and our willingness to follow Him. He will always be in the lead, for *'One is your Leader'*. Yet He will never lead us further than the extent of our willingness to obey what He has already revealed to us.

'Again he measured a thousand and led me through the water, water reaching the knees'. This increased depth of the water of the divine life will be the result of our deepening commitment to follow and obey Jesus. It will be evidenced by our growth in grace and in our increasing enjoyment of Him. Those that reach this stage are resolute in their faith, giving glory to God.

'Again he measured a thousand and led me through the water, water reaching the loins'. Progress in our spiritual walk will require no exams or earthly qualifications to prove it. When we are led *'through the water, water reaching the loins'* we shall be feeling the buoyancy of the water to support us. Our reliance on keeping our feet touching the river bed will give way to a desire to be launched forever upward into that precious state of utter dependence on the Lord Jesus. If we will determine to simply abandon ourselves and our all upon Him we shall surely find ourselves among the few that find the narrow gate that leads to the narrow way that leads away to life. Matthew 7:13-14.

'Again he measured a thousand; and it was a river that I could not ford, for the water had risen, enough water to swim in, a river that could not be forded'. Surely this major stage will come as an answer to our heartfelt cry *'that I may know Him and the power of His resurrection and the fellowship of His sufferings, being conformed to His death'*. Philippians 3:10.

At the early stage of our journey when we were led into *'water reaching the ankles'* we found many companions rejoicing in what the Lord had done for them. We and they seemed so care free in the wonder of the Lord's forgiveness and the assurance of eternity with Him. Now, at this much later stage, it may cause us surprise at the inner stillness, peace and lack of striving we experience, yet the comparative scarcity of companion hearts with whom to share our deepest joys and revelations of Jesus.

Notably, it will be His will we desire with all our heart to do; His pleasure we seek to fulfill; His sufferings we find it a privilege to share. In experience we will discover the truth found in Colossians 3:3. *'For you have died and your life is hidden with Christ in God'.* Colossians 3:3.

When we found 'the narrow gate' we will have discovered the Lord Jesus waiting to usher us through it. All we had counted important in our life before; all the gifts we had hitherto received from Him; all we had set so much store upon were no longer things to be grasped or held onto compared to our fixed desire *'that I may know Him'*.

When the writer was around eight years old he recalls staying with his godly grandmother. At one point she handed him a phonograph record to listen to. It contained two hymns sung by a mighty man of God named Gypsy Smith. Both hymns had been composed by him. They have for more than seventy years remained treasured favourites. Two verses of one of these hymns are very relevant to the topic of this chapter.

> Christ, the Transforming Light,
> Touches this heart of mine,
> Piercing the darkest night,
> Making His glory shine.
>
> Chorus:
> Oh, to reflect His grace,
> Causing the world to see
> Love that will glow,
> 'Till others shall know
> Jesus revealed in me.
>
> Life is no longer mine,
> I yield it all to Thee;
> Fill me, that I may shine,
> Until Thy face I see.

From that time was planted in the writer's young and still unregenerate heart an unquenchable desire to know the Jesus of Gypsy Smith. However, the living flame of that desire was to be lit only many decades later. The Lord Jesus is so patient with us and He will only lead us in accordance with the degree of our desire for Him. Yet, once that flame has been lit it will, in His time, accomplish its complete work of purification of the life devoted to Jesus. Then at last our deepest desire will have been met; *'that I may know Him'*.

'Then he said to me, "These waters go out toward the eastern region and go down into the Arabah; then they go toward the sea, being made to flow into the sea, and the waters of the sea become fresh'. Ezekiel 47:8. We note that when the waters finally enter the sea that *'the waters of the sea become fresh'*.

The length of time it may take for a soul to be lost in the ocean of God's love will depend on its degree of willingness to rest in the gracious hands of He who is, who was and who is to come.

As has been previously stated; those who enter in Jesus through the narrow gate and enter upon the narrow way that leads away to life have come to Him; been yoked together with Him; been betrothed to Him and are moment by moment learning of He who is *'meek and lowly of heart'*. They will have entered into the rest promised in Hebrews 4:9-10. *'So there remains a Sabbath rest for the people of God. For the one who has entered His rest has himself also rested from his works, as God did from His'*.

Once a heart has been caught up into Him, to live in Him, to know with the deepest certainty its destiny in Him, its utmost yearning will be to participate fully forever in *'the bride, the wife of the Lamb'*.

CHAPTER 41
TO HIM WHO OVERCOMES

Scripture references: Luke 3:21-22, Luke 4:1-14, James 1:12 NKJV, John 16:32-33, 1 John 5:4-5, Hebrews 2:11-15, Romans 6:6-7, Galatians 2:20.

When Jesus was baptised in the River Jordan by John the Baptist *'the Holy Spirit descended upon Him in bodily form like a dove, and a voice came out of heaven, "You are My beloved Son, in You I am well-pleased." Luke 3:22.* Such an endorsement by His Father leaves no doubt that *'without controversy....God was manifested in the flesh, Justified in the Spirit'.* 1 Timothy 3:16 NKJV.

"For He whom God has sent speaks the words of God; for He gives the Spirit without measure." John 3:34. The words of Jesus recorded in the gospels are unparalleled in all the annals of the human race. How well this was expressed by the officers sent by the Pharisees to seize Jesus, *"Never has a man spoken the way this man speaks."* John 7:46.

'Jesus, full of the Holy Spirit, returned from the Jordan and was led around by the Spirit in the wilderness for forty days, being tempted by the devil'. Luke 4:1-2. The Lord Jesus overcame Satan and all his temptations because He was constantly under the absolute direction and control of the Holy Spirit, as surely it must be for us if we would be overcomers in Him.

In the second of three temptations the devil *'led Him up and showed Him all the kingdoms of the world in a moment of time. And the devil said to Him, "I will give You all this domain and its glory; for it has been handed over to me, and I give it to whomever I wish. "Therefore if You worship before me, it shall all be Yours." Luke 4:5-7.* From this statement of the devil it is apparent that God had given him authority to rule over the earth when he was formerly Lucifer. Following his rebellion against God he became Satan, meaning 'adversary'.

'Blessed is the man who endures temptation; for when he has been approved, he will receive the crown of life which the Lord has promised to those who love Him'. James 1:12 NKJV. As Jesus

overcame temptation and endured every trial, so He intends that, in Him, we who believe should take our stand against all the wiles of the devil and overcome all his temptations. That we be approved by Him and receive the crown of life is surely the mark of an overcomer.

"These things I have spoken to you, so that in Me you may have peace. In the world you have tribulation, but take courage; I have overcome the world." John 16:33. Peace and tribulation might seem to be impossible of co-existence yet the secret is that we rest in Him. It is *'in Me you may have peace'*. When Jesus yielded Himself unconditionally to obey His Father He had already overcome Satan's 'cosmos', the world. The good news is that as the Lord Jesus has overcome the world so we too through faith in Him will also overcome the world, *'For whatever is born of God overcomes the world; and this is the victory that has overcome the world - our faith'*. 1 John 5:4.

Embodied in Jesus when He appeared for a time on earth was another kingdom, *'the kingdom of heaven'*. All who have been born again into this kingdom have become the enlargement of it as members individually of the body of Christ, the church.

Jesus proclaimed to His disciples and to a great multitude, *"Blessed are those who have been persecuted for the sake of righteousness, for theirs is the kingdom of heaven."* Matthew 5:10. Tribulation and persecution may be the pathway down which the Lord chooses to lead His own yet, what a glorious outcome for those who *'overcome the world'* in Him, *"for theirs is the kingdom of heaven."*

'Therefore, since the children share in flesh and blood, He Himself likewise also partook of the same....' Hebrews 2:14. The children mentioned here are the seed of Adam who share with him *'in flesh and blood'*. The incarnate Christ also, as the Seed promised in the Garden of Eden, *'partook of the same that through death He might render powerless him who had the power of death, that is, the devil'*. The death of the Lord Jesus on the cross nullified and brought to naught the works of the devil because, through His sacrifice of Himself, the sin of the world was dealt with, so that freedom from the power and authority of Satan was obtained for all

those *'who do not walk according to the flesh but according to the Spirit'*. Romans 8:4. As they walk *'according to the Spirit'* those who overcome celebrate and exhibit Jesus' complete and eternal victory over sin and death.

The *'power of death'* mentioned is not simply physical death but is more significantly what the Bible describes as the second death, the death of the soul, for *'The soul who sins will die'*. Ezekiel 18:4. *'....it is appointed for men to die once and after this comes judgment'*. Hebrews 9:27. The death of the body is inevitable except for those still alive who receive *'the prize of the upward call of God in Christ Jesus'* or those *'who are alive and remain until the coming of the Lord'*. But for everyone who has received by faith God's great salvation, an incorruptible body will be theirs at His coming as King of kings and Lord of lords.

Then, each one who has believed unto salvation must appear before the judgment seat of Christ. With the exception of one other special group, all others will participate in the judgment of the great white throne at the close of the thousand year reign on this earth of the Lord Jesus with His overcoming saints. Those who are judged and condemned, whose names are not found written in the book of life, and they alone, will suffer the second death. *'Then death and Hades were thrown into the lake of fire. This is the second death, the lake of fire'*. Revelation 20:14.

Jesus also partook of flesh and blood that He *'might free those who through fear of death were subject to slavery all their lives'*. Hebrews 2:15. The conscience that God has imparted to every human being immediately disturbs our peace whenever we speak or act in a way that is contrary to what we know to be right. Many may override their conscience and it may become hardened by sin, but none can entirely deny its promptings.

God's answer in Christ is provided in Romans 6:6-7; *'knowing this, that our old self was crucified with Him, in order that our body of sin might be done away with, so that we would no longer be slaves to sin for he who has died is freed from sin'*. Unfortunately, many who read these words fail to realize that the part that Jesus played in freeing us from the slavery of sin requires our response of abandonment to Him of all our rights. As with Paul we must be able to say *'I count all things to be loss in view of the surpassing value of knowing Christ Jesus my Lord, for whom I have suffered the loss of all things, and count them but rubbish so that I may gain Christ'*. Philippians 3:8. It is this state of absolute surrender of ourselves to Jesus as Lord that will qualify us to be overcomers in Him.

How vital it is for all who love the Lord Jesus to know the true significance of these words, *'knowing this, that our old self was crucified with Him....'* Ultimately it is the *'old self'* that keeps multitudes of Bible believing and apparently devout Christians from paying the price that they may overcome.

We may recall the incident when Jesus spoke candidly to His disciples about how He was going to suffer in Jerusalem; that He would be killed and would rise on the third day. In response to Peter's rebuke, "*God forbid it, Lord! This shall never happen to You,*" Jesus had *'turned and said to Peter, "Get behind Me, Satan! You are a stumbling block to Me; for you are not setting your mind on God's interests, but man's."* Matthew 16:22-23. The self, man's fleshly nature, is ever Satan's instrument to resist the will of God.

The flesh became our ruler in the Garden of Eden when Eve and her husband Adam swallowed Satan's lie and ate of the fruit of the tree of the knowledge of good and evil. Jesus, who had been their frequent companion in the Garden, had His rightful lordship set aside in favour of the self. Satan had said, *"....you will be like God, knowing good and evil."* Genesis 3:5. Not only did they commit sin and thus come to know evil but, through their complicity, the way to the tree of life was barred from them and the fatherhood of God was lost to them.

God had formerly given Adam and his wife Eve *"dominion over the fish of the sea, over the birds of the air, and over every living thing that moves on the earth."* Genesis 1:28. NKJV. This included the serpent, Satan, within the category of the creeping things. It had been the Creator's desire that man should take of the fruit of the tree of life and defeat and depose Satan as *'the god of this world'*. The son of God, Adam, failed, so the flesh ruled in him and in all the seed of the woman, Eve, except in the promised One, the Son of God, Jesus.

In Him, those who overcome Satan will enter into the freedom that Adam surrendered. They will re-assert the sovereignty of God over the great red dragon *'because of the blood of the Lamb and because of the word of their testimony, and they did not love their life even when faced with death'*. Revelation 12:11. The life referred to here is not primarily their physical life but rather the life of their soul or self.

When finally realized and apprehended, Paul's cry of release from the curse of self and slavery to sin will reverberate with great joy and relief around the human heart. With joy we will be free to exclaim, *"I am crucified with Christ; and it is no longer I who live, but it is Christ who lives in me; and the life which I now live in the flesh I live in faith, the faith of the Son of God, who loved me and gave Himself up for me."* Galatians 2:20. Recovery Version. May this become the real and living experience and the victory cry of the writer and of those who shall read, that we may together become overcomers in Christ.

CHAPTER 42
THE UPWARD CALL OF GOD

Scripture references: Philippians 3:4-15, 1 Corinthians 9:24-27, Hebrews 12:1-2, Revelation 19:7-9, Philippians 1:27-30, 1 Corinthians 1:26-31.

Soon after the birth of the church, almost two thousand years ago, the apostle Paul was filled with a consuming desire to know Christ. The *'surpassing value of knowing Christ Jesus'* led him to suffer *'the loss of all things and count them as rubbish'* so that he might gain Christ and be found in Him, not having a righteousness of his own but *'the righteousness which comes from God on the basis of faith'*. Paul had received understanding that this goal of gaining and knowing Christ would qualify him *'for the prize of the upward call of God in Christ Jesus'*. Today, the same pathway which lay before Paul lies ahead of all those lovers of the Lord Jesus who willingly pay the price for this prize.

'Do you not know that those who run in a race all run, but only one receives the prize?' 1 Corinthians 9:24. In the race of life there has only been one winner and He has rightfully received the prize; that one is Jesus. In Him alone was it possible for Paul to win the prize and in Him alone will it be possible for us to win this same prize also. We shall only win by running our individual race *'fixing our eyes on Jesus, the author and perfecter of faith'*. Hebrews 12:2.

It will be to the victorious ones in Christ that an invitation will be given to the marriage supper of the Lamb. He Himself will be their ultimate prize. At the marriage supper the Lamb will receive His wife and His wife will receive her Husband. *"Let us be glad and rejoice and give Him glory, for the marriage of the Lamb has come, and His wife has made herself ready....Write: 'Blessed are those who are called to the marriage supper of the Lamb!'" And he said to me, "These are the true sayings of God."* Revelation 19:7,9. NKJV.

In the verses quoted from Paul's letter to the church in Philippi there are several important pointers concerning how we too may qualify for *'the prize of the upward call of God in Christ Jesus'*.

We shall willingly suffer *'the loss of all things'* for the sake of our Beloved, Christ. *'For to you it has been granted for Christ's sake, not only to believe in Him, but also to suffer for His sake'*. Philippians 1:29. We shall also be willing to share in the fellowship of His sufferings. Surely, at the very centre of suffering loss is our willingness to deny our independent self. In our flesh is the root of the desire to be important; to gain and to possess more material things and gratifications; money, security, comfort – the list is long. Our fallen nature always desires to be more or to possess more.

Even if our natural attributes and giftedness may seem very small compared with those of the apostle Paul, nevertheless, we must *'count them as rubbish'* as he did. It is not a matter of the size of our gifts but of the immensity of who Christ is.

One small phrase provides the answer to surrendering our all to Jesus, *"Your will be done."* Matthew 6:10. As many as are our thoughts, our words and our actions, so many are the times we will repeat this phrase *"Your will be done"* for love of He Who willingly became the ultimate sacrifice, through which each one of us must be saved.

'For consider your calling, brethren, that there were not many wise according to the flesh, not many mighty, not many noble'. 1 Corinthians 1:26. The hierarchical concepts we grew up with in our multi-layered, status-conscious society must be set aside if we would clearly perceive what the apostle Paul is conveying to us by the Spirit in these verses. It is not a matter of our prominence or giftedness but the greatness of Christ. It is not our degree of influence but His supreme and omnipotent power and authority. It is not what we can do but what He can accomplish through us. *'I am able to do all things in Him who empowers me'*. Philippians 4:13, Recovery Version.

Perhaps the greatest barrier to our understanding and acceptance of this truth is the organization of the church on earth as it is in our day. There are those who have been ordained and there are the common or lay people, as they are often referred to. There are those with spiritual authority and there are those who must follow their dictates. There are methods and systems of worship in place that all who attend must simply follow along with. There is the Lord's rightful authority and supremacy and there is authority usurped by man. *'....but God has chosen the foolish things of the world to shame the wise, and God has chosen the weak things of the world to shame the things which are strong, and the base things of the world and the despised God has chosen, the things that are not, so that He may nullify the things that are, so that no man may boast before God'.* 1 Corinthians 1:27-29.

In the Scriptures there are four identifiable companies of believers who will qualify to receive the prize of *'the upward call of God in Christ Jesus'*.

- Those who represent the church in Philadelphia. *'Because you have kept the word of My perseverance, I also will keep you from the hour of testing, that hour which is about to come upon the whole world, to test those who dwell on the earth'.* Revelation 3:10.
- Those who are included within the male child. *'And she gave birth to a son, a male child, who is to rule all the nations with a rod of iron; and her child was caught up to God and to His throne'.* Revelation 12:5.
- Those who follow the Lamb wherever He goes. *'Then I looked, and behold, the Lamb was standing on Mount Zion, and with Him one hundred and forty-four thousand, having His name and the name of His Father written on their foreheads'.* Revelation 14:1.
- Those *'who had been beheaded because of their testimony of Jesus'* during the great tribulation. These *'came to life and reigned with Christ for a thousand years'.* Revelation 20:4.

Regardless of worldly wisdom or importance, or of the lack of both; or of any seeming significance, or the lack of it; all lovers of Jesus may become qualified to receive *'the upward call of God in Christ Jesus'*. These will be Christ's overcoming saints who have overcome in Him alone. To them will be granted the highest honour and privilege; that of being *'invited to the marriage supper of the Lamb'*. These will also reign with Him for a thousand years.

May we heed the words of Paul. *'Brethren, I do not regard myself as having laid hold of it yet; but one thing I do: forgetting what lies behind and reaching forward to what lies ahead, I press on toward the goal for the prize of the upward call of God in Christ Jesus. Let us therefore, as many as are perfect, have this attitude; and if in anything you have a different attitude, God will reveal that also to you'*. Philippians 3:13-15.

May this be the unchangeable determination of our heart, *'I press on toward the goal for the prize of the upward call of God in Christ Jesus'*.

CHAPTER 43
THE CHURCH IN PHILADELPHIA

Scripture references: 1 John 3:14, Revelation 3:7-13, John 10:1-10, John 6:57-63, Isaiah 22:20-23, Hebrews 3:5-6, James 1:12-13, John 17:1-26, Ephesians 4:1-6.

'We know that we have passed out of death into life, because we love the brethren'. 1 John 3:14. Which 'brethren' is the Holy Spirit speaking about? All those who are in Christ Jesus are brothers in Him. *'Therefore if anyone is in Christ, he is a new creature; the old things passed away; behold, new things have come'.* 2 Corinthians 5:17. Whether that 'anyone' believes exactly as I do; wears uniform or robes in which he or she worships; accepts teachings differing from mine; follows rituals strange to me; *'if anyone is in Christ'* that one is my brother. My new nature will spontaneously love that one's new nature.

In Revelation chapters 2 and 3 we have descriptions of the character and condition of seven churches that existed at the time of the apostle John. These churches are depicted as seven golden lampstands. Each description is also applicable to church characteristics historically from Pentecost to the present day. The first three, Ephesus, Smyrna and Pergamum came and went long ago. The last four, Thyatira, Sardis, Philadelphia and Laodicea will persist until close to the end. All except two of the seven are admonished by the Lord for shortcomings. Smyrna (the suffering church), and Philadelphia (brotherly love) receive no reprimand. The church in Smyrna is descriptive of the period when the church went through much persecution under the Roman emperors and during which many believers were martyred. However, the church in Philadelphia is descriptive of a great movement of God which was quite recent in time. It came into prominence in about 1825 to grow into a worldwide movement known simply as 'the Brethren'.

Although, sadly, much division came about over a period of time among the Brethren, many other gatherings of believers have met in a similar way under the sole direction and sovereignty of the Holy Spirit with no presiding pastor, reverend or priest. The glory of such gatherings unto Jesus may be hard to describe to those who have never experienced it, yet the dangers and difficulties that assemblies that meet in this way face from the subtleties of Satan are many. Satan targets all who choose to meet in unity around our beloved Lord Jesus, for by them he is put under the Lord's feet.

John 10 is full of enlightenment concerning the form, function and content of God's ekklesia and its perfect unity in constitution and operation. In the two parts of Jesus' parable He is first *'the Good Shepherd'* and later He identifies Himself also as *'the door of the sheep'*. Because Jesus asks the doorkeeper to be let into the fold then the doorkeeper must be God the Father.

We may recall that Jesus presented Himself before His Father after His resurrection as the fulfilment of the Old Testament type of the first fruits. The Father only recognizes His Son and those who are in Him. Jesus is the only one who may enter the kingdom of heaven which, in this illustration, is the sheepfold, which we who believe unto salvation must enter in Him.

A hireling is one who must be paid to care for the sheep but does not have their real interests at heart. Whereas Jesus gave His life for the sheep, a hireling will only care for them if he receives payment. Should Satan threaten the sheep, the hireling will fail to protect them and they will be scattered. The one flock consists of the whole company of those who are in Christ Jesus; Jew and Gentile; master and servant; male and female; young and old; five talent and one talent.

The Lord Jesus alone can lead His own in and out of the sheepfold. He is also their green pastures. He is the complete food for the life-giving health of His sheep. *"As the living Father sent Me, and I live because of the Father, so he who eats Me, he also will live because of Me."* John 6:57.

Those of Philadelphia have undivided hearts. They follow one Good Shepherd and they refuse to acknowledge or pay attention to hirelings. They receive with love and they recognize and welcome all who have entered the kingdom through Jesus, the one door. Their heart is His throne. Their focus is upon Him alone. They encourage any of His own who are wandering in the wilderness to return to the

Good Shepherd and to find perfect peace and rest as members of His one flock.

Isaiah 22:20-22 *'Then it shall be in that day, That I will call My servant Eliakim the son of Hilkiah; I will clothe him with your robe And strengthen him with your belt; I will commit your responsibility into his hand. He shall be a father to the inhabitants of Jerusalem And to the house of Judah. The key of the house of David I will lay on his shoulder; So he shall open, and no one shall shut; And he shall shut, and no one shall open.* In this passage from Isaiah, Eliakim the son of Hilkiah (who had responsibility over the household of King Hezekiah) is described as a type of the Lord Jesus who truly has 'the key of David' who opens *'and no one shall shut'*, and that shuts *'and no one shall open'*.

Satan constantly seeks to create disagreement and dissension, yet true Philadelphians will have none of it. It is to such that Jesus promises, '*I know your deeds. Behold, I have put before you an open door which no one can shut, because you have a little power, and have kept My word, and have not denied My name'*. Revelation 3:9. These Philadelphians are the ones to whom God gives His full authority to preach the gospel of the kingdom to all nations that shall usher in the sure return of the Lord Jesus.

And Moses indeed was faithful in all His house as a servant, for a testimony of those things which would be spoken afterward, but Christ as a Son over His own house, whose house we are if we hold fast the confidence and the rejoicing of the hope firm to the end. Hebrews 3:5-6. Here we see the connection between Eliakim the type and Jesus the reality. The Father gave His Son the key of David and His Son has placed an open door *'which no one can shut'* before these ones of Philadelphia because He has found them to be faithful. They have kept His word and have not denied His name.

We are reminded of the response of Jesus to Satan's suggestion *"If You are the Son of God, command that these stones become bread."* And of Jesus reply, *"It is written, 'Man shall not live by bread alone, but by every word that proceeds from the mouth of God.'"* The ones who meet together as 'brothers' under the sovereignty of the Lord Jesus care for no word of man but only the anointed word *'that *proceeds from the mouth of God'* through whomever and whenever the Holy Spirit shall speak. Thus their meetings are held in mutuality with no man presiding – no pastor, no reverend, nor priest.

John 6:63 *It is the Spirit who gives life; the flesh profits nothing. The words that I speak to you are spirit, and they are life.* The anointed words of the Holy Spirit bring the very life of God to those who will meet simply with Jesus uplifted as Lord in their midst. Among those of Philadelphia all who belong to the Lord Jesus may contribute in the meetings as and when prompted by the Holy Spirit. *What is the outcome then, brethren? When you assemble, each one has a psalm, has a teaching, has a revelation, has a tongue, has an interpretation. Let all things be done for edification* (building up). 1 Corinthians 14:26.

And the disciples were first called Christians in Antioch. Acts 11:26. This word from the Book of Acts gives us who believe in Jesus the right to call ourselves Christians, but the Scriptures allow no other designation or title. His name is Jesus 'Jehovah saves'. As the Christ He is 'Messiah'. All who belong to the Lord Jesus are Christians and are members of the one body of Christ.

Blessed is a man who perseveres under trial; for once he has been approved, he will receive the crown of life which the Lord has promised to those who love Him. James 1:12-13. Those who dare in Christ to stand against the tide of division and human opinion will suffer because of their steadfastness. *'Because you have kept My command to persevere, I also will keep you from the hour of trial which shall come upon the whole world, to test those who dwell on the earth'.* Revelation 3:10 This promise to the church in Philadelphia is a most precious one. Those of Philadelphia who will be living on the earth during the first three and a half years of the tribulation will be caught away to God just before the commencement of the great tribulation.

What sets those of Philadelphia apart as a remnant who will escape the great tribulation is that they satisfy the heart of God by answering the prayer of the Lord Jesus. *"The glory which You have given Me I have given to them, that they may be one, just as We are one."* John 17:22. The Holy Spirit, who is *'the Spirit of glory and of God'*, has been gifted to all believers in Jesus that they might individually be perfected and also be brought collectively into perfect unity. Perfect unity is the oneness that the Father has with the Son and the Son has with the Spirit. This unity of the Holy Trinity is what Jesus prayed to His Father might be displayed on the earth by those who are His own and *'against the rulers, against the powers, against the world forces of this darkness, against the spiritual forces of wickedness in the heavenly places'*. Ephesians 6:12.

"I in them and You in Me, that they may be perfected in unity, so that the world may know that You sent Me." John 17:23. This testimony to Jesus of unity among those of Philadelphia will shut every mouth of the unbelieving who will be obliged to admit that the Father did indeed send His Son into the world.

It is fitting to close our deliberation on this topic with the words of the apostle Paul in Ephesians 4:1-6. *'I, therefore, the prisoner of the Lord, beseech you to walk worthy of the calling with which you were called, with all lowliness and gentleness, with longsuffering, bearing with one another in love, endeavoring to keep the unity of the Spirit in the bond of peace. There is one body and one Spirit, just as you were called in one hope of your calling; one Lord, one faith, one baptism; one God and Father of all, who is above all, and through all, and in you all'*.

May the Lord have mercy on he who writes these words and on all those who will read them, that we may together in *'the unity of the Spirit'* be counted among those overcoming ones who answer the great prayer of Jesus.

CHAPTER 44
THE MALE CHILD

Scripture references: Genesis 1:26-28, Acts 17:24-26, Ezekiel 28:13-15, Genesis 3:1-6, 1 Peter 4:12-13, Colossians 1:24, Revelation 12:1-12, 2 Thessalonians 2:7, Psalms 8:2,4-5.

A whole book might be written in response to the title of this chapter, but the purpose at this time will be to highlight the role and significance of a company of overcoming saints who together forward the plan and purpose of God; a great company of those who will receive *'the prize of the upward call of God in Christ Jesus'*.

'In the beginning....God created man in His own image, in the image of God He created him; male and female He created them'. Genesis 1:1,27. The creation of Adam was God's concluding act of bringing all things into being. To Adam was accorded the supreme place among all God's creation, for he was made in the image of the One who was, who is and who forever will be the image of the eternal and omnipotent God, Jesus. When Adam was created, Eve was already included within him awaiting God's unique creative act of building her from a rib or part of the side of the man.

"*The God who made the world and all things in it....made from one man every nation of mankind to live on all the face of the earth....*" Acts 17:24,26. Eve and all human beings who have ever lived had their origin in Adam. God's intention in creating Adam was that the man would exercise the authority bestowed upon him by his Creator to defeat and bring to naught the power and the works of His enemy Satan.

"*You were in Eden, the garden of God....*""*You were the anointed cherub who covers, and I placed you there....*""*You were blameless in your ways from the day you were created until unrighteousness was found in you.*" Ezekiel 28:13-15. When exactly did Satan's unrighteousness occur? We are not informed about this. All we know from the Scriptures is that Lucifer, morning star, was one of three archangels and that he was given specific authority from God to administer the earth. God placed Lucifer in Eden where, because of his rebellion against God he became the 'adversary', Satan, who confronted Eve with a plausible lie.

Genesis 3:1,6. *Now the serpent was more crafty than any beast of the field which the Lord God had made. And he said to the woman, "Indeed, has God said, 'You shall not eat from any tree of the garden'?"....When the woman saw that the tree was good for food, and that it was a delight to the eyes, and that the tree was desirable to make one wise, she took from its fruit and ate; and she gave also to her husband with her, and he ate.* First the woman, then the man succumbed to Satan's temptation and the flesh, the self, became the directing and controlling element in our human existence. If, instead of partaking of the forbidden fruit, they had eaten of the fruit of the tree of life, they would have placed themselves forever under the rule of God. God Himself would have been their one and only source of guidance, direction and authority.

In the face of failure or setbacks God never alters His intention or His plan and purpose. He always has a contingency plan. *'The Son of God appeared for this purpose, to destroy the works of the devil'.* 1 John 3:8. The Son of God was incarnated to be the Son of Man. He lived the human life, that through His sacrificial death He might *'destroy the works of the devil'*. Through the cross Jesus brought to naught all that Adam's sin had brought upon mankind. However, the Lord has also determined that from Adam's race He will raise up a great company of the faithful, who shall withstand and overcome Satan, where Adam and Eve failed.

'Beloved, do not be surprised at the fiery ordeal among you, which comes upon you for your testing, as though some strange thing were happening to you; but to the degree that you share the sufferings of Christ, keep on rejoicing, so that also at the revelation of His glory you may rejoice with exultation'. 1 Peter 4:12-13. For those whom the Lord chooses to face Satan and to withstand him He gives to share in a portion of His sufferings. Peter reminds us that this is not to be considered strange but is to be a source of continual rejoicing now and even more so when Christ is revealed in glory.

'Now I rejoice in my sufferings for your sake, and in my flesh I do my share on behalf of His body, which is the church, in filling up what is lacking in Christ's afflictions'. Colossians 1:24. To Paul and to all God's overcomers the Lord has given a portion of His

sufferings, not only to fill up *'what is lacking'* in His afflictions but to do so *'on behalf of His body, which is the church'*. To suffer on behalf of other believers was a source of joy for the apostle Paul and it will be also for all those who are given to fill up *'what is lacking in Christ's afflictions'*. Those who do so will not only greatly please Him but their willing obedience will also be of benefit to multitudes of His own who may not be called upon or enabled to do so.

In the passage in Revelation 12:1-12 are four beings and four outcomes. There is a woman about to give birth, a great red dragon, a male child, and Michael the archangel. The outcomes are that the woman, after giving birth *'fled into the wilderness where she had a place prepared by God'*, the male child was caught up *'to God and to His throne'*, there was war in heaven, *'Michael and his angels waging war with the dragon'* and *'the great red dragon was thrown down, the serpent of old who is called the devil and Satan'*.

'A great sign appeared in heaven: a woman clothed with the sun, and the moon under her feet, and on her head a crown of twelve stars; and she was with child; and she cried out, being in labour and in pain to give birth'. Revelation 12:1-2. Who is this woman who is in labour to give birth? The woman described here is noteworthy. She is *'clothed with the sun, and the moon under her feet, and on her head a crown of twelve stars...'* Surely she represents those who died in faith prior to the death and resurrection of the Lord Jesus, and those among both the Jews and Gentiles who have come to salvation since then. The moon under the woman's feet represents the age of law which began from Adam and ended with the sacrifice of the Lord Jesus on the cross. The moon has no light of its own and must depend on the light of the sun. *'Therefore the Law has become our tutor to lead us to Christ, so that we may be justified by faith'*. Galatians 3:24. The sun that clothes the woman represents Christ's *'so great salvation through faith'*, including all He is. The twelve stars represent the twelve sons of Israel from whom issued the twelve tribes. Thus the woman is inclusive of all believers of all the ages. She represents the fullness of God's 'ekklesia'.

When Adam and Eve were confronted by Satan in the Garden of Eden they were drawn away into sin and Satan was permitted to continue as *'the god of this world'* 2 Corinthians 4:4, and *'the accuser of our brethren....who accuses them before our God day and night'*. Revelation 12:10. However, since that utter failure, God has been gathering a company of people who during their lifetime have resisted and overcome Satan. *'Submit therefore to God. Resist the devil and he will flee from you'*. James 4:7. This great company of overcomers will have others added to them until the total attains to God's requirement. At that point the male child will be given birth from the woman.

And the woman *'gave birth to a son, a male child, who is to rule all the nations with a rod of iron; and her child was caught up to God and to His throne'*. Revelation 12:5. That the male child will be composed of many believers is apparent because we are informed that it was *'they* (who) *overcame him* (Satan – the great red dragon) *because of the blood of the Lamb and because of the word of their testimony, and they did not love their life even when faced with death.'* Revelation 12:11.

Paul writes to those of his day in Thessalonica, *'For the mystery of lawlessness is already at work; only he who now restrains will do so until he is taken out of the way'*. 2 Thessalonians 2:7. Who is *'he who now restrains'* and *'will do so until he is taken out of the way'*? Surely this is another reference to the male child. Those who represent the male child who have been restraining Satan are *'taken out of the way'* to the throne of God.

God had given Adam authority over all living things and He desired that Adam would resist Satan and would overcome him. He had given instruction to them, both male and female, that they *"Be fruitful and multiply; fill the earth and subdue it; have dominion over the fish of the sea, over the birds of the air, and over every living thing that moves on the earth."* Genesis 1:28. During all the ages since then there have been many who have indeed resisted and overcome the evil one.

The world has always exalted the naturally gifted, the wealthy and the powerful. This is not so with God for we read in Psalms 8:2,4-5,

'From the mouth of infants and nursing babes You have established strength Because of Your adversaries, To make the enemy and the revengeful cease'. Who exactly are these ones who *'make the enemy and the revengeful cease?'* In this Psalm they are described as *'infants and nursing babes'*. We cannot help but ask, can this really be so? How wrong are our concepts if we look to so called experts and professionals to 'establish strength'. Matthew 18:19. All it will take will be two seemingly insignificant saints of God who, in unity in the Spirit, will call upon the mighty power of the Godhead *'to make the enemy and the revengeful cease'*.

May we be accounted worthy to be among those *'infants and nursing babes'* who, in faith, take up their God-given authority over all the power of the enemy; who, in company together as the male child will provide the Lord with what He requires that Satan may be cast forever out of heaven.

CHAPTER 45
FIRST FRUITS TO GOD AND TO THE LAMB

Scripture references: Hebrews 1:1-4, Mark 9:2-8, Matthew 4:1-4, Revelation 14:1-5, Revelation 3:12, 1 Corinthians 9:5.

'God, after He spoke long ago to the fathers in the prophets in many portions and in many ways, in these last days has spoken to us in His Son, whom He appointed heir of all things, through whom also He made the world. Hebrews 1:1-2. How easy it can be simply to think of the Bible as a divinely-inspired book, filled with amazing accounts and revelations, yet not perceive its urgent personal messages to each and every inhabitant of this world at this very moment in time. In fact, the Bible is God's up to the minute newscast and messaging system.

'In these last days' God is all the more urgently speaking *'to us in His Son'*. On the mount of His transfiguration the voice of God made forever certain that it is Jesus and He alone who issues forth the word from the Father, *'Then a cloud formed, overshadowing them, and a voice came out of the cloud, "This is My beloved Son, listen to Him!"* Mark 9:7.

"It is written, 'man shall not live on bread alone, but on every word that proceeds out of the mouth of God.'" Matthew 4:4. It was Jesus who spoke these words in response to Satan's suggestion that He turn stones into bread that He might satisfy His hunger. Jesus lived by every word His Father spoke to Him and thereby lived the perfect and blameless life before God and before mankind. Our Father's will for us is that we listen to Jesus and that we live on His every word.

In all circumstances and in every place Jesus must always be the speaker and the Holy Spirit will be the transmitter. For this purpose we who believe were gifted with the forever indwelling Holy Spirit, *'For all who are being led* continually *by the Spirit of God, these are sons of God'*. Romans 8:14.

There is much symbolism in the account of the woman who is *'in labour and in pain to give birth'* to the male child: Whereas, in the account of *'the ones who follow the Lamb wherever He goes'*, their exaltation before God and their deeds and character are described very precisely. Throughout all the ages there have been some who have listened more closely and obeyed with more dedication. Revelation 14:1-5 describes a company of overcomers such as these.

'Then I looked, and behold, the Lamb was standing on Mount Zion, and with Him one hundred and forty-four thousand, having His name and the name of His Father written on their foreheads'. Revelation 14:1. When or how these so highly spoken of ones arrived on Mount Zion we are not informed here. Yet, because the company of Philadelphians and those who comprise the male child will be taken up to God prior to the commencement of the great tribulation, it is entirely reasonable to suppose that this company of one hundred and forty-four thousand will receive *'the upward call of God'* during the same time period. Who might they be?

We may recall that all those of Philadelphia are overcomers for they already have the crown. They are cautioned against letting anyone take their crown. However, even among this company are a select group of overcomers to whom very great promises are made including these, *'He who overcomes....I will write on him the name of My God....and My new name'.* Revelation 3:12. Surely then this company of *'one hundred and forty-four thousand'* on Mount Zion must be the overcomers of the church in Philadelphia for they are described as *'having His name and the name of His Father written on their foreheads'.*

All those of the church in Philadelphia are approved of God. They are a faithful remnant who *'accept one another, just as Christ also accepted'* each one of them. They display that condition of unity that answers the prayer of Jesus to His Father recorded in John 17. Yet it appears that the ones on Mount Zion are yet more diligent and precise in their discernment of God's will and in their obedience to Him. They are a very select company of overcomers.

It is said of these one hundred and forty-four thousand that *'they follow the Lamb wherever He goes'.* May we pause right now where we are, in inner silence, and ponder upon this deepest desire of our Father and our Lord Jesus Christ. This is what the call to discipleship really involves and it is what Jesus meant when He called out to those He chose, *"Follow Me!"* To follow Jesus is to follow Him *'wherever He goes'*.

'And I heard a voice from heaven, like the sound of many waters and like the sound of loud thunder, and the voice which I heard was like the sound of harpists playing on their harps'. Revelation 14:2. We are reminded of the description of Jesus in Revelation 1:13-16. In which is stated that *'His voice was like the sound of many waters'*. On that occasion the apostle John *'fell at His feet as a dead man'*. Now, on the heavenly Mount Zion, John says *'the voice which I heard was like the sound of harpists playing on their harps'*. Fear and dread is no longer evoked by that great voice but it possesses the soothing qualities of the sweetest music.

The music of the Lord's voice transitions into the singing of a unique song rendered by the one hundred and forty-four thousand. *'And they sang a new song before the throne and before the four living creatures and the elders; and no one could learn the song except the one hundred and forty-four thousand who had been purchased from the earth'*. Just as the wedding dress in which the wife of the Lamb will be displayed before her Bridegroom was created stitch by stitch by the righteous acts of the saints, Revelation 19:7-9, so this song, only known to these overcoming saints, was created by their acts of devotion performed by them for Jesus sake. They had been purchased as earth-dwellers at the highest price possible; the blood of the Lamb. Their response to what He has done for them has been to *'follow the Lamb wherever He goes'*.

'These are the ones who have not been defiled with women, for they have kept themselves chaste'. This statement appears to apply to men only in regard to women, yet it may be applied also to women in regard to men also. The key expression here is *'they have kept themselves chaste'*. The writer in Hebrews 13:4 states *'Marriage is to be held in honor among all, and the marriage bed is to be undefiled; for fornicators and adulterers God will judge'*. The apostle Paul was never married yet many, if not all of the other first apostles were married. *'Do we not have a right to take along a believing wife, even as the rest of the apostles and the brothers of*

the Lord and Cephas'? 1 Corinthians 9:5. Surely then to be *'defiled with women'* must mean to be *'fornicators or adulterers'*.

'But now Christ has been raised from the dead, the first fruits of those who are asleep'. 1 Corinthians 15:23. After the Lord Jesus rose from the dead, Mary Magdalene sought to hold on to Him by the garden tomb. His response to her was *'"Stop clinging to Me, for I have not yet ascended to the Father; but go to My brethren and say to them, 'I ascend to My Father and your Father, and My God and your God.'"* John 20:17. Jesus' immediate and brief ascension was to present Himself as the first fruits from the grave before His Father. That same afternoon He joined the two the road to Emmaus.

'These have been purchased from among men as first fruits to God and to the Lamb'. The ones on Mount Zion are presented as *'first fruits to God and the Lamb'*.

'And no lie was found in their mouth; they are blameless'. These few significant words provide the assurance that this company who are presented as the first fruits have also overcome Satan for *'Whenever he speaks a lie, he speaks from his own nature, for he is a liar and the father of lies'*. John 8:44. The Lord finds these one hundred and forty-four thousand completely free of all Satan's entanglements, thus they are blameless.

The past three chapters have unveiled significant information about three companies of overcoming saints who have paid the price in their lives to meet the Lord's requirements.

- Those of the church in Philadelphia
- The ones who together form the male child
- Those who follow the Lamb wherever He goes

Before time was, God formed His eternal purpose and plan in which mankind was to play an essential part. May he who has been privileged to write these words and may those who shall read them be moved and encouraged to *'press on toward the goal for the prize of the upward call of God in Christ Jesus'*.

CHAPTER 46
THERE WAS WAR IN HEAVEN

Scripture references: Ezekiel 28:12-19, Isaiah 14:12-15, John 12:31-32, James 1:13-15, Job 1:6-12, Revelation 12:7-12.

As dwellers in this fallen world in which there is so much division, hatred and darkness it is almost impossible for us to imagine conditions in which there is absolute unity, love and light. Yet that is what existed unchanged and unchallenged until Lucifer, 'bright star', allowed a desire to take possession of him to be in competition with God. Immediately this desire took hold he became Satan, 'the adversary' and he became the antithesis of God. All God's attributes were lost to him. *'"You were blameless in your ways From the day you were created Until unrighteousness was found in you'.* Ezekiel 28:15.

At his creation God gave Lucifer free will to act, as He has given to mankind and to all His created beings. What then was the basis of Satan's sin? He was tempted by no one. Lucifer became overwhelmed with a desire to be equal with God; that is to elevate his status above all the angelic beings and be able to rule over and control them instead of simply serving God and following His desires and directions.

We may well ask, what is the nature of heaven's rule? The answer is simple. It is found in the prayer Jesus taught His disciples to pray. *'Your kingdom come. Your will be done, On earth as it is in heaven'.* Matthew 6:10. Heaven's rule is transmitted from the Triune God to all His created beings, absolute in purpose and in righteousness. When heaven rules none of His created beings speaks or acts independently. There is simply whole hearted and willing obedience.

Hebrews 1:14 speaks of the role of angels thus, *'Are not the angels all ministering spirits (servants) sent out in the service [of God for the assistance] of those who are to inherit salvation'?* AMP. All the angels are servants of God created specifically to perform His will.

*"You had the seal of perfection, Full of wisdom and perfect in beauty...."You were in Eden, the garden of God"....*Ezekiel 28:12-

13. Lucifer was a perfect and beautiful being in his creation. God bestowed on him the fullness of His wisdom, the wisdom that comes alone from God. James 1:5. *'But if any of you lacks wisdom, let him ask of God, who gives to all generously and without reproach, and it will be given to him'.*

'You said in your heart, I will....I will....I will....I will....I will....' Isaiah 14:13-14. There were five actions that Lucifer decided he would take in independence of the Most High God. God's response was, *"Nevertheless you will be thrust down to Sheol, To the recesses of the pit."* Isaiah 14:15. *'Now judgment is upon this world; now the ruler of this world will be cast out. "And I, if I am lifted up from the earth, will draw all men to Myself."* John 12:31-32. Lucifer became Satan and he, *'the ruler of this world will be cast out'.*

'Let no one say when he is tempted, "I am being tempted by God"; for God cannot be tempted by evil, and He Himself does not tempt anyone. But each one is tempted when he is carried away and enticed by his own lust. Then when lust has conceived, it gives birth to sin; and when sin is accomplished, it brings forth death'. James 1:13-15. Just as the original sin of independence from God caused the fall of Lucifer, so it was an act of independence that caused sin to come upon the whole human race through Adam in the Garden of Eden.

We know that, when God created the heavens and the earth and all things, He also created time for we read for instance in Genesis 1:3-5, *'"Let there be light"; and there was light. God saw that the light was good; and God separated the light from the darkness. God called the light day, and the darkness He called night. And there was evening and there was morning, one day'.* At the instant that God put Lucifer in Eden, the garden of God, he became bound by time.

'Now there was a day when the sons of God came to present themselves before the Lord, and Satan also came among them. The Lord said to Satan, "From where do you come?" Then Satan answered the Lord and said, "From roaming about on the earth and walking around on it." Job 1:6-7. The word 'day' is the same Hebrew word used in this phrase *'there was evening and there was*

morning, one day' in Genesis 1:5. Satan left his *'roaming about on the earth and walking around on it"* on a certain day that he might appear before God. We note that, despite having become the embodiment of all evil, Satan is still referred to as 'a son of God'.

No patriarchal figure of the Old Testament appears to have been tested more severely than the Lord's servant Job. To God's assessment of Job *"Have you considered My servant Job? For there is no one like him on the earth, a blameless and upright man, fearing God and turning away from evil."* Satan responded *"Does Job fear God for nothing?"* God permitted Satan to bring upon Job, not only terrible loss of family and possessions, but the criticism and misunderstanding of his dear friends. Because of his unwavering trust in the Lord, Job overcame Satan and, thus, he will be among those who participate in the male child. Job looked ahead to his redemption with a great cry of faith, *"As for me, I know that my Redeemer lives, And at the last He will take His stand on the earth. "Even after my skin is destroyed, Yet from my flesh I shall see God...."* Job 19:25-26.

In Revelation 12:10 we read, *'the accuser of our brethren has been thrown down, he who accuses them before our God day and night'*. Satan's accusations against those who believe in the Lord Jesus is constant before the throne of God yet this is also expressed in terms of time – *'day and night'*. But as we shall shortly find out Satan's appearing in heaven is about to be terminated.

'And there was war in heaven, Michael and his angels waging war with the dragon. The dragon and his angels waged war, and they were not strong enough, and there was no longer a place found for them in heaven. And the great dragon was thrown down, the serpent of old who is called the devil and Satan, who deceives the whole world; he was thrown down to the earth, and his angels were thrown down with him'. Revelation 12:7-9. This war, waged by Michael and his angels, will open the door to the final tide of unfettered evil to be launched upon mankind for a short while before Jesus returns to reign forever. For three and a half years the world will have suffered under the antichrist and the false prophet; now, Satan will not only join these two on earth but he will endow

the antichrist (also known as the beast) and the false prophet with his authority. Thus the world will be ruled by a trinity begotten in Hell. These events will usher in 'the great tribulation'.

"....Woe to the earth and the sea, because the devil has come down to you, having great wrath, knowing that he has only a short time." Revelation 12:12. Satan knows the timetable of God very well. The short time he has before Jesus returns will be *'one thousand two hundred and sixty days'*, or forty two lunar months, which is three and a half years.

'Now to Him who is able to keep you from stumbling, and to make you stand in the presence of His glory blameless with great joy, to the only God our Savior, through Jesus Christ our Lord, be glory, majesty, dominion and authority, before all time and now and forever. Amen'. Jude 24-25. To many, these words are familiar as a benediction. May they also be our prayer and our source of endless praise.

CHAPTER 47
NIGHT IS COMING

Scripture references: 1 John 1:5, Genesis 1:1-5, John 1:1-5, Luke 22:52-53, Colossians 1:13-14, 1 Peter 2:9-10, John 9:4-5, Matthew 24:21-22, Revelation 13:1-18, Daniel 7:1-8, Revelation 21:23-25, Romans 13:12.

When and how did darkness come to exist? *God is Light, and in Him there is no darkness at all'.* 1 John 1:5. Surely darkness came to be when Lucifer rebelled against God and became the antithesis of God. Everything that God represented was lost forever to him and he became Satan, the adversary. He now rules over all who, through sin and disobedience, reside in *'the domain of darkness'*.

'In the beginning God created the heavens and the earth. The earth was formless and void, and darkness was over the surface of the deep, and the Spirit of God was moving over the surface of the waters. Then God said, "Let there be light"; and there was light. God saw that the light was good; and God separated the light from the darkness. God called the light day, and the darkness He called night'. Genesis 1:1-5. We are not informed about how or why darkness was present *'over the surface of the deep'.* All that we are told is that the Spirit of God was moving over the surface of the waters ready to execute God's command. *"Let there be light"; and there was light'.* In the context of this chapter we also note, that *'the darkness He called night'.*

'In the beginning was the Word, and the Word was with God, and the Word was God. He was in the beginning with God; all things were made through him, and without him was not anything made that was made. In him was life, and the life was the light of men. The light shines in the darkness, and the darkness has not overcome it'. RSV. John 1:1-5. These verses unequivocally establish that it was the great creator, Jesus, who spoke the words *"Let there be light"; and there was light.* The inspired word assures us, *'and the darkness has not overcome it':* And it never will.

'Then Jesus said to the chief priests and officers of the temple and elders who had come against Him, "Have you come out with swords and clubs as you would against a robber? "While I was with you

daily in the temple, you did not lay hands on Me; but this hour and the power of darkness are yours." Luke 22:52-53. How unimaginably awful it was that those who were leaders among *'His own'* should embrace the power of darkness in order to condemn and pass sentence on their Messiah. Yet, through what He suffered, the stranglehold of sin was broken forever. Our Lord's words from the cross on behalf of those who cried out for His crucifixion, though they cried out in ignorance, echo down the ages *"Father, forgive them; for they do not know what they are doing."* Luke 23:34.

'....For He rescued us from the domain of darkness, and transferred us to the kingdom of His beloved Son, in whom we have redemption, the forgiveness of sins'. Colossians 1:13-14. Through His redemptive sacrifice we, who have come to Jesus in repentance and faith, were transferred *'from the domain of darkness'* into *'the kingdom of His beloved Son'*. Now, having rescued us from the domain of darkness the Lord's intention is to remove the darkness out of us.

'But you are a chosen race, a royal priesthood, a holy nation, a people for God's own possession, so that you may proclaim the excellencies of Him who has called you out of darkness into His marvelous light'. 1 Peter 2:9. The abundance of what we who believe unto salvation have entered into is gloriously expressed in these verses. At the heart of what Peter is revealing to us is the purpose of our calling, *'that you may proclaim the excellencies of Him who has called you out of darkness into His marvelous light'*.

We can only proclaim *'the excellencies of Him'* if we bear His testimony with such transparency that both other believers and the worldly folks will see His image, hear His words and behold His deeds expressed through us. Paul reminds those of the assembly in Ephesus *'....for you were formerly darkness, but now you are Light in the Lord; walk as children of Light'*. Ephesians 5:8.

"We must work the works of Him who sent Me as long as it is day; night is coming when no one can work. "While I am in the world, I am the Light of the world." John 9:4-5. Now we have come to the main point of this chapter, which is that there will very shortly come

upon the whole earth a time when it will be impossible to spread the good news of the gospel of the kingdom. The night that the Lord Jesus is referring to will be the great tribulation of three and a half lunar years, during which time the triumvirate of Satan, the antichrist and the false prophet will have absolute control on the earth until Jesus returns in glory.

After the male child, *'he who now restrains'*, has been taken out of the way, Satan's full fury will be unleashed upon all those who dwell on the face of the earth. This will create the conditions spoken of by Jesus as *'night....when no one can work'*. Every individual found to be a disciple of Jesus will be martyred. *"For then there will be a great tribulation, such as has not occurred since the beginning of the world until now, nor ever will. "Unless those days had been cut short, no life would have been saved; but for the sake of the elect those days will be cut short."* Matthew 24:21-22. These most dreadful days will be cut short by the coming to reign forever of the Lord Jesus.

Revelation 13:1-18 is devoted to a description of the night that will come upon the dwellers of the earth following the fall of Satan and his angels from heaven. At the start of this vision John saw *'the dragon* (Satan) *stood on the sand of the seashore'* and *'coming up out of the sea'*, the Mediterranean Sea, was the beast.

Only in complete dependence on the Holy Spirit may we approach the unknown and unrevealed in Scripture. All our human reasoning and imagination must be subordinated to the readiness of the Lord to reveal His mysteries. *'For we know in part and we prophesy in part. But when that which is perfect has come, then that which is in part will be done away'*. 1 Corinthians 13:9-10.

Revelation 13:1-2. *Then I stood on the sand of the sea. And I saw a beast rising up out of the sea, having seven heads and ten horns, and on his horns ten crowns, and on his heads a blasphemous name. Now the beast which I saw was like a leopard, his feet were like the feet of a bear, and his mouth like the mouth of a lion. The dragon* (Satan) *gave him his power, his throne, and great authority.* These three carnivores are mentioned in reverse order to their first appearance out of the great sea in Daniel's dream.

Daniel 7:1-7. *Daniel spoke, saying, "I saw in my vision by night, and behold, the four winds of heaven were stirring up the Great Sea.* Verse 7 indicates that the times in which this dream applies will be dark and turbulent; the seven years of the tribulation and great tribulation.

Out of this Mediterranean Sea Daniel in his vision observed four beasts arising one after another, their description is awesome and disturbing, especially the description of the fourth beast. Without going into great detail we may note that *the first was like a lion....the second like a bear....another like a leopard. The fourth was different from all the beasts that were before it, and it had ten horns.*

Surely by the time of the prophecy of Revelation 13 the fourth beast of Daniel 7 has acquired the characteristics of the first three beasts. He, the fourth beast, has taken away their power and has assumed absolute authority over them.

Now we come to the one who wields the power of this fourth beast; the little horn *'before whom three of the first horns were plucked out by the roots. And there, in this horn, were eyes like the eyes of a man, and a mouth speaking pompous words'*. Daniel 7:8 NKJV.

We do not know exactly who are represented by the ten horns, except that they are ten kings, Revelation 17:12. However, we may assume that the three that *'were plucked out by the roots'* are the first three beasts – *'the first was like a lion....the second like a bear....another like a leopard'*. This is all quite mysterious. Only by the unveiling of this mystery by the Holy Spirit, and as He will, may we know what all this has in store for this world in the end times.

From Daniel 2, then Daniel 7 and on to Revelation 13 we are shown a gradual unfolding and enlargement of what God is revealing to us about the end times. The feet and toes of Nebuchadnezzar's image transition into the ten horns. From these ten horns three are *'plucked out by the roots'* before a fourth horn which grows up to replace the three. In Daniel's dream the four beasts are merged together to become the composite beast of the Apostle John's revelation. Out of this fourth beast emerges a little horn that rules them all. This little horn has *'eyes like the eyes of a man, and a mouth speaking pompous words'*. This is the beast. He is none other than the antichrist.

'Then I saw another beast coming up out of the earth; and he had two horns like a lamb and he spoke as a dragon'. Revelation 13:11-17. In these verses is described the manifestation of the false prophet who completes this triumvirate from Hell. He also is endowed with the authority of the dragon, Satan, because he is the dragon's mouthpiece.

Recent history is replete with dictators and autocrats whose time on the world stage has caused untold suffering to millions under their sphere of influence. Yet, in comparison with any of them the three and a half year reign of terror brought about by the dragon, the antichrist and the false prophet will be completely beyond human endurance. Add to this that the wrath of God will be let loose in catastrophic events of nature to test the human race.

Jesus....for the joy set before Him endured the cross, despising the shame'. Hebrews 12:2. Just as our dear Lord Jesus looked ahead to the joy that lay beyond the awful suffering of the cross so, in these rapidly darkening days may we see beyond this approaching night to the day that shall dawn with the greatest joy; joy which shall continue forever.

'And the city has no need of the sun or of the moon to shine on it, for the glory of God has illumined it, and its lamp is the Lamb. The nations will walk by its light, and the kings of the earth will bring their glory into it. In the daytime (for there will be no night there) its gates will never be closed'. Revelation 21:23-25. When the bride, the wife of the Lamb is displayed before an entirely new creation *'there will be no night there'*. Satan, the antichrist, the false prophet and all those who have followed them will have been consigned to the pit of Hell forever. Henceforth the glory of God will illumine the holy city and the Light of the world, Jesus, will be the constantly shining lamp for the nations who will inhabit the new earth.

In a travelogue published in 1650 the English theologian and historian Thomas Fuller coined the well-known phrase 'the darkest hour is just before the dawn'. This 'darkest hour' will certainly be true about the period known as the great tribulation. Yet this grave event will usher in the dawn of the reign forever and ever of our Lord and Saviour Jesus Christ.

A final encouragement to us is found in Romans 13:12. *'The night is almost gone, and the day is near. Therefore let us lay aside the deeds of darkness and put on the armor of light'.*

CHAPTER 48
THOSE WHO ARE WITH HIM

Scripture references: Revelation 22:12-13, Genesis 15:1 NKJV, Ezekiel 44:15-16, 23, 28, 2 Peter 1:3-4, John 6:57-58, Song of Solomon 2:4, 2:16, 6:3, 7:10, Revelation 17:14, Revelation 19:7-9 NKJV.

"Behold, I am coming quickly, and My reward is with Me, to render to every man according to what he has done. "I am the Alpha and the Omega, the first and the last, the beginning and the end." Revelation 22:12-13. These words of Jesus spoken to the apostle John are a strong admonition and encouragement that our life be lived utterly for Him. Never have they carried more weight than now as the end of the age draws so near. For during His earthly sojourn Jesus had also said, *"For this reason you also must be ready; for the Son of Man is coming at an hour when you do not think He will."* Matthew 24:44. He's coming for you. He's coming for me. The serious question that confronts each one of us is this: Am I ready?

'For I am confident of this very thing, that He who began a good work in you will perfect it until the day of Christ Jesus'. Philippians 1:6. We have His absolute assurance that Jesus will perfect His work in each one who is absolutely surrendered to Him. Just as He was our Alpha, so He will be our Omega. As assuredly as He was our beginning so He will as surely be our end. *'He who began a good work in you will perfect it'*. The serious consideration that faces each one of us is this: Will I let Him?

'After these things the word of the Lord came to Abram in a vision, saying, "Do not be afraid, Abram. I am your shield, your exceedingly great reward." Genesis 15:1 NKJV. What wonderful assurance did the Lord provide to His faithful servant Abram. This was spoken to him even before the Lord renamed him Abraham, *'a father of many nations'*. He told him, *"I am....your exceedingly great reward."* The Lord Himself is Abram's reward.

"But the Levitical priests, the sons of Zadok, who kept charge of My sanctuary when the sons of Israel went astray from Me, shall come near to Me to minister to Me; and they shall stand before Me to *offer Me the fat and the blood," declares the Lord God...."They shall enter My sanctuary; they shall come near to My table to minister to Me and keep My charge...."Moreover, they shall teach My people the difference between the holy and the profane, and cause them to discern between the unclean and the clean. "And it shall be with regard to an inheritance for them, that I am their inheritance; and you shall give them no possession in Israel - I am their possession.* Ezekiel 44:15-16, 23, 28. In the midst of an appalling state of apostasy among the people of Judah and Jerusalem there existed, in the time of the prophet Ezekiel, a division of the Levitical priests who remained steadfastly faithful to the Lord; namely the sons of Zadok. The Lord describes details of their ministry to Him and their role as teachers to His people. Then He pronounces upon them their very great reward. *"And it shall be with regard to an inheritance for them, that I am their inheritance; and you shall give them no possession in Israel - I am their possession."* Can we really grasp the significance of these last few words? Because of their devoted faithfulness, as surely as the sons of Zadok (as with Abram) belong to God so He belongs to them. Right now may we pause in utter astonishment at the enormity of these promises, because they are available to us also.

Are there perhaps comparable promises such as these that may apply to us today? Indeed there are. 2 Peter 1:3-4. *'His divine power has granted to us everything pertaining to life and godliness, through the true knowledge of Him who called us by His own glory and excellence. For by these He has granted to us His precious and magnificent promises, so that by them you may become partakers of the divine nature, having escaped the corruption that is in the world by lust'.* Right at the heart of these two verses is the avenue through which His precious and magnificent promises will come to us. They are made available *'through the true knowledge of Him who called us by His own glory and excellence'.* Surely that is why Paul cried out *'that I may know Him'*; that is Jesus. So that we too may know Him ours must be an undivided and utterly devoted seeking heart.

Why does the Lord desire that we *'become partakers of the divine nature?'* So that we may participate in *'the bride, the wife of the*

Lamb', that we may be with Him and enjoy Him and He us forever and ever. Not only are Abram and the sons of Zadok assured that the Lord will be their possession but to all who come to *'the true knowledge of Him'* are *'His precious and magnificent promises'* given.

The prime example in the Bible of a bride coming into an ever deeper knowledge and appreciation of her future husband is found in Song of Solomon. Truly, this little book contains a description of the stages through which the betrothed is led to be *'ready as a bride adorned for her husband'*.

The short quotations chosen from Song of Solomon somewhat parallel the stages that the Lord leads us through which were identified from Ezekiel 47:1-12. The location that marks the beginning of the journey taken by the Shulamite is found in Song of Solomon 2:4. *"He has brought me to his banquet hall, And his banner over me is love."* God's provision for every true seeker after Him is that they may feed luxuriously upon His Son, the Lord Jesus Christ. *"As the living Father sent Me, and I live because of the Father, so he who eats Me, he also will live because of Me. "This is the bread which came down out of heaven; not as the fathers ate and died; he who eats this bread will live forever."* John 6:57-58.

When we take Jesus in by the living word we are taking in all that He is. We thereby *'become partakers of the divine nature'*. The Father desires that we feast upon His Son and His Son has brought us into His banquet hall for that very purpose. In this private place of preparation and growth in the divine life He will spread over us His banner of unchanging and unchangeable love.

The love her Beloved has planted within her heart causes her to exclaim, *"My beloved is mine, and I am his...."* At this early stage of her betrothal her consciousness is upon her possession of Him. Her self-absorption at this early stage is evident in an incident in which the Beloved comes to the Shulamite's door and knocks, *'Open to me, my sister, my darling, My dove, my perfect one! For my head is drenched with dew, My locks with the damp of the night.'* *"I have taken off my dress, How can I put it on again? I have washed my feet, How can I dirty them again?* Song of Solomon 5:2-3. Rather than open to her beloved whose 'head is drenched with dew and his locks with the damp of the night' (which indicates deep suffering), the Shulamite considers the inconvenience of putting on the clothes she has taken off. She is more concerned about herself than Him. When she does open the door, her Beloved has disappeared and she cannot find Him.

"I am my beloved's and my beloved is mine." Song of Solomon 6:3. After many experiences the Shulamite has been led to a deeper appreciation of her divine suitor. Now His right to her has been put before her right to Him. She has been learning of Him who is *'gentle and humble in heart'*. She has also been learning through some suffering that He has led her through.

"I am my beloved's, And his desire is for me." Song of Solomon 7:10. During the period before this final expression of delight in her betrothal, the narrative is all about the Beloved's appreciation of her transformation into His perfect bride. She has made herself ready. Now her concern is all about Him and the delight that she is bringing to His heart. A holy flame of love for Him has been forever ignited in her heart.

The Shulamite in this allegorical account represents the bride undergoing the process of transformation to become the wife of the Lamb. She is composed of many individuals throughout the ages upon whom grace has been given to display a devoted heart for Jehovah and His Son, the Lord Jesus Christ. These are the overcoming saints that form the central theme of this book. The suffering the Lord has led this great company of saints through has qualified them to reign with Him.

Before the kingdom of this world becomes *'the kingdom of our Lord and of His Christ'* there will be warfare with the forces of evil that have been keeping the nations under their rule in an iron grip. *"These will wage war against the Lamb, and the Lamb will overcome them, because He is Lord of lords and King of kings, and those who are with Him are the called and chosen and faithful."* Revelation 17:14.

Those who compose together the Shulamite are described here as *'the called and chosen and faithful'*. All who have come to Jesus in repentance and faith are the called. *"For many are called, but few are chosen."* Matthew 22:14. The chosen are those few who find and enter in Jesus through the narrow gate. Surely then those who also prove to be faithful are the ones that walk unhesitatingly the narrow way that leads to life yoked to He who is *'gentle and humble of heart'*. These are the ones who will compose the wife of the Lamb who *'has made herself ready'*. Their exceeding great reward will be awaiting them in the marriage supper in the person of the Lamb of God. She will be His and He will be hers thereafter forever and ever.

'Let us be glad and rejoice and give Him glory, for the marriage of the Lamb has come, and His wife has made herself ready." And to her it was granted to be arrayed in fine linen, clean and bright, for the fine linen is the righteous acts of the saints. Then he said to me, "Write: 'Blessed are those who are called to the marriage supper of the Lamb!'" And he said to me, "These are the true sayings of God." Revelation 19:7-9 NKJV.

CHAPTER 49
THE WIFE OF THE LAMB

Scripture references: Genesis 1:26-28, Genesis 2:7-8, Acts 17:26, Luke 3:38, Genesis 22:16-18, Revelation 21:9-11, John 11:47-53, Revelation 19:7-9, Philippians 2:12-13, Romans 8:38-39, Matthew 25:1-13, Ephesians 2:8-10.

When the Triune God, Elohim, counselled together to create mankind, the three Persons spoke as One, *"Let Us make man in Our image, according to Our likeness...."* Genesis 2:7 describes how God created Adam in the image of Jesus, who Himself *'is the image of the invisible God'*. Colossians 1:15.

The passage from Genesis 1 reveals that God's intention in creating man was that ultimately a race of people, composed of male and female, should populate the whole earth and rule over all living things.

'....He made from one man every nation of mankind to live on all the face of the earth, having determined their appointed times and the boundaries of their habitation....' Acts 17:26. Firstly Eve, then every single human being who has ever lived was contained within this magnificent creation of God; namely Adam, the man. They that built the great pyramid and all the ancient wonders of the world were the descendants of no primitive hominid.

'....the son of Enosh, the son of Seth, the son of Adam, the son of God'. Luke 3:38. Our human minds cannot grasp, nor even imagine the amazing character and qualities of that first man. The fact that he is described as being *'in the image of God'* and *'the son of God'* conjures up a superman that no Hollywood director could ever portray on the screen. He was perfect, sinless and in communion with God. He, and those who came forth from him, were given God's full authority to rule over all created things. We note that Satan did not confront Adam with his deceit but chose Eve as his target. Yes, Adam also fell into sin but by then the damage had already been done.

We must never fall for the impression that Adam was pretty much like one of us. We were born in sin with corruptible bodies from countless generations who have served their own interests, having our minds blinded by Satan, who is *'the god of this world'*. Adam before he sinned was a glorious being with unimaginable gifts.

That which began in Adam later became refocused in the person of faithful Abraham. God chose and set him apart to be *'a father of many nations'*. Romans 4:17-18. From Abraham came forth the nation of Israel who were, and will continue to be, the apple of God's eye. From him too came forth a multitude of peoples through Ishmael, who became the father of all the Arab nations.

Furthermore He promised Abraham that in him all nations of the earth would be blessed. God called to him from heaven, *"By Myself I have sworn, declares the Lord, because you have done this thing and have not withheld your son, your only son, indeed I will greatly bless you, and I will greatly multiply your seed as the stars of the heavens and as the sand which is on the seashore; and your seed shall possess the gate of their enemies. "In your seed all the nations of the earth shall be blessed, because you have obeyed My voice."* Genesis 22:16-18. What glorious and amazing promises are contained within this message to Abraham. *'In your seed'* of course refers to Christ. First the Jews and then the Gentiles have entered into the blessing as the seed of faithful Abraham.

God's intention for all those who have believed unto salvation is that every individual be perfectly recovered to God's design from the distortions brought about through sin. David expressed our former condition so well, *'Behold, I was brought forth in iniquity, And in sin my mother conceived me'*. Psalms 51:5. Yet God's intention for mankind in the death of our dear Lord Jesus was not simply to recover what had been lost through disobedience, but to make all things new and to provide for Him a spotless bride to be brought to Him, as Eve was brought to Adam, created out of His very substance.

The bride, the wife of the Lamb will be composed of all those recovered and perfected members of Adam's seed, both Jew and Gentile, brought together to be the ultimate centrepiece of the new heavens and new earth where forever she will display the glory of God. It all started with one perfect and magnificent man; namely

Adam. It will end with that which was shown to the apostle John; the new Jerusalem, the eternal dwelling place of God. *'Then one of the seven angels who had the seven bowls full of the seven last plagues came and spoke with me, saying, "Come here, I will show you the bride, the wife of the Lamb." And he carried me away in the Spirit to a great and high mountain, and showed me the holy city, Jerusalem, coming down out of heaven from God, having the glory of God....'* Revelation 21:9-11.

In the ages that lie between Adam and the new Jerusalem there have been two monumentally important turning points. Firstly the coming of the promised seed in the person of the Lord Jesus and all that He accomplished through His death on the cross; secondly the gift of the Holy Spirit to dwell within all who believe unto salvation and His power and authority given to the church, the body of Christ, which will one day be His bride, His wife.

Somewhat hidden away in John's gospel is a statement which the Holy Spirit gave the apostle which adds far deeper significance to the prophecy of Caiaphas the high priest. *'Now he* (Caiaphas) *did not say this on his own initiative, but being high priest that year, he prophesied that Jesus was going to die for the nation, and not for the nation only, but in order that He might also gather together into one the children of God who are scattered abroad'.* John 11:52-53. God's ultimate goal is that just as all mankind came from one, Adam, so all those of Adam's perfected seed will be brought together to compose the one wife of the Lamb. The means and process by which this is achieved is central within the eternal plan and purpose of God.

In the book of Revelation are described two phases of this gathering *'together into one'*. The first phase is found in Revelation 19:7-9 in connection with the marriage supper of the Lamb, in which those of all the ages who have been perfected by the Holy Spirit will participate. *"....His wife has made herself ready."* Revelation 19:7, NKJV. The essential qualification for anyone to be invited is that we 'have made ourselves ready'.

How much misinformation or lack of understanding of what the Lord requires exists today among believers in Jesus. So adamant are many that all our works are in vain that their faith rests on false hopes. Jesus has done it all on the cross they say. *'Thy will be done on earth'* is prayed by such as these as a general and distant hope rather than as an acknowledgment of *'Thy will be done'* right now in me. Progress in readiness is a moment by moment issue of critical importance. Our frequent prayer must be "Thy will be done in my thoughts." "Thy will be done in my words." "Thy will be done in all my deeds and actions." "Thy will be done in my behaviour and my deportment." These works wrought in Jesus are the ones we must perform in order to 'make ourselves ready'.

The following admonition of the apostle Paul must be comprehended and obeyed, *'So then, my beloved, just as you have always obeyed, not as in my presence only, but now much more in my absence, work out your salvation with fear and trembling; for it is God who is at work in you, both to will and to work for His good pleasure.* Philippians 2:12-13. Note that the word says *'work out your salvation'* not 'work for your salvation'. The latter is futile and worthless. Have we yet made it our irrevocable decision to live each moment *'with fear and trembling'* because of the Majesty within who is at work in us? He, the Spirit of Truth, can only perform His work if He has complete freedom to do so and that must be the reason for our frequent, yea constant prayer, *"Thy will be done."*

The evidence of our commitment to the Lord Jesus is the peace we have within, the joy in us that cannot be suppressed and the love that burns in our heart for Him. *'For I am convinced that neither death, nor life, nor angels, nor principalities, nor things present, nor things to come, nor powers, nor height, nor depth, nor any other created thing, will be able to separate us from the love of God, which is in Christ Jesus our Lord'.* Romans 8:38-39.

Matthew 25:1-13 records a parable of the Lord Jesus that will help to clarify what we have been presenting in this chapter. The parable of the ten virgins is well known, yet perhaps less well understood. Five of the virgins are prudent and five others are foolish. There is no difference in their situation. They all have had their lamps lit. They all have slept because the bridegroom is delayed in his coming. They all hear the *'shout, 'Behold, the bridegroom! Come out to meet him.'* They all awake and trim their lamps. What qualifies the prudent to be ready to meet the bridegroom is one thing and one thing only, they have an extra portion of oil. We read *'....the prudent took oil in flasks along with their lamps'*. Matthew 25:5. Meanwhile the lamps of the foolish virgins were going out and they were told by the prudent virgins that they must go and buy oil. While the foolish virgins were seeking to buy oil the bridegroom came and the prudent virgins went in with the bridegroom to the marriage supper – *'and the door was shut'*. When the Lord shuts the door no one can open it.

The lamps of all ten virgins were lit. *'The spirit of man is the lamp of the Lord, Searching all the innermost parts of his being'*. Proverbs 20:27. To have their lamp lit surely means that their spirit has been made alive. Thus all ten virgins are born again of the Spirit of God. The issue wasn't that the foolish virgins had no oil but that they did not have enough oil.

"Now while the bridegroom was delaying, they all got drowsy and began to sleep." Matthew 25:5. Sleep here indicates that all ten virgins had experienced the sleep of physical death.

"But at midnight there was a shout, 'Behold, the bridegroom! Come out to meet him.'" Matthew 25:6. This will be a critical moment for these virgins for they must have enough oil to keep their lamp burning brightly until the bridegroom arrives. A flask full of oil bespeaks a soul fully transformed by the Holy Spirit; a life that has been made ready during the time of diligent preparation. Five were found ready and five were unprepared; their lamps were going out. Those who have made themselves ready comprise the wife spoken of in Revelation 19:7 who thus receive an invitation to *'the marriage supper of the Lamb'*.

Of the seed of Adam all those who have overcome, both of the Old and the New Testament eras, will have made themselves ready and thus, as perfectly completed works of God, are invited to attend the marriage supper. They will be ushered in with their Bridegroom as individual precious stones ready to be fitted together to be made an eternal being who, at this great event, will be displayed as the wife of the Lamb, dressed in *'fine linen, bright and clean'*. The material of her wedding garment has been put together stitch by stitch; each stitch represents a righteous act of one of those who comprise His wife.

We might use an analogy with the building of Solomon's temple in Jerusalem. The stones were prepared in the quarry. When perfectly completed they were taken to the temple site where they found their foreordained place in the structure. No stone left the quarry until it was perfect. In the same way no foolish virgin will be included in the new Jerusalem, the eternal dwelling place of God, until the full price for the oil has been paid. We are not informed in Scripture how this will be accomplished but we do know the location; *'in outer darkness; in that place there is weeping and gnashing of teeth'*.

'For by grace you have been saved through faith, and this not of yourselves; it is the gift of God; not of works that no one should boast. For we are His masterpiece, created in Christ Jesus for good works, which God prepared beforehand in order that we would walk in them'. Ephesians 2:8-10, Recovery Version. Verses 8 and 9 are well known and treasured by countless individuals who have found living faith in Jesus, yet verse 10 which continues the theme is somewhat overlooked. The whole passage taken together is very important to understand because it contains some vital truths for all who desire to follow the Lord fully.

To have been *'saved through faith'* is *'not of works'*. Likewise, that *'we are His masterpiece created in Christ Jesus'* is *'for good works which God prepared beforehand in order that we would walk in them'*. According to these verses the only works that God desires from us are the ones planned for us when we were foreknown as being His own before the foundation of the world. How amazing this is. There is no possible way that any individual could 'walk in these works' except by the indwelling Holy Spirit in utter submission to the will of God.

What or who is God's masterpiece? The short answer is *'we are'*. But this question deserves a fuller and more complete explanation. At the dawn of eternity future, His masterpiece will be unveiled before all the new creation in the second and final phase in which all the now perfected ones will be *'gathered together into one'* to be *'the bride, the wife of the Lamb'*. At the dawn of eternity future she will have been *'made ready'* as the new Jerusalem which will descend out of heaven from God. Those who one thousand years earlier had comprised *'the wife of the Lamb'* will be greatly increased in number by those who, back then, were foolish virgins who will now have paid the full price for the oil they had failed to acquire during the time allotted to them on earth.

To the human mind the Trinity of the Father, Son and Holy Spirit being One God cannot be comprehended, yet it is so. This is the expression of God's very nature and being. Under the same principle may we most humbly propose that the wife of the Lamb will be one wife, yet built together from many individual parts. Each individual who comprises her, having been *'built up in Him'* to be His one wife will have full awareness of being His wife.*

When all the many parts have been fused together the size of each part, whether smaller or greater will be irrelevant. The size of each part will be as the size of the whole, whether of the wife of the Lamb at the marriage supper or of *'the bride, the wife of the Lamb'* at the dawn of eternity.

Our ascendancy from the deepest pit of sin and depravity to the unimaginable heights of glory as the wife, the beloved of the Lamb of God, has been made possible by the greatest act of love that will ever be expressed – that of the incarnation of God's Son and the awful horror of having all mankind's sin and corruption laid upon Him.

May the writer, and all who shall read these words enter deeply into the import of this fact and never allow it to leave our highest consciousness until we shall meet Jesus our Saviour, Lord and Husband and rest forever in His embrace.

---

*See 'Addendum 'B' – Ultimate Unity' at the back of the book.

CHAPTER 50
BEHOLD A WHITE HORSE

Scripture references: Matthew 20:20-28, Matthew 23:10-12, Revelation 19:7-9,11-21.

In our fallen society and culture the self is constantly striving to have power and control over others; to possess more than others; to be recognized as more gifted or more important than others. There is no end to its insatiable appetite for more.

Matthew 20:20-28. *'Then the mother of the sons of Zebedee came to Jesus with her sons, bowing down and making a request of Him. And He said to her, "What do you wish?" She said to Him, "Command that in Your kingdom these two sons of mine may sit one on Your right and one on Your left." But Jesus answered, "You do not know what you are asking. Are you able to drink the cup that I am about to drink?" They said to Him, "We are able." He said to them, "My cup you shall drink; but to sit on My right and on My left, this is not Mine to give, but it is for those for whom it has been prepared by My Father." And hearing this, the ten became indignant with the two brothers. But Jesus called them to Himself and said, "You know that the rulers of the Gentiles lord it over them, and their great men exercise authority over them. "It is not this way among you, but whoever wishes to become great among you shall be your servant, and whoever wishes to be first among you shall be your slave; just as the Son of Man did not come to be served, but to serve, and to give His life a ransom for many."*

This passage of Scripture is quoted in full because it reveals some vital principles concerning the kingdom of heaven. As we approach the end of Gentile rule on earth and the sure return of Jesus Christ is so near we must heed the words proclaimed by John the Baptist, Jesus and later by His disciples, *'the kingdom of heaven is at hand'*. The kingdom of this world will soon become the kingdom of our God and of His Christ. This eternal kingdom came to earth in the person of Jesus and it has expanded as every new believer in Jesus has entered it through the new birth.

The unfulfilled ambitions of parents are often reflected in what they desire for their children. The mother of James and John came with them to Jesus to ask that her two sons be the most prominent in His coming kingdom. Jesus answer was simply to the affect that it will be His Father's decision. The remaining ten disciples became indignant because they also wanted to be the greatest. Even though we may be *'able to drink the cup'* of suffering Jesus spoke about, it will be He who will receive the glory and we who will *'be glorified with Him'*. Romans 8:17.

What a contrast there is between what we experience during our time on earth under the hierarchical structures of power and authority, wielded often heavy-handedly and unjustly, compared with the application of authority and greatness in the kingdom. For, *'whoever wishes to become great among you shall be your servant, and whoever wishes to be first among you shall be your slave; just as the Son of Man did not come to be served, but to serve, and to give His life a ransom for many."* Matthew 20:27-28.

"Do not be called leaders; for One is your Leader, that is, Christ. "But the greatest among you shall be your servant. "Whoever exalts himself shall be humbled; and whoever humbles himself shall be exalted". Matthew 23:10-12. From the moment an individual is born again, that new creature in Christ has a new Master who has absolute authority over every thought, word and deed. However, He does not demand obedience but He waits for the soul to surrender all its rights and simply to acknowledge *'Your will be done'*.

A bond slave of Jesus Christ will have surrendered all his choices in favour of performing the will of God, in all circumstances, out of love for Him. Such is the condition and expression of the lives of those who have overcome in Jesus. Responsible alone to Him their constant gaze is on no other.

At the marriage supper of the Lamb His wife, composed of all these overcoming saints, will be presented to her Husband and He will be presented to her as her eternal very great reward. This amazing fact and the wonder of it must surely melt our hearts with love at His feet as we reflect upon so unimaginably wondrous a prize.

The wedding garment in which His wife is adorned will proclaim to Him her readiness, for it will have been fabricated stitch by stitch by each righteous act of every saint of those composed together as His wife. Her Bridegroom's all-seeing eyes will perceive every single stitch of obedience in her wedding garment. He will know what righteous act created it and which saint it was who performed His will because of love for Him. What a moment to be recalled forever that will be, to be wholly approved and adored by the gaze of God.

One wonders how many of those, whose seemingly small acts of obedience worked their contribution into this wonderful garment, will be filled with astonishment that, what they regarded as so little done for Jesus sake, was rewarded with so much. With much reluctance we must now move on beyond that unspeakable moment and the unimaginable joy and celebration of the marriage supper.

He who was so lately a husband has now in Revelation 19:11-13 taken the role of the commander of an army, for we read as follows. *'And I saw heaven opened, and behold, a white horse, and He who sat on it is called Faithful and True, and in righteousness He judges and wages war. His eyes are a flame of fire, and on His head are many diadems; and He has a name written on Him which no one knows except Himself. He is clothed with a robe dipped in blood, and His name is called The Word of God'*. The final act of the dark night of the great tribulation is about to give way to a day of victory whose ray of hope and righteousness shall know no end. But, before that, those who have held the earth in dreadful bondage must be defeated and dealt with.

'Behold, a white horse....' How dramatic will be the appearance of this white horse out of an opened heaven. *He who sat on it is called Faithful and True'*. The same eyes as *'a flame of fire'* that the apostle John saw are now turned towards Satan and His cohorts to bring their reign of terror to a final conclusion. His robe is dipped in the precious blood that cleanses from every sin yet, displayed in the face of the evil one, Satan, the blood will provide the evidence of his final defeat wrought long before on the cross. The One before whom every knee must bow will be appropriately adorned with many diadems and what He speaks will bring hope eternal to His own and everlasting doom to those who have opposed His will.

'And the armies which are in heaven, clothed in fine linen, white and clean, were following Him on white horses'. Revelation 19:14.

'The wife of the Lamb,' so recently enjoying the marriage supper, is now following her Bridegroom as a company on white horses of *'the called and chosen and faithful'*. They are *'clothed in fine linen white and clean'*. The wedding garment of testimony to their righteous acts has now been individualized as a testimony of their purity in the face of ultimate evil. In their life they had withstood Satan. Now, as a company of the faithful, they follow their husband to confront and deal with the enemy and all who follow him.

'And I saw the beast and the kings of the earth and their armies assembled to make war against Him who sat on the horse and against His army. And the beast was seized, and with him the false prophet who performed the signs in his presence, by which he deceived those who had received the mark of the beast and those who worshiped his image; these two were thrown alive into the lake of fire which burns with brimstone. And the rest were killed with the sword which came from the mouth of Him who sat on the horse, and all the birds were filled with their flesh'. Revelation 19:19-21. Just as the Lord Jesus had withstood the forty days temptation in the wilderness and had once and for all destroyed the works of the devil on the cross, so now the Victor over sin and death will be unrelenting in bringing judgment upon Satan, the beast and the false prophet and death to all those who chose the rule of evil in deliberate defiance of God and His holiness. The latter must face the judgment of the great white throne. The beast and the false prophet will be *'thrown alive into the lake of fire which burns with brimstone'*.

As to those *'called and chosen and faithful'* their role as warriors with their divine husband had been made sure long before, when they had deliberately made their irrevocable choice to become bond slaves of Jesus Christ.

HAST THOU HEARD HIM

Hast thou heard Him, seen Him, known Him!
Is not thine a captured heart?
Chief among ten thousand own Him;
Joyful choose the better part.

Chorus
Captivated by His beauty,
Worthy tribute haste to bring;
Let His peerless worth constrain thee,
Crown Him now unrivalled King.

Idols once they won thee, charmed thee,
Lovely things of time and sense;
Gilded thus does sin disarm thee,
Honeyed lest they turn thee thence.

What has stripped the seeming beauty
From the idols of the earth?
Not a sense of right or duty,
But the sight of peerless worth.

Draw and win and fill completely,
Till the cup o'erflow the brim;
What have we to do with idols
Who have companied with Him?

Ora Rowan, 1834-1879

CHAPTER 51
THOSE WHO HAD BEEN BEHEADED

Scripture references: Genesis 4:3-12, Hebrews 11:4, Genesis 4:25-26, John 12:27-32, John 8:44, Acts 7:51-53, Revelation 6:9-11, Revelation 20:4, Hebrews 12:3-4.

Immediately following the account of Adam and Eve being cast out of the Garden of Eden, right at the beginning of Genesis chapter 4, we are informed that they became parents to two sons, Cain and Abel. Details of their childhood are not recorded. The first information we are given about them is that each brought an offering to God.

Genesis 4:3-5. *'So it came about in the course of time that Cain brought an offering to the Lord of the fruit of the ground'*. Cain's sacrifice resulted from the work of his hands, by the sweat of his brow, and the Lord *'had no regard'* for Cain's offering. *'So Cain became very angry and his countenance fell'*.

'Abel, on his part also brought of the firstlings of his flock and of their fat portions'. *'And the Lord had regard for Abel and for his offering;* Abel presented to the Lord that of which He approved. Hebrews 9:22 informs us that *'without shedding of blood there is no forgiveness'*. The shed blood of an unblemished firstling from Abel's flock prefigured the shed blood of the Lamb of God on the cross for the sin of the whole world.

Genesis 4:8. *'Cain told Abel his brother'* that God had rejected his offering. *'And it came about when they were in the field, that Cain rose up against Abel his brother and killed him'*. Once sin came upon all mankind it did not take long for death to follow. Resentment that his younger brother Abel's sacrifice was accepted by the Lord and his was rejected caused such hatred and jealousy in Cain that he rose up and killed his brother and thereby committed the first murder.

'By faith Abel offered to God a better sacrifice than Cain, through which he obtained the testimony that he was righteous, God testifying about his gifts, and through faith, though he is dead, he still speaks. Hebrews 11:4. Abel's name is among those of the faithful overcoming saints of Hebrews chapter 11. Indeed, Abel had

become the first martyr. His testimony of righteousness still lives on, for *'through faith, though he is dead, he still speaks'*.

As soon as unrighteousness was found in Satan, He became utterly unrighteous. When the love of God became totally absent from him, Satan became the embodiment of hatred. When the light of God was taken from him, Satan became impenetrable darkness. Cain was his first tool to do away with righteous Abel.

However, the Lord gave Adam and his wife Eve another son and she *'named him Seth, for, she said, "God has appointed me another offspring in place of Abel, for Cain killed him."* Once to Seth a son was born named Enosh, *'Then men began to call upon the name of the Lord'*. Genesis 4:25-26. The line from Adam to Jesus was established through Seth, thus those righteous ones living at that time were confident in the Lord that the promised seed would certainly come that would 'bruise the serpent's head'. We are told that calling upon the name of the Lord brings salvation. *'For there is no difference between Jew and Gentile - the same Lord is Lord of all and richly blesses all who call on him, for, "Everyone who calls on the name of the Lord will be saved."* Romans 10:12-13, NIV.

'But when the fullness of the time came, God sent forth His Son, born of a woman, born under the Law....' Galatians 4:4. Soon after the birth of Jesus, following the visit of the magi, *'an angel of the Lord appeared to Joseph in a dream and said, "Get up! Take the Child and His mother and flee to Egypt'*. Matthew 2:13. After they had departed for Egypt Herod *'sent and slew all the male children who were in Bethlehem and all its vicinity, from two years old and under, according to the time which he had determined from the magi'*. In the foreordained plan and purpose of God, Jesus was destined to die, but it was to be in God's chosen manner and in accordance with His timing.

It was more than thirty years later that Jesus became acutely aware that, in the plan and purpose of His Father, the time was approaching that He would be offered as the ultimate sacrifice for the sin of all mankind. His words were, "Now My soul has become troubled; and what shall I say, 'Father, save Me from this hour'? But for this purpose I came to this hour. "Father, glorify Your *name." Then a voice came out of heaven: "I have both glorified it, and will glorify it again." So the crowd of people who stood by and heard it were saying that it had thundered; others were saying, "An angel has spoken to Him." Jesus answered and said, "This voice has not come for My sake, but for your sakes. "Now judgment is upon this world; now the ruler of this world will be cast out. "And I, if I am lifted up from the earth, will draw all men to Myself."* John 12: 27-32.

Satan saw the condemnation and crucifixion of Jesus as his final blow to thwart God's will and purpose. All those of a pure heart see it for what it was – murder of Him who was and is and ever shall be the epitome of righteousness and innocence. To serve his ends, Satan instilled the deepest hatred for Jesus in the hearts of the Pharisees. Jesus confronted them, discerning exactly what was in their hearts, *"You are of your father the devil, and you want to do the desires of your father. He was a murderer from the beginning...."* John 8:44. It had been Satan who instigated Cain to slay his righteous brother Abel.

The first documented Christian martyr was Stephen who, after he had regaled the Jewish leaders with a dissertation of God's grace and provision for the nation of Israel, brought home to them the awfulness of their rejection of Jesus. He boldly told them, *"You men who are stiff-necked and uncircumcised in heart and ears are always resisting the Holy Spirit; you are doing just as your fathers did." Which one of the prophets did your fathers not persecute? They killed those who had previously announced the coming of the Righteous One, whose betrayers and murderers you have now become; you who received the law as ordained by angels, and yet did not keep it."* Acts 7:51-53. Those who heard these words gnashed their teeth at Stephen, *'But being full of the Holy Spirit, he gazed intently into heaven and saw the glory of God, and Jesus standing at the right hand of God; and he said, "Behold, I see the heavens opened up and the Son of Man standing at the right hand of God."* Acts 7:55-56. Yes! When Stephen was about to be martyred Jesus arose from His throne and stood *'at the right hand of God'* to honour His faithful servant.

God bestows special recognition and honour upon those who become martyrs because of their faith and their testimony to Him. *'When the Lamb broke the fifth seal, I saw underneath the altar the souls of those who had been slain because of the word of God, and because of the testimony which they had maintained; and they cried out with a loud voice, saying, "How long, O Lord, holy and true, will You refrain from judging and avenging our blood on those who dwell on the earth?" And there was given to each of them a white robe; and they were told that they should rest for a little while longer, until the number of their fellow servants and their brethren who were to be killed even as they had been, would be completed also'*. Revelation 6:9-11.

Against the testimony of God and His Son, the Lord Jesus Christ, Satan has the bitterest hatred. The cry of all those martyred for their faith throughout all the ages rings out *"How long, O Lord, holy and true, will You refrain from judging and avenging our blood on those who dwell on the earth?"*

God will have a special reward for those who have been beheaded during the great tribulation. *'Then I saw thrones, and they sat on them, and judgment was given to them. And I saw the souls of those who had been beheaded because of their testimony of Jesus and because of the word of God, and those who had not worshiped the beast or his image, and had not received the mark on their forehead and on their hand; and they came to life and reigned with Christ for a thousand years.* Revelation 20:4. These ones are destined to join with all those martyrs throughout all the ages back to Abel, and with all the other overcoming saints, to reign with Jesus on the earth during His millennial kingdom.

Many believers who will have been left behind on earth will choose to pay the price to be overcomers by willingly accepting martyrdom for their faith in Jesus during the final three and a half years of the great tribulation. Although this choice may seem terrifying to us, it demonstrates on the one hand the grace of God to those who had not made themselves ready and thus did not receive the earlier upward call of God; on the other hand it emphasizes our Lord's demand that we give our all now during our earthly life.

'For consider Him who has endured such hostility by sinners against Himself, so that you will not grow weary and lose heart. You have not yet resisted to the point of shedding blood in your striving against sin; Hebrews 12:3-4. The writer and perhaps most of those who will read these words may not yet have *'resisted to the point of shedding blood'.*

May we pause in silent gratitude before passing beyond this chapter that we may honour in our hearts our dearest Lord Jesus Christ for His greatest of all sacrifice. May we also give thanks to God for all those, from righteous Abel onwards, who have *'resisted to the point of shedding blood in striving against sin'.*

CHAPTER 52
THE JUDGMENT SEAT OF CHRIST

Scripture references: Galatians 6:7-9 AMP, Psalm 119:9-11, Galatians 6:8-9 AMP, 2 Corinthians 5:9-10, 1 Corinthians 3:11-15, Matthew 25:30, 2 Corinthians 6:1-2 NKJV.

'Do not be deceived and deluded and misled; God will not allow Himself to be sneered at (scorned, disdained, or mocked by mere pretensions or professions, or by His precepts being set aside.) [He inevitably deludes himself who attempts to delude God.] *'For whatever a man sows, that and that only is what he will reap'*. Galatians 6:7, AMP. The Amplified Version brings out the real impact and finer points of this verse. It leaves no middle ground in which anyone may find temporary relief. If a believer or indeed an unbeliever sets God's precepts aside then this is tantamount to treating the Almighty with contempt.

'Your word I have treasured in my heart, That I may not sin against You'. Psalms 119:11. Surely we must be familiar with and believe the Scriptures in their entirety and live by their precepts in the light freely given to us by the Holy Spirit. We cannot simply rely on being spoon fed portions of Scripture provided on a Sunday morning or indeed at any other time. Jesus told the Pharisees, *'You search the Scriptures because you think that in them you have eternal life; it is these that testify about Me; and you are unwilling to come to Me so that you may have life'*. John 5:39-40. If we would have life, His divine life, then we must come to Jesus, diligently searching the Scriptures for *'in them you have eternal life'*.

'For whatever a man sows, that and that only is what he will reap'. For so many, life on earth today is a matter of 'scraping through' or 'getting by' and it may be a severe challenge to accept that no slippage from God's standards and precepts is permissible. What each of us sows during our brief sojourn on the earth will be the evidence presented at the judgment seat of Christ. There will be no observers on that unique occasion. He will be the judge and each one who has come to Him for salvation through faith will take their turn as the plaintiff. That will be the all-important occasion when what we have sown, and that only, will determine whether we will

receive His invitation to the marriage supper of the Lamb or have the door shut against us.

For he who sows to his own flesh (lower nature, sensuality) will from the flesh reap decay and ruin and destruction, but he who sows to the Spirit will from the Spirit reap eternal life'. Galatians 6:8, AMP. Surely these words could not be more specific. Overcomers are those who find and enter in Christ through the narrow door that leads away to life. Matthew 7:13-14. May the Lord's grace be upon us that we be among those who deliberately make it their choice to 'sow to the Spirit'. *'And let us not lose heart and grow weary and faint in acting nobly and doing right, for in due time and at the appointed season we shall reap, if we do not loosen and relax our courage and faint'.* Galatians 6:9, AMP.

'Therefore we also have as our ambition, whether at home or absent, to be pleasing to Him'. 2 Corinthians 5:9. That which Paul states to be *'our ambition'* is both God's requirement from His created beings and their greatest joy to fulfil. Each redeemed soul was created for the enjoyment of its Creator and its foreordained purpose is to please Him.

We may receive Jesus as our Saviour yet it is only as we acknowledge Him as Lord that we shall enter our true destiny in Him. At the judgment seat of Christ no doubt will remain as to whether He has reigned as undisputed Lord of our life. The *'deeds in the body'* will reveal exactly what have been our heart's decisions. If our ambition has been as Paul's *'to be pleasing to Him'* then our *'deeds in the body'* will testify to the strength of our desire to please Jesus and of our submission to Him as Lord.

For no man can lay a foundation other than the one which is laid, which is Jesus Christ. 1 Corinthians 3:11. Every thought we have indulged; every word we have spoken; every action we have taken; all will comprise the evidence of the foundation of them. All our sins and shortcomings are under the cleansing blood of Jesus and will be remembered no more. Yet even our best of intentions will amount only to *'wood, hay, straw'.* For our deeds in the body 'according to what we have done', if built on the foundation of

Christ, will attest to the fact that His will has consistently been performed in and through us.

There is a direct connection between the passage of Scripture we have just quoted from 1 Corinthians and that quoted earlier from 2 Corinthians. The *'deeds in the body'* directly relate to the fruit, *'gold, silver, precious stones, wood, hay, straw'*. There will be no excuses at the judgment seat of Christ. The fire will do its work and what is left will reveal what our life has amounted to. But we note especially that whatever is approved, whatever is precious and fireproof has been built on the one and only true foundation, which is Christ Jesus the Lord.

Sadly, for countless numbers of those who have come to salvation by faith there may be little to show for it at the judgment seat of Christ. Worldliness, complacency and indolence will have consumed vast amounts of time which will have been lost for the one who wasted it, lost for the kingdom and, above all, lost for Jesus. All foolish virgins will be compelled to buy the oil of the Holy Spirit and be denied participation in the marriage supper of the Lamb. They will be turned away at the door. The Lord Jesus only recognizes those who have been transformed into His likeness. Wise virgins will qualify because they paid the full price for an extra portion of the oil of the Holy Spirit during their time on earth and thereby they have been perfected. All those who are invited and welcomed to the marriage supper will also rule with the Lord for a thousand years on the earth.

Many who have received one or more talents from the Lord may have been deceived into believing that, just as the entry into salvation is free, so the entry into eternity's full enjoyment with Jesus is also without cost. Yet the Lord requires a return from His gifting. Many after entering the gates of salvation through grace may have simply warmed a pew, bench or chair, week after week and have never experienced the glory of anointed speaking on behalf of Jesus; their part in building up the body of Christ will have been largely or completely neglected. Their sentence will amount to being cast *'into outer darkness; in that place there will be weeping and gnashing of teeth'*. Matthew 25:30. However, because God's grace is so great there is yet hope, for *'If any man's work is burned up, he will suffer loss; but he himself will be saved, yet so as through fire'*. 1 Corinthians 3:15.

Our lifespan of three score years and ten, or even four score years and more, is given us that we may abandon ourselves to the Lord Jesus that He may transform us into His likeness. For this very purpose we who believe unto salvation were given the indwelling Holy Spirit. The alternative of spending every moment of every day for a thousand years in outer darkness, separated from the Lord, is truly an awful prospect.

The *'weeping and gnashing of teeth'* will arise from the torment of having seen and experienced the Lord Jesus *'just as He is'* when appearing before His judgment seat. Those in such dreadful pain and sorrow will be filled with the deepest regret not to have responded to His great love by doing His will instead of serving their own desires. Such ones will realize too late how much of their time was spent on self-serving and meaningless activity and will acknowledge the justice of their sentence.

May the Lord be gracious to us that we may open our eyes to the issues of this life. In these last days, the Lord is urgently reminding His own what He desires of them; that they may obey Him, live for Him and please Him. *'Behold, now is the accepted time; behold, now is the day of salvation'*. 2 Corinthians 6:1-2. Transformation into the perfect likeness of Jesus is the goal of salvation. Built together in seamless unity, all the transformed ones will one day comprise *'the bride, the wife of the Lamb'*.

The hymn that follows is a deep reminder of the critical importance of fully surrendering our life, every moment of it, to the Lord Jesus. At the judgment seat of Christ it will be absolutely apparent that *'there is no creature hidden from His sight, but all things are open and laid bare to the eyes of Him with whom we have to do'*. Hebrews 4:13.

ONLY ONE LIFE

Only one life, yes only one,
Soon will its fleeting hours be done;
Then, in 'that day' my Lord to meet,
And stand before His Judgement seat;
Only one life, 'twill soon be past,
Only what's done for Christ will last.

Only one life, a few brief years,
Each with its burdens, hopes, and fears;
Each with its days I must fulfill,
Living for self or in His will;
Only one life, 'twill soon be past,
Only what's done for Christ will last.

Give me Father, a purpose deep,
In joy or sorrow Thy word to keep;
Faithful and true whate'er the strife,
Pleasing Thee in my daily life;
Only one life, 'twill soon be past,
Only what's done for Christ will last.

Only one life, yes only one,
Now let me say, "Thy will be done";
And when at last I'll hear the call,
I know I'll say "'twas worth it all";
Only one life, 'twill soon be past,
Only what's done for Christ will last.

C.T.Studd

1860 – 1931

CHAPTER 53
THE STONE THAT STRUCK THE STATUE

Scripture references: Matthew 16:13-18, Luke 20:17-18, Daniel 2:1-49, Revelation 11:15-18, Revelation 20:6, Ephesians 5:25-32.

Now when Jesus came into the district of Caesarea Philippi, He was asking His disciples, "Who do people say that the Son of Man is?" Matthew 16:13. In their response His disciples gave examples of what people were saying about Him. Jesus followed that up with a more penetrating question. *'He said to them, "But who do you say that I am?" Simon Peter answered, "You are the Christ, the Son of the living God." And Jesus said to him, "Blessed are you, Simon Barjona, because flesh and blood did not reveal this to you, but My Father who is in heaven.* Matthew 16:15-17. This divinely inspired answer from Peter allowed Jesus the opportunity to inform Peter and all His disciples what is His role and position in the plan and purpose of God and what would be Peter's role in relation to His.

Jesus continued, *'And I tell you, you are Peter* [Greek, Petros - a large piece of rock], *and on this rock* [Greek, petra - a huge rock like Gibraltar] *I will build My church, and the gates of Hades* (the powers of the infernal region) *shall not overpower it* [or be strong to its detriment or hold out against it]. Matthew 16:18 AMP. If we did not have access to the Greek text it would be very difficult for us to understand this profound statement that Jesus was making to His disciples. He was telling them all, *'I will build My church'*, and I am the foundation upon which Peter and all others will be built.

One day, Jesus was teaching a crowd of people in the temple precincts when a company of Jewish leaders and elders approached Him. They asked Him by what authority He was teaching the people. He responded with a question that they dared not answer and then He recounted a parable about the owner of a vineyard that went on a journey and leased his vineyard while he was away. During his absence he sent them servants whom they beat and mistreated and then he finally sent his son in anticipation that they would surely receive him. However they cast his son out of the vineyard and killed him.

Those who listened to this story were dismayed. They agreed that severe retribution by the owner would be justified. *'But Jesus looked at them and said, "What then is this that is written: 'the stone which the builders rejected, this became the chief corner stone'? "Everyone who falls on that stone will be broken to pieces; but on whomever it falls, it will scatter him like dust."* Luke 20:17-18.

As we read accounts such as this we are in awe at the way Jesus was able to deflect a demanding question and use the opportunity to present an important divine truth. In effect He told them "I am the cornerstone that you builders have rejected. If you fall on that stone you will be broken, but if it falls on you, you will be crushed to dust and the wind will blow you away." We can understand from Jesus' statement that He, as 'a huge rock like Gibraltar', is the cornerstone of God's building. The Jewish leaders who should have been co-builders with God had rejected Jesus as the cornerstone.

In Daniel chapter 2 is an account of a dream given to Nebuchadnezzar, the great ruler of Babylon. This dream describes kingdoms and events during what Jesus would later describe as *'the times of the Gentiles'*. The dream started at the time of Nebuchadnezzar and ended with the setting up of *'the kingdom of our God and of His Christ'*.

'Nebuchadnezzar had dreams; and his spirit was troubled and his sleep left him'. The king gathered together his many advisors who represented a wide range of worldly wisdom. Even if they had been told the dream in detail it is doubtful whether the Chaldeans could have come up with an interpretation. In response to his request that they tell him both the dream and its interpretation they responded, *"there is no one else who could declare it to the king except gods, whose dwelling place is not with mortal flesh."* In this they were right of course, except that those they termed gods would have been as impotent to declare the dream as were these magicians and conjurors.

In his fury at the failure of his counsellors to recall for him his dream, the king ordered Arioch, his bodyguard, to round up all the wise men of Babylon and put them to death. Although Daniel and his friends had not been included among those called to advise the king they were not excluded from Nebuchadnezzar's edict. But Daniel persuaded Arioch to bring him before Nebchadnezzar and Daniel respectfully declared to the king *'there is a God in heaven who reveals secrets'*. Then Nebuchadnezzar granted Daniel the time he requested.

Daniel called together his three companions to beseech the Lord to disclose the dream and to provide a revelation of its meaning. *'Then the mystery was revealed to Daniel in a night vision. Then Daniel blessed the God of heaven'*. Daniel's expression of thanks to God is so eloquent. It reads like a psalm of David. What a man of God was Daniel! As we read and re-read his prayer our heart is full of praise to the Lord.

Daniel went in to Arioch...and spoke to him as follows: "Do not destroy the wise men of Babylon! Take me into the king's presence, and I will declare the interpretation to the king." How pleased and relieved must Arioch have been to present Daniel before King Nebuchadnezzar with the answer to the king's desperate desire to recall his dream and to receive its interpretation. How pleased also are we, at the end of times, to know the content of this defining dream and to be assured of its ultimate impending fulfilment.

No man could interpret this dream. *"However, there is a God in heaven who reveals mysteries, and He has made known to King Nebuchadnezzar what will take place in the latter days."* What a testimony to this pagan potentate! To God alone be the glory for every word that He gives us to speak on His behalf! Daniel now unveiled both the dream and its interpretation to the king, assuring him that the purpose of the revelation was that the king might understand the thoughts of his mind. This dream was no ordinary dream. It was given to Nebuchadnezzar by God and to all generations, including ours today.

Daniel's description of the great statue which Nebuchadnezzar saw in front of him was precise in every detail down to the *'feet partly of iron and partly of clay'*.

So awesome was the sight that, in his dream, Nebuchadnezzar continued looking, *until a stone was cut out without hands, and it struck the statue on its feet of iron and clay and crushed them.* Note that the stone, cut out by no visible means, struck the image on the feet. This caused the whole image, from the feet upwards to the head of gold to become like dust and it was blown away in the wind with not a trace left of it. May we again recall the words of Jesus quoted earlier in this chapter, *"Everyone who falls on that stone will be broken to pieces; but on whomever it falls, it will scatter him like dust."*

What or who then is the stone *'cut out without hands'* which strikes the image on the feet and which causes it to shatter into such tiny particles that the wind carries them away? Surely it is not a created object. It must be divine. *'Then the seventh angel sounded; and there were loud voices in heaven, saying, "The kingdom of the world has become the kingdom of our Lord and of His Christ; and He will reign forever and ever."* Revelation 11:15. The stone that falls from the heavens brings to an end all earthly authorities and establishes the rule of God *'forever and ever'*. This stone is none other than our mighty Saviour and Lord, Jesus Christ. At the instant of His coming all power and authority will be accorded to Him.

Yet there is more to be shown to us, for is Christ not the Head and is not His body the church? We read, *'But the stone....became a great mountain that filled the whole earth'*. The stone that *'was cut out without hands'* represents the complete Christ. It will be Christ and those who are His at His coming. *'Blessed and holy is the one who has a part in the first resurrection; over these the second death has no power, but they will be priests of God and of Christ and will reign with Him for a thousand years'*. Revelation 20:6. The full authority of God is expressed through Christ and shared with those who have *'a part in the first resurrection'*. This is the essence and substance of the mountain that fills the whole earth. Christ and the church is the *'great mystery'* of God.

'....because we are members of His body. For this reason a man shall leave his father and mother and shall be joined to his wife, and the two shall become one flesh. This mystery is great; but I am speaking with reference to Christ and the church'. Ephesians 5:30-32. Those who comprise the *'wife of the Lamb'* will reign with Him for a thousand years. During the millennial kingdom they, together

with their Lord, will be the expression of the *'great mystery'* which is described in Nebuchadnezzar's dream as *'a great mountain that filled the whole earth'*.

We are living in, or very close to, the days of the feet of the great image. Very soon the stone cut out without hands will do away with and replace forever man's authority and *"The kingdom of the world will become the kingdom of our Lord and of His Christ; and He will reign forever and ever."* Hallelujah!

May the Lord who reveals secrets make perfectly clear His message given through dreams and visions to those who humbly wait upon Him in simple trust.

CHAPTER 54
THE THOUSAND YEARS

Scripture references: Isaiah 24:1-23, Matthew 24:21-22, Revelation 6:1-12, Revelation 11:15-19, , Revelation 16:17-21, Isaiah 65:17-25, Romans 8:16-25.

Isaiah 24 is wholly concerned with catastrophic events that will come upon the world because of mankind's irresponsible and destructive behaviour. *'The earth is also polluted by its inhabitants, for they transgressed laws, violated statutes, broke the everlasting covenant. Therefore, a curse devours the earth, and those who live in it are held guilty. Therefore, the inhabitants of the earth are burned, and few men are left'.* Isaiah 24:5-6.

As we start to comprehend in this our day the appalling and seemingly irreversible damage mankind has inflicted upon our wondrous planet, our God provided home, we are aghast. The air, the land and the seas are heavily polluted and are steadily becoming more so.

However, we must remove our focus from the widespread and devastating effects of mankind's selfishness and greed so that we may uncover and identify the underlying reasons for these conditions. The words of Isaiah 24:5 are concise and damning, *'for they transgressed laws, violated statutes, broke the everlasting covenant'.* The root cause for the pollution and desecration of the earth is mankind's flagrant disregard for the laws and statutes of Almighty God and their rejection of His *'everlasting covenant'* of salvation to be found alone in Jesus Christ.

In one of the best loved verses of Scripture, John 3:16, is most clearly expressed God's side of His everlasting covenant and man's required response to this covenant. *"For God so loved the world, that He gave His only begotten Son, that whoever believes in Him shall not perish, but have eternal life."* God's provision through the voluntary death of His Son is eternal life which is made available to all who will believe in Him.

To believe in Jesus is not simply an act or event that provides a believer with eternal security. It demands from every believer a full and final commitment henceforth to follow Jesus alone, to follow no other, and persistently to do His will. In other words, to believe in Jesus as Saviour must result in absolute obedience to Him as Lord.

There are two categories of individual who break the everlasting covenant; believers who walk *'according to the flesh'* and those unsaved who reject the person and authority of Jesus Christ. Those who walk *'according to the Spirit'* are, and always have been, a very small minority.

Immediately before the return of our Lord and Saviour to reign forever and ever, that dreadful event will have occurred known as the *'great tribulation'*. The words of Jesus graphically describe this time. *"For then there will be a great tribulation, such as has not occurred since the beginning of the world until now, nor ever will. "Unless those days had been cut short, no life would have been saved; but for the sake of the elect those days will be cut short".* Matthew 24:21-22.

Not only will the earth have been polluted and desecrated by mankind, but a series of catastrophic disasters will have been let loose upon the whole world during those final forty two lunar months, or three and a half years. The earth to which Jesus returns will indeed by then be in a state of unimaginable desecration and destruction; all this having come about as a result of the sin of mankind.

The book of Revelation describes the judgments of God in three phases – seven seals, seven trumpets and seven bowls. There is a pattern of ever increasing intensity between these three as the return of the Lord Jesus grows closer. Contained within the seventh seal are the seven trumpets. Contained within the seventh trumpet are the seven bowls. Seven is a divine number showing without doubt that all these judgments come from God Himself.

The first four seals represent four riders on four horses. Each horse and its rider is descriptive of something major that characterizes the time period in which it occurs.

The first is a rider on a white horse *'and he who sat on it had a bow; and a crown was given to him, and he went out conquering and to conquer.* Revelation 6:2. This first horse and its rider represent the preaching of the *'gospel of the kingdom'*. The bow is symbolic of the divine power that is embodied in the message and the crown given to the rider is symbolic of the victory that is assured as its outcome. No arrows are mentioned because God's arrows are the messengers He chooses and sends forth to spread His message to all the nations. Without the power of the bow the message will not reach the target. *"This gospel of the kingdom shall be preached in the whole world as a testimony to all the nations, and then the end will come."* Matthew 24:14.

The *'gospel of the kingdom'* tries men's hearts to see if they will repent of their evil condition and receive God's great salvation through Christ. *"He who believes in Him is not judged; he who does not believe has been judged already, because he has not believed in the name of the only begotten Son of God."* John 3:18.

The second is a rider on a red horse, *'and to him who sat on it, it was granted to take peace from the earth, and that men would slay one another; and a great sword was given to him'*. Revelation 6:4. This horse and its rider surely represent war, conflict and the shedding of blood.

The third is *'a black horse; and he who sat on it had a pair of scales in his hand'*. Revelation 6:5. This black horse and its rider represent famine. *'And I heard something like a voice .... saying, "A quart of wheat for a denarius, and three quarts of barley for a denarius; and do not damage the oil and the wine."*

The fourth is *'an ashen horse; and he who sat on it had the name Death; and Hades was following with him. Authority was given to them over a fourth of the earth, to kill with sword and with famine and with pestilence and by the wild beasts of the earth'*. Revelation 6:8. The great multitude whose destiny is Hades are all those who have *'not believed in the name of the only begotten Son of God'*. How aptly it is said of this vast unregenerate throng that *'they transgressed laws, violated statutes, broke the everlasting covenant.* These are deliberate acts of rebellion.

From the great day of Pentecost, when that first company of believers in Jesus were clothed with power from on high, the bow in the hand of the first rider has been thrusting forth chosen and empowered messengers into His harvest to proclaim to the ends of the earth the great *'gospel of the kingdom'*. Wherever this message has come it has brought peace, abundance and the shared life of God to those who have received it, yet often in the face of much persecution. But wherever this divine life has been refused and rejected there has followed war, famine and death. What despoiling and destruction of our God-provided earth has occurred as a result of the willfulness and selfishness of mankind.

These first four seals, commonly known as 'the four horses of the apocalypse', have continued over a large stretch of history. They will continue until the middle of the seven year tribulation period. From the commencement of the great tribulation the gospel will no longer be able to be proclaimed. To quote the words of Jesus *'night is coming when no one can work'*. John 9:4.

The fifth seal directs attention to the martyred saints whose souls are underneath the altar. These are they who have been slain for bearing unwavering testimony to the truth of God. As with the repentant thief they must surely be in Paradise. The united cry to God of the martyred saints is to request that He judge and avenge their blood.

The sixth seal launches the outpouring of the great wrath of God, which will be unimaginable in its horror upon the population of the whole earth and so destructive that the world, as we now know it, will become unrecognizable. This sixth seal will consist of one event and two signs *'....there was a great earthquake; and the sun became black as sackcloth made of hair, and the whole moon became like blood'*. Revelation 6:12.

The initial objective of this chapter has been to show that the earth that Jesus will one day return to as King of kings and Lord of lords will firstly have been destroyed by its inhabitants and secondly by a series of devastating judgments that are released upon it by God.

After the Lamb opens the seventh seal, *'there was silence in heaven for about half an hour'*. Revelation 8:1. What sobering words of awful portent of what is about to be unleashed.

Now might be the time to pause in reading further and to open the Book of Revelation and read chapters 8 through to the end of chapter 11 and Revelation 16:18-21. Note all the events which will have impact upon the physical earth and try to imagine what will be its appalling condition at the time of our Lord's return with His overcoming saints.

"And the nations were enraged, and Your wrath came, and the time came for the dead to be judged, and the time to reward Your bondservants the prophets and the saints and those who fear Your name, the small and the great, and to destroy those who destroy the earth." Revelation 11:18. After announcing the eternal reign of the Lord Jesus Christ these words summarize the outcome. However, note the closing words *'the time came.... to destroy those who destroy the earth'*. The destruction that has occurred throughout the ages and now especially in our day in the name of enjoying the 'good life' will bring a terrible penalty.

It is surely inconceivable that the Lord, who together with His overcoming saints will rule the nations with a rod of iron, will not employ the huge numbers of people still remaining on the earth to remove all that offends Him and to restore the earth to the state that He intended for man *'to cultivate and to keep it'*.

Satan will have been bound for a thousand years. The world system over which Satan ruled will be no more. Nevertheless, the earth dwellers will have been steeped in the cultures and ways of the world so that it will be imperative that all manifestations of the past be eradicated. The iron rule of Jesus and His overcoming saints will make quite sure of that.

People will still die during this period of a thousand years but life will be extended. *"No longer will there be in it an infant who lives but a few days, Or an old man who does not live out his days; For the youth will die at the age of one hundred And the one who does not reach the age of one hundred Will be thought accursed."* Isaiah 65:20. Although, previous to this in verse 17 it stated *"For behold, I create new heavens and a new earth...."* the restoration described must be progressive in that Revelation 21:4 informs us *'there will no longer be any death'* when the new heavens and new earth are brought into being..

Creatures will no longer devour each other. *"The wolf and the lamb will graze together, and the lion will eat straw like the ox; and dust will be the serpent's food. They will do no evil or harm in all My holy mountain," says the Lord."* Isaiah 65:25. As we have noted earlier *'My holy mountain'* will be Christ and His overcoming saints who together become the mountain that fills the whole earth.

'For the anxious longing of the creation waits eagerly for the revealing of the sons of God. For the creation was subjected to futility, not willingly, but because of Him who subjected it, in hope that the creation itself also will be set free from its slavery to corruption into the freedom of the glory of the children of God. For we know that the whole creation groans and suffers the pains of childbirth together until now'. Romans 8:19-22. The *'revealing of the sons of God'* mentioned here will be God's display of His overcomers who have come to reign as *'joint heirs with Christ'*.

For those who participate in the restoration of the world to recover it to the state that God desires, this will surely prove to be an amazing experience and a profound enjoyment. It will be like rolling back history to the beginning. The world will be brought back to its condition in the time of Methuselah. *'The Son of God appeared for this purpose, to destroy the works of the devil'.* 1 John 3:8.

From the moment of His return, Jesus will usher in a new order of peace and wellbeing for mankind. The way of life experienced under the foul and totally evil influence of Satan will recede in the memory and will scarcely be brought to mind. We cannot speculate about the process that will restore the earth to a pristine condition for we are not told anything about events during these one thousand years. We do know that all individuals and companies of people will be under God's absolute authority and control.

How we thank God that what He has purposed from eternity past cannot be thwarted or delayed. Just as *'when the fullness of the time came, God sent forth His Son'* so, in the fullness of time His Son shall come to reign forever and ever in glorious majesty, together with all those who will pay the price now to rule with Him then.

CHAPTER 55
SATAN RELEASED FROM HIS PRISON

Scripture references: Revelation 20:7-10.

We live in a world of compromise. This has come about because of the choice made and the decision taken by our first parents to disobey God by eating of the tree of the knowledge of good and evil. During the Millennium, as it is sometimes referred to, the world's inhabitants will still be living under this constraint, to choose what is good and to reject what is evil. However, Satan, who will have been bound for a thousand years, will be powerless to influence the choices and decisions of those inhabiting the earth during this lengthy period of time.

The overcoming saints will be directing mankind to carry out precisely the will of God. His kingdom will have come. His will *'will be done on earth as it is in heaven'*. Some of earth's inhabitants will obey out of a willing heart while others will be compelled to do so.

Although there is no indication from the Scriptures of the purposes of God planned for the Millennium it must seem that, by its close, life on earth will be idyllic compared with the conditions on earth at the coming of Jesus. The world itself will be in a state unimaginable to us living in these days. For one thing, surely it will become an agrarian lifestyle with every man living under his own fig tree and under his own vine as was God's promise to the nation of Israel after they had entered into the 'promised land'.

God had given the man, Adam, and through him his wife Eve, His authority to rule the world and over every living thing. This stewardship of man was in no way negated by the fall. Thus it is entirely reasonable to suppose that, under the pervasive and all-seeing supervision of the overcomers, all conditions on the earth will be recovered to the state the Lord intended and ordained.

It should be noted that the overcomers collectively will be the wife of the Lamb. Their words, deeds and behaviour will be in perfect harmony with His desires and character. They will be absolute in executing His authority, yet His love also will be perfectly expressed through them as they ensure that His will is done.

*'When the thousand years are completed, Satan will be released from his prison....*Revelation 20:7. God will imprison Satan for His purpose so that His rule on earth shall suffer no interference while His will is fully carried out by its inhabitants. God will release Satan for a short while, also for His purpose, that he may again deceive and tempt mankind at the close of the thousand years. By this means the condition of the hearts of all those living on the earth at that time will be revealed.

Will those who are alive on earth and have known the rule of Jesus be loyal to Him? Apparently not, for when Satan is released from his prison he will again deceive and great numbers will be shown to be rebels at heart.

Satan *'will come out to deceive the nations which are in the four corners of the earth, Gog and Magog, to gather them together for the war; the number of them is like the sand of the seashore.'* Great multitudes of the earth's inhabitants will join Satan in rebellion against God as soon as they are given the opportunity. During their time on earth they will have merely accepted the rule of Jesus and those with Him because they were compelled to do so. Does it not seem amazing that such countless numbers, having experienced the rule of Christ; having also experienced such a wonderful renewal of the earth; yet through all this will have rejected and hated Him in their hearts?

'And they came up on the broad plain of the earth and surrounded the camp of the saints and the beloved city'. The broad plain of the earth or, as otherwise translated, 'across the breadth of the earth' seems to indicate a great convergence towards the location from which the Lord Jesus will rule the whole earth; the city of Jerusalem with its re-built temple.

'....and fire came down from heaven and devoured them. And the devil who deceived them was thrown into the lake of fire and brimstone, where the beast and the false prophet are also; and they will be tormented day and night forever and ever'. Hell was prepared for the devil and his angels. The beast and the false

prophet were immediately consigned there at the time of the return of Jesus. Those who now are condemned to accompany Satan to the place of eternal torment will have deliberately chosen to do so. How unspeakably evil a condition of heart that must be!

What a great honour and blessing it will be for the overcoming saints to serve the eternal purpose and plans of God throughout the Millennium. For those earth dwellers who have a good heart, how blessed it will be to enjoy a consistent and perfect reflection of Jesus displayed with absolute faithfulness by these ruling overcomers.

It appears that the company of His overcoming saints will be seen and realized by the Lamb as His wife in all her perfection of beauty, yet to all the earth's inhabitants she will be visible and experienced only as individual members of a great company who bear His authority.

Will the marriage supper have been an entirely unique and private display of His wife to the Lamb and of the Lamb to His wife? It appears that the public, immense and full disclosure of God's eternal purpose in Christ will not occur until *'the bride, the wife of the Lamb'* descends from God out of heaven at the dawn of eternity as the centrepiece of the vastness of His new heavens and new earth wherein righteousness will dwell forever.

CHAPTER 56
THE BOOK OF LIFE

Scripture references: Matthew 25:31-46, Revelation 20:10-15, Acts 9:1-20, Matthew 10:40-42, John 13:20, Romans 1:18-32, Job 1:8, Job 9:25-27, Job 42:8-9, 1 Peter 3:18-20, John 16:13-14.

Although this chapter and topic may not appear to be strictly in keeping with the theme of this book, its purpose will be to address some questions arising from the previous chapter. Those which concern the destiny of vast numbers who will have been too late to receive salvation by grace through faith, as well as the vast majority of earth's inhabitants, throughout the ages, who have never heard or had opportunity to receive the message of God as recorded in the Scriptures.

It will attempt to provide a better understanding of the mercy and grace of God in dealing with a question which many loving hearts ask constantly: What will be the destiny of countless numbers of people who have demonstrated earnest intentions to do good and to reject evil?

So, what is God's full, clear and final answer to this seemingly great dilemma? Is there to be found provision in His mercy and grace for countless individuals to enjoy an alternative destiny to that of accompanying the devil and his angels forever into the fires of hell?

To very many believers in the Lord, the writer included, there formerly have seemed to be only two destinies for mankind; heaven forever with Jesus or eternal separation from God. The prevailing message that most believers have been given is that each individual during their time on earth must choose to accept God's offer of forgiveness and redemption in Christ, or face a lost eternity.

The ultimate statement concerning the eternal destiny of mankind is to be found in Revelation 20:15, *'And if anyone's name was not found written in the book of life, he was thrown into the lake of fire'*. What these words tell us unequivocally is that if our name is *'not found written in the book of life'* we will certainly be cast into the fires of hell. However, by inference, all whose name is *'found written in the book of life'* will be approved of God and will enjoy a blessed destiny.

There are three judgments of mankind referred to in the Scriptures:

- The judgment seat of Christ at which all believers will be judged (which is the subject of an earlier chapter)
- The judgment presided over by Christ of those categorized as *'sheep'* and *'goats'*.
- The final judgment of the great white throne, also presided over by Christ.

Matthew 25:31-46 provides an account of the judgment of those dwelling on the earth at the time of Christ's return. All the believers of all the ages will have appeared before the judgment seat of Christ so those under judgment on this occasion cannot have been born again of the Spirit of God. The judgment made by the Lord Jesus, the judge of all men, is on the basis of their treatment of Christians during the great tribulation.

Those who fail to care for *'My brethren'* are classified as *'goats'*. The judgment handed down by Jesus is that the goats *'will go away into eternal punishment'*. Those classified as *'sheep'*, because they cared for *'My brethren'*, are rewarded with these words of Jesus, *'Come, you who are blessed of My Father, inherit the kingdom prepared for you from the foundation of the world. 'For I was hungry, and you gave Me something to eat; I was thirsty, and you gave Me something to drink; I was a stranger, and you invited Me in; naked, and you clothed Me; I was sick, and you visited Me; I was in prison, and you came to Me.'*

What Jesus is saying to this great company referred to as *'sheep'* is summed up in these words, *"'Truly I say to you, to the extent that you did it to one of these brothers of Mine, even the least of them, you did it to Me.'"* Matthew 25:40.

The *'sheep'* must surely be those who will continue to dwell on the earth as their inheritance, who will populate it from the commencement of the Millennium. If these referred to as the *'blessed of My Father'* who *'inherit the kingdom prepared for you from the foundation of the world'*, how can their names not be *'found written in the book of life"*?

Let us now consider the population living on the earth during the thousand year reign of the Lamb with His overcomers. These will continue to marry and be given in marriage and thus will bear children. Over this long period the earth will be re-populated. Many individuals will live and die during this lengthy period and will be among those who must appear at the final judgment of the great white throne.

'Then I saw a great white throne and Him who sat upon it, from whose presence earth and heaven fled away, and no place was found for them. And I saw the dead, the great and the small, standing before the throne, and books were opened; and another book was opened, which is the book of life; and the dead were judged from the things which were written in the books, according to their deeds'. Revelation 20:11-12. During the Millennium every single one of earth's inhabitants will be obliged to give obedience to the delegated authorities of Jesus; namely the overcomers. These too will be *'My brethren'*. To these must be added all members of the Jewish nation living on the earth at that time. They also will be *'My brethren'* for as Paul writes in Romans 11:25-26 AMP. *'....a hardening* (insensibility) *has* [temporarily] *befallen a part of Israel* [to last] *until the full number of the ingathering of the Gentiles has come in, And so all Israel will be saved'*.

To receive those who are sent by Him is tantamount to receiving Jesus Himself. *"Truly, truly, I say to you, he who receives whomever I send receives Me; and he who receives Me receives Him who sent Me."* John 13:20. On the other hand, to persecute or reject those who are His own is equivalent to persecuting or rejecting Jesus. *'As he was traveling, it happened that he was approaching Damascus, and suddenly a light from heaven flashed around him; and he fell to the ground and heard a voice saying to him, "Saul, Saul , why are you persecuting Me?" And he said, "Who are You, Lord?" And He said, "I am Jesus whom you are persecuting."* Acts 9:3-5.

'....the dead were judged from the things which were written in the books, according to their deeds'. There will be those who will treat

these brethren with respect and welcome their instruction. There will be those who will resent these brethren yet be forced to accept their instruction. The latter will demonstrate by their choice to join Satan in his last rebellion that they hated their rightful overseers. Their choice will have been made irrevocably and thus they will be *'cast into the lake of fire'*.

Surely the names of those who have treated their overseers with respect and have welcomed their instruction will be *'found written in the book of life'*. Such ones will deliberately choose not to participate in Satan's final battle against God. These descendants of the inheritors of the earth will join their blessed forebears in populating the new earth when time is no more and eternity ushers in the new heavens and new earth with the new Jerusalem as its centrepiece as the dwelling place of God.

There will also be a huge number of individuals who will appear at the judgment of the great white throne, who have lived and died without opportunity to hear or know of the living God and His Son Jesus Christ. In regard to these, the words that wonderfully express the heart of Jesus ring down through the corridors of time, He *'is not willing that any should perish but that all should come to repentance'*. 2 Peter 3:9 NKJV.

Romans 1:18-32 contains an indictment against the rebellious heart of man and, at the same time, it expresses the fact that no excuses can justify their behaviour. *'For since the creation of the world His invisible attributes, His eternal power and divine nature, have been clearly seen, being understood through what has been made, so that they are without excuse'*. Since the creation of the world surely not all individuals will have rejected this irrefutable evidence of the natural world?

Job appears in no genealogy, nor do his three friends, yet throughout their conversations all of them pay tribute and deep respect to Almighty God. Job himself is described by the Lord to Satan thus, *"Have you considered My servant Job? For there is no one like him on the earth, a blameless and upright man, fearing God and turning away from evil."* Job 1:8. The Lord implanted in Job a great hope which he expressed in the midst of his grave trials, a hope that all who believe unto salvation find greatly encouraging. He exclaimed *"As for me, I know that my Redeemer lives, And at the last He will take His stand on the earth. "Even after my skin is destroyed, Yet from my flesh I shall see God; Whom I myself shall behold, And whom my eyes will see and not another."* Job 19:25-27.

After admonishing his three friends because of their failure to speak rightly about Him the Lord gave them instruction as to what they must do, *"Now therefore, take for yourselves seven bulls and seven rams, and go to My servant Job, and offer up a burnt offering for yourselves, and My servant Job will pray for you. For I will accept him so that I may not do with you according to your folly, because you have not spoken of Me what is right, as My servant Job has." 'So Eliphaz the Temanite and Bildad the Shuhite and Zophar the Naamathite went and did as the Lord told them'.* Job 42:8-9. Will not the names of these three be *'found written in the book of life'*?

1 Peter 3:18-20, *'For Christ also died for sins once for all, the just for the unjust, so that He might bring us to God, having been put to death in the flesh, but made alive in the spirit; in which also He went and made proclamation to the spirits now in prison, who once were disobedient, when the patience of God kept waiting in the days of Noah, during the construction of the ark, in which a few, that is, eight persons, were brought safely through the water'.* If this great multitude of people who had died during the flood needed to receive such a proclamation from the Lord Jesus, it was surely for a very significant purpose. They were in prison in Hades, not in Paradise, the place where the repentant thief was promised that he would be with Jesus. Will these have been given opportunity to have their names *'written in the book of life'*? God never utters a word that returns to Him void or purposeless.

One thing remains certain, which is expressed succinctly in Hebrews 9:22, *'....without shedding of blood there is no forgiveness'*. While the deeds of all those *'found written in the book of life'* may speak eloquently on their behalf, it will be on account of the blood of the Lamb that their names will be found there.

Truth silences opinion as faith silences speculation. Always must we, in submission to God and in humility, approach our journey into eternal truth with fear and trepidation lest we lead ourselves and others into false hope.

In taking an attitude of total dependence on Him we are assured by the words of Jesus *"But when He, the Spirit of truth, comes, He will guide you into all the truth; for He will not speak on His own initiative, but whatever He hears, He will speak; and He will disclose to you what is to come. "He will glorify Me, for He will take of Mine and will disclose it to you."* John 16:13-14. The words *'guide you into all truth'* leave no doubt that being led into all the truth is a process. There may be errors and failures along the way but the Spirit of truth will guide us into *'all the truth'* as we are yielded to Him.

From this and previous chapters we may fairly draw the following conclusions. All those who have come to salvation by grace through faith, including all who put their faith in God's promise of a coming redeemer, will participate in *'the bride, the wife of the Lamb'*. When God has completed this immense work, with and through those who obey Him, the new Jerusalem will be displayed as the focal point within the immensity of the new heavens and new earth. She, as God's masterpiece, will be the eternal dwelling place of God and the Lamb. All others who will have been judged and approved by God will surely inherit and inhabit forever the new earth.

May what is unveiled to us, of what shall be, ever deepen our commitment to follow Jesus until faith shall at last be lost in sight.

CHAPTER 57
THE CITY WHICH HAS FOUNDATIONS

Scripture references: Hebrews 11:8-10, 1 Chronicles 21:1-30, 1 Chronicles 28:1-19, 2 Chronicles 3:1, 1 Kings 6:7, Ephesians 2:10-22, 2 Timothy 4:7-8.

The consistency of Scripture never ceases to amaze; the types provided in the Scriptures that accurately depict ultimate truth; the parables of Jesus that so clearly explain spiritual realities. All these unveil to the trusting heart the very nature, character and purposefulness of Almighty God and His provision for mankind in and through His Son Jesus Christ.

Long ago, in an act of faith, a man named Abraham departed with his whole family from the great city of Ur of the Chaldees to take possession of a land he had no knowledge of and to live as a tent dweller within that land. *'By faith Abraham, when he was called, obeyed by going out to a place which he was to receive for an inheritance; and he went out, not knowing where he was going. By faith he lived as an alien in the land of promise, as in a foreign land, dwelling in tents with Isaac and Jacob, fellow heirs of the same promise; for he was looking for the city which has foundations, whose architect and builder is God.* Hebrews 11:8-10.

In order to reveal His eternal purpose to Abraham, God removed him from the realm of human wisdom and separated Abraham unto Himself. Not only so, but in and through Abraham's seed God told him that He intended to display His testimony to all the nations that they too might receive the promises God made to him. Centrally within this land that God gave to Abraham He planned to make His dwelling place; a temple in which His presence would reside.

Abraham and his household lived in tents in the land promised to him by God, as would his son Isaac and grandson Jacob. This was significant because possession of the whole territory by their descendants would take place many centuries in the future. Until the city of Jerusalem should be built and a site for the temple be identified by God, only then would He dwell among His people in a house of stone. That they were tent dwellers also reminds us of the words of Hebrews 13:14, *'For here we do not have a lasting city, but we are seeking the city which is to come'*. This world is not our home.

God also revealed to Abraham that His ultimate dwelling place will be *'the city which has foundations, whose architect and builder is God'*. This city that Abraham *'was looking for'* will be the subject of this final chapter.

Around a thousand years later, from the seed of Abraham, came forth David who became King and ruler of God's people Israel. Through David, Israel captured and acquired in battle all the territory that God had promised to Abraham long before. One special conquest was the capture of Mount Zion from the Jebusites.

King David, in whose heart had been framed the question, *'From whence comes my help?* And who had answered it with conviction, *'My help comes from the Lord'* was, in a moment of forgetfulness, tempted by Satan to take a census of his fighting men. Joab, who was charged with the responsibility of carrying out this task, cautioned David with these words, *"May the Lord add to His people a hundred times as many as they are! But, my lord the king, are they not all my lord's servants? Why does my lord seek this thing? Why should he be a cause of guilt to Israel?"* 1 Chronicles 21:3-4. We read, *'Nevertheless, the king's word prevailed against Joab'*. Despite Joab's sound advice, David was determined to go ahead to satisfy his own pride. Can we imagine standing before an army as commander in chief of around 1,500,000 men?

What a lesson this was for David, as it is also a lesson for us today. David's and our *'help comes from the Lord'* only as we accord Him absolute sovereignty and authority over ourselves and over our every situation.

In numbering the warriors of Israel and Judah David gravely sinned. The prophet Gad was dispatched by God to David with an ultimatum. Gad presented David with three choices, *'either three years of famine, or three months to be swept away before your foes, while the sword of your enemies overtakes you, or else three days of the sword of the Lord, even pestilence in the land, and the angel of the Lord destroying throughout all the territory of Israel'*. David chose the third option and God sent His destroying angel throughout the land. *'70,000 men of Israel fell. And God sent an angel to Jerusalem to destroy it; but as he was about to destroy it, the Lord saw and was sorry over the calamity, and said to the destroying angel, "It is enough; now relax your hand." And the angel of the Lord was standing by the threshing floor of Ornan the Jebusite'.* 1 Chronicles 21:12-15. In awe and great fear David saw the angel of the Lord standing between earth and heaven with a drawn sword in his hand stretched out over Jerusalem.

'Then the angel of the Lord commanded Gad to say to David, that David should go up and build an altar to the Lord on the threshing floor of Ornan the Jebusite'. Ornan offered David the oxen for a sacrifice, the threshing sledges for wood and the wheat for a grain offering and David purchased the threshing floor and all that Ornan offered him for an agreed price.

'Then David built an altar to the Lord there and offered burnt offerings and peace offerings. And he called to the Lord and He answered him with fire from heaven on the altar of burnt offering'. Not only did God answer with fire from heaven but on this very site God revealed to David that His permanent dwelling place on earth, the temple, was to be built.

'Then David gave to his son Solomon the plan of the porch of the temple, its buildings, its storehouses, its upper rooms, its inner rooms and the room for the mercy seat....' 1 Chronicles 28:11. David not only prepared the site for the temple but he gathered much of the material that would be required in its construction. We are reminded of what God had told Moses when he was about to erect the tabernacle; for, *"See,"* He says, *"that you make all things according to the pattern which was shown you on the mountain."* Hebrews 8:5. The dwelling place of God must be constructed exactly according to His revealed plan.

'Then Solomon began to build the house of the Lord in Jerusalem on Mount Moriah, where the Lord had appeared to his father David, at the place that David had prepared on the threshing floor of Ornan the Jebusite'. 2 Chronicles 3:1. It had been on Mount Moriah that Abraham had shown his willingness to slay his son and it was on that exact location that Ornan had established his threshing

floor. There Solomon faithfully commenced the building as his father David had directed.

'The house, while it was being built, was built of stone prepared at the quarry, and there was neither hammer nor axe nor any iron tool heard in the house while it was being built'. 1 Kings 6:7. Each stone had its place in the temple structure according to the plan. All the work to ensure it fitted perfectly in its chosen place was *'prepared at the quarry'.*

The process and principles that applied to the preparation and building of Solomon's temple provide significant insight into the process that the Lord is following in building and bringing to perfection the City of God in the heavens. The site in the heavens needs no solid base for, unlike this world, God Himself is heaven's base and everything He builds is aligned with the Father's cornerstone, Jesus. From eternity past this cornerstone has been laid, but the sin of mankind created a delay in building upon it.

Just as Satan led Adam to deny the sovereignty of God and to rely on fleshly power, so was David led by Satan into denying the rightful sovereignty of God and to rely upon the strength of his army. The Lord not only gave David a remedy for the forgiveness of his sin but, at the same time, He also purified the site of Ornan's threshing floor by sending fire from heaven to consume the sacrifice, thus demonstrating that He accepted the offering. Likewise, before God could commence building His ultimate dwelling place the Father's beloved Son must be sacrificed that the sin of man might have the means of forgiveness and that the works of Satan might be destroyed.

Many perfected precious stones had been prepared in the quarry of the lives of Old Testament saints who had looked forward to the coming Saviour; Abraham and David being two of them. However, no building work could commence until the price for man's sin was fully paid and Jesus had risen victorious from the grave.

'So then you are no longer strangers and aliens, but you are fellow citizens with the saints, and are of God's household, having been built on the foundation of the apostles and prophets, Christ Jesus Himself being the corner stone, in whom the whole building, being

fitted together, is growing into a holy temple in the Lord, in whom you also are being built together into a dwelling of God in the Spirit'. Ephesians 2:19-22. In his letter to the church in Ephesus Paul informed these largely Gentile believers that, through the death of God's Son on the cross, the middle wall of partition between believing Jews and believing Gentiles has forever been broken down. Both groups are now fellow members of God's household. Their future in the holy temple of God is assured yet, as we have been shown, only finished stones can fit together in God's building. Thus, it is quite evident that God's full work in each believer must be completed before being given its appointed place in the building. On the building site in the heavens only finished stones will be found, ready to be put in place.

It seems, therefore, an inescapable fact that all the other stones will not be ready to take their place until the thousand years have passed. *"Buy* (oil) *for yourselves"*, as the prudent virgins exhorted the foolish ones to do, may well mean that those who have not made themselves ready will be required to undergo the tough process of shaping hereafter. How this will be accomplished we have not been informed.

Built on the foundation stone are the apostles and prophets. To these, the company of all others who have overcome in Jesus must surely be added. As these are brought together and placed into God's building there will come forth the wife of the Lamb who will be given to be arrayed in linen, bright and pure, readied to meet her bridegroom at the marriage supper of the Lamb.

The master stone mason in the quarry of life is the blessed person of the Holy Spirit. It is He who is given as a pledge, or down payment, to every believer in Jesus at the instant of the new birth. We read that whereas the first Adam *'became a living soul'*, the last Adam, namely Jesus, *'became a life-giving Spirit'*. As such, He is the One who will complete His transforming work in us if we will simply allow Him the freedom to do so. Over every thought we must seek His guardianship. Over every word and action we must murmur "Your will be done!" As we make this our habitual way of living, every second of every minute, every hour of every day, of every week, of every month and of every year, we shall effortlessly be embraced into an endless and eternal experience of Jesus.

Does the writer believe there is a way in which even the most seemingly ungifted believer may be constituted an overcomer in Jesus; thus a perfected stone for the building? Yes! And it is indeed simple for any truly seeking heart to understand.

Life in the Spirit is lived without strain. How blessed it is when our ego yields to submit wholly to Jesus and thereby finds the promised peace that passes understanding. As the thoughts, words and actions come from Jesus so, that which is displayed through our behaviour and deportment will be Jesus too. There will follow the deepest and most overwhelming sense that He is pleased with His creature and that His blessing rests unceasingly upon that one. What can provide greater assurance than that, that all is forever settled in Him.

What better way can there be to end this concluding chapter than with the Spirit-inspired words of the apostle Paul. He, as a perfected foundation stone, could confidently assert *'I have fought the good fight, I have finished the course, I have kept the faith; in the future there is laid up for me the crown of righteousness, which the Lord, the righteous Judge, will award to me on that day; and not only to me, but also to all who have loved His appearing'*. 2 Timothy 4:7-8. What a statement of encouragement are Paul's closing words to all who have it as their great desire to be constituted perfected stones for God's ultimate temple - the bride, the wife of the Lamb and dwelling place of God.

ADDENDUM 'A' - OUTER DARKNESS

In humility and dependence on the Holy Spirit let us consider this matter of outer darkness. *'This is the message we have heard from Him and announce to you, that God is Light, and in Him there is no darkness at all. If we say that we have fellowship with Him and yet walk in the darkness, we lie and do not practice the truth'.* 1 John 1:5-6. From these two verses we understand that God Himself is light, there is no darkness in Him. Likewise, if we walk in darkness we are living a lie and are not practicing the truth.

Paul in Philippians 3:18-20 expresses deep sorrow when he writes, *'For many walk, of whom I often told you, and now tell you even weeping, that they are enemies of the cross of Christ, whose end is destruction, whose god is their appetite, and whose glory is in their shame, who set their minds on earthly things'.* How aptly this describes those whom Jesus described as unfruitful. *"And the one on whom seed was sown among the thorns, this is the man who hears the word, and the worry of the world and the deceitfulness of wealth choke the word, and it becomes unfruitful."* Matthew 13:22.

'....for you were formerly darkness, but now you are Light in the Lord; walk as children of Light'. Ephesians 5:8-10. It is God's intention that there be no darkness remaining in us. If we will walk as children of light the Holy Spirit will remove all traces of darkness out of our being then, as He is holy, so we also shall be holy. Revelation 20:6. *'Blessed and holy is the one who has a part in the first resurrection; over these the second death has no power, but they will be priests of God and of Christ and will reign with Him for a thousand years'.*

By definition, these verses inform us that the second death does have power over those who do not have *'a part in the first resurrection'*. Satan will still have a claim on those in whom darkness remains at the close of their life on earth. They will not be ready for they will not be like Jesus.

The fate of all in whom darkness remains will be that they be cast into outer darkness so that all traces of darkness may be eliminated from them. That we make ourself ready is the choice facing each and every believer in the Lord and it is a most serious one.

Where might be this place of outer darkness into which these careless ones will be cast? We are not told, yet we may find a clue in the words of Psalms 97:1-2, *'The Lord reigns, let the earth rejoice; Let the many islands be glad. Clouds and thick darkness surround Him; Righteousness and justice are the foundation of His throne'*. David in his psalm of deliverance states, *'He made darkness His hiding place, His canopy around Him, Darkness of waters, thick clouds of the skies'*. Psalm 18:11.

We are reminded of the situation prevailing at the beginning as recorded in Genesis 1:2-3, *'darkness was over the surface of the deep, and the Spirit of God was moving over the surface of the waters. Then God said, "Let there be light"; and there was light.* Surely then, to be in outer darkness means that the Lord Jesus is not visible or consciously realized to those cast out into it.

Yet He, the Holy Spirit, is there nevertheless. At the end of this agonizing experience, when the full price has been paid, each believer who has been consigned to that outer darkness will be brought into the fullness of the light of God which will know no end. All those who had not 'made themselves ready' will have been *'made ready'*.

'And there will no longer be any night; and they will not have need of the light of a lamp nor the light of the sun, because the Lord God will illumine them; and they will reign forever and ever'. Revelation 22:5. Satan and his domain of darkness and all who have chosen to follow him will have been cast into the lake of fire, so *'there will no longer be any night';* no more darkness.

For all who have believed their ultimate destiny will be to reign with their beloved Jesus, the Lamb of God, *'forever and ever'*.

ADDENDUM 'B' – ULTIMATE UNITY

When Adam became a created being he became self-aware. When Eve was formed out of his rib or a part of his side, she possessed a separate self-awareness. All those born through Eve, including the Lord Jesus as Son of Man, have also possessed self-awareness. Yet He, Jesus, could rightly assert that *"I and the Father are One"*

Jesus maintained an unbroken unity with His Father. He willingly laid aside all self-awareness. His awareness was wholly of His Father, that His Father's will would be accomplished unhindered through Him.

As members of the body of Christ we each possess self-awareness, yet it is God's desire that, in utter surrender to the Lord Jesus, we lay aside our self-awareness in order to live in the awareness of Him, that His perfect will may be performed unhindered through us.

The greatest expression of love is that we lay aside our self-awareness in order to be lost in the awareness of the object of our love, in doing what is pleasing to that one.

Song of Songs contains an allegorical love story of a Shulamite who is being courted by her divine lover. Her adjustment in self-awareness is expressed in three very telling statements. In chapter 2:16 she is largely self-aware for she says *"My beloved is mine and I am his"*. Following a number of tests of her love she is able to exclaim *"I am my beloved's and my beloved is mine."* Song of Solomon 6:3. Her awareness of her beloved has grown to be of greater significance than her own self-awareness. Following still deeper adjustments she has clearly laid aside her self-awareness to be aware only of him, her beloved, for she joyously confesses, *"I am my beloved's, And his desire is for me."* Song of Solomon 7:10. After many experiences and because of her deep love for her beloved, *'His wife has made herself ready'*. Revelation 19:7.

At the dawn of eternity, when all the countless saved, sanctified and glorified ones have been built up and fused together to be the bride, the wife of the Lamb, all individual self-awareness will have been lost forever in a unified, cohesive awareness of our Bridegroom and how we may please Him in everything forever.

COMMUNICATION

The writer warmly welcomes comments and feedback from the readers of this book. Should you wish to question or critique any statements or perspectives he would simply request that different or other points of view be supported by relevant quotations from Scripture.

We are all journeying together towards that finishing line where faith will at last be lost in sight. 'And we shall see Him face to face….' May the Lord bless you and keep you.

My email address:

shampurgate@gmail.com

Made in the USA
Lexington, KY
29 March 2018